Norman Borlaug's is the greatest life story never told.

Peter McPherson, President, Michigan State University

When Norman Borlaug came to the University of Minnesota as a student athlete in 1934, his ability to do university work was questioned. Today we are proud to have named a building in his honor. Dr. Borlaug's life story should be an inspiration to everyone.

Mark G. Yudof, President, University of Minnesota

Norman Borlaug is one of the most honored Members of the National Academy of Sciences. Some credit him with saving more human lives than any other person in history.

Bruce Alberts, President, National Academy of Sciences

Norman Borlaug is such a charming and humble man, even though he has saved millions of lives through his genius and perseverance as an agricultural humanitarian.

Michelle Riley, the Carter Center

Norman Borlaug is the world's most important peacemaker. There can be no peace when millions are hungry. Dozens of nations would have faced turmoil during recent decades had the food supply not risen so dramatically.

E.C.A. Runge, Head, Soil & Crop Sciences Dept., Texas A&M University

I believe that Norman Borlaug will eventually be recognized as one of the 10 greatest contributors to humankind of the 20th century.

Bruce Chassy, University of Illinois, Champaign-Urbana

Norman Borlaug has shown how agriculture can solve immense problems in society. His story will heighten public appreciation for farmers and food production. And that is one of the most vital needs as the new, and probably hungrier, century begins.

Earl L. Butz, Former U.S. Secretary of Agriculture

Norman Borlaug's concern for the small-scale farmers of the world never wavers. His highly successful efforts to help them access improved food production technologies have saved millions of lives and may one day end our global hunger crisis.

Former U.S. President Jimmy Carter

The signal posts of Norm's life were hard work, a clear focus on worthy goals, and science directed at solving problems. He continually stressed the need to tackle problems rather than pursue disciplinary knowledge.

Robert W. Herdt, The Rockefeller Foundation

Food is an essential element of life. Those who help make it more abundant and more widely available perform an invaluable service to their fellow man. They deserve to be recognized and rewarded.

Robert McNamara, Former President of the World Bank

Borlaug's work seemed the product of benevolent destiny, though on close analysis it appears that destiny undertakes few ventures of her own; she awaits the actions of the bold and courageous.

Donald Paarlberg, U. S. Department of Agriculture

Norm Borlaug is not only a great scientist; he's a great guy.

Former U.S. President George H. W. Bush

BOOKS BY NOEL VIETMEYER

For Bracing Books
Borlaug: Right off the Farm. 1914 – 1944*
Borlaug: Wheat Whisperer. 1944 – 1959*
Borlaug: Feeding the Millions. 1960 – 1970 [in preparation]
Liquid Life Savers: The Fluid-Food Revolution [in preparation]

For the National Academy of Sciences
NEW CROPS
Lost Crops of Africa: Volume 1 – Grains*
Lost Crops of Africa: Volume 2 – Vegetables*
Lost Crops of Africa: Volume 3 – Fruits*
Lost Crops of the Incas
Underexploited Tropical Plants
Tropical Legumes
The Winged Bean: A High-Protein Crop for the Humid Tropics
Amaranth: Modern Prospects for an Ancient Crop*
Jojoba: A New Crop for Arid Lands*
Quality-Protein Maize*
Triticale: A Promising Addition to the World's Cereal Grains*
Vetiver: A Thin Green Line Against Erosion*
Guayule: An Alternative Source of Natural Rubber
Neem: A Tree for Solving Global Problems
Leucaena: Promising Forage and Tree Crop for the Tropics
Mangium and Other Fast-Growing Acacias*
Calliandra: A Versatile Tree for the Humid Tropics*
Casuarinas: Nitrogen-Fixing Trees for Adverse Sites*
Firewood Crops: Shrub and Tree Species for Energy*

ANIMAL RESOURCES
Water Buffalo: New Prospects for an Underutilized Animal*
Butterfly Farming *
Crocodiles as a Resource for the Tropics*
Little-Known Asian Animals with Promising Economic Futures*
Microlivestock*

OTHER
Ferrocement: Applications in Developing Countries
Making Aquatic Weeds Useful
Mosquito Control: Perspectives for Developing Countries
More Water for Arid Lands
Sowing Forests from the Air*
Producer Gas: Another Fuel for Motor Transport*

* Available (while supplies last) from **BracingBooks.com**, see p276

BORLAUG

VOLUME 1

Right off the Farm, 1914 - 1944

NOEL VIETMEYER

BRACING BOOKS
LORTON, VIRGINIA

BORLAUG; Volume 1, Right off the Farm. 1914 - 1944. Copyright © 2004, 2008 by
Noel Vietmeyer

Version 1.1: October 2009. Compared with Version 1.0, this printing omits the
subtitle [The Mild-Mannered Maverick who fed a Billion People] and incorporates
many minor modifications that illuminate or enrich the text.

LIBRARY OF CONGRESS CATALOGUING-IN-PUBLICATION DATA

Vietmeyer, Noel Duncan, 1940-

ISBN 978-0-578-04125-4

Biography & Autobiography/Science & Technology

For more information on Norman Borlaug as well as on Volumes 2 and
3 please visit **BracingBooks.com**. There also you can preview other
books providing provocative, practical and perhaps priceless tools and
methods helpful for reducing hunger and other planetary problems
such as child malnutrition, deforestation, soil erosion, malaria, and
atmospheric overheating.

BRACING BOOKS
5921 River Drive
Lorton, VA 22079-4128
USA

Printed in the United States of America

Signature Book Printing, www.sbpbooks.com

CONTENTS

List of Illustrations x

Preface xii

Introduction 1

Prologue 13

Chapter 1   1914-17, Hostage 17

Chapter 2   1918-19, Mortality 33

Chapter 3   1920-27, Awakening 53

Chapter 4   1928-29, Dreamy Days 79

Chapter 5   1930-33, Nightmares 101

Chapter 6   1933-34, Hunger Pains 121

Chapter 7   1934-35, Margaret 135

Chapter 8   1936, Heavy Weather 161

Chapter 9   1937, Wilderness 181

Chapter10   1938, Course Correction 203

Chapter 11   1938-41 National Service 219

Chapter 12   1941-44, Wartime 237

Afterword by Norman Borlaug 257

Author's Note 261

Acknowledgements 267

Picture Credits 270

Further Reading 272

Notes 274

ILLUSTRATIONS

Iowa (map) 16

Samaritan (Herbert Hoover) 22

Supplicant (Belgian girl) 23

The Day the Old Diet Died 25

Hell on Wheels (Hinckley Fire) 30-31

Forebears Recalled 34

The School 38

Heartbreak Home (polio) 42-43

Healthcare Heroes (1918 influenza) 46-47

Survival Shelter 55

Mud Matters 60

Little Norway 65

Willing Workforce 67

Best of Buddies 72-73

The Super Bowl of Corn Picking 76-77

Career Saver #1 (Sina Borlaug) 80

A Kid's Dream ... (hybrid corn) 92-93

Henry Ford's Greatest 96

Career Saver #2 (David Bartelma) 102

Problem-Solving Trainee 103

Outlaws in Overalls 108

Capital Chaos 112-3

Career Saver #3 (George Champlin) 119

The Real Depression 124

Career Saver #4 (Frederick Hovde) 127

Food Fight (Teamster's strike) 130-1

University of Minnesota map 132-3

Career Saver #5 (Margaret Gibson) 136

Career Saver #6 (White Castle) 139

Career Saver #7 (Alpha Omicron Pi) 141

Career Saver #8 (Eleanor Roosevelt) 143

ILLUSTRATIONS (cont.)

Medicine Man (Gerhard Domagk)...148

Rookie Reformer (Henry Wallace)...152

Famine (USSR)..155

Workout Place (U-Minn Wrestlers)..158

Workplace (U-Minn St Paul)..159

Brown Blizzard...164-5

The Guide (Raphael Zon)...168

Career Saver #9 (Edward Behre)...172

Idyllic Interlude...174

Freedom From Cant...176

Power To the People..178-9

Firefighter..184

Work Site (Fire Lookout)..186

Living Quarters, Summer 1937...187

The View From the Top...190-1

Miracle Site..194

Miracle Worker (Ed Pulaski)..195

Idaho Mountains...198

Tying a Lifetime Knot...201

Career Saver #10 (Hank Shank)..208

Rust Never Sleeps...210

Career Saver #11 (E.C. Stakman)..211

The Fungus that Fashioned our Lives...214

"Ocean City"..222-3

Before & After (Harvard Forest)..226-7

Lumber Jills..228

Home at Last...231

Dusting the Drawers..243

Wartime Digs...249

Career Saver #12 (George Harrar)...253

Norman Borlaug and the author...278

FAREWELL TO FAMINE

Children of my generation were constantly pressed to eat everything on their plate. Our mothers seemed to be forever barking: "Think of all the starving children in China [or India]!"

Modern mothers cannot exploit that handy inducement. Despite doubling their populations during the past half-century, China and India grow all the grain their billion-plus populations can eat.

BORLAUG; Right off the Farm is the first in a series of books telling why this miraculous transformation almost didn't occur. Without one little-known scientist's charmed career and myriad hairbreadth rescues from professional ruination, China, India and scores of other nations would still be synonymous with famine. And today's world would be much worse off.

Great lessons can be learned from this heretofore hidden history. Indeed, this humble man's endeavors provide a blueprint for countering today's resurgence in global hunger.

At heart, however, his story highlights the immense power of the human spirit. To that end, it can entertain and inspire everyone, whatever their mission or motivation in life.

You see, no one has ever done more to lessen human misery or to increase human happiness than Norman Borlaug.

Noel Vietmeyer

INTRODUCTION

B efore the Twentieth Century childhood was a gauntlet run through the Valley of Death. Of all the newborns only a fortunate few completed the passage. Like malevolent scythes, malnutrition and its attendant ills mercilessly felled babies by the millions.

No household was immune: in cottage, commune, country house and castle births and deaths followed each other with a rapidity that seemed preordained. Life's comings and goings often occurred with dreadful regularity, honeycombing human happiness with horror and repeated stabs of pain. Most families got to bury a baby; many suffered that worst of all agonies seven times over . . . or more.

Each person remained Destiny's plaything right up until the 1920s, a decade when public-health interventions initiated stunning advances against malnutrition and associated child-killing contagions. It was a seminal change in the human condition; for the first time children could be diverted from miserable ends. Soon twice as many were surviving than ever before in history.

Clearly this was the greatest humanitarian achievement—the closure of the Age of Pain that had begun with the species. Fearsome old child killers—quinsy, pleurisy, rheumatic fever, scarlet fever, infantile paralysis, tonsillitis, "adenoids," catarrh, rickets, beriberi, pernicious anemia, sprue and many more—began disappearing from the public lexicon. Also fatalism and the fear of epidemics began retiring from the public consciousness, retreating into the shadows of forgetfulness.

Surprisingly, though, the new broom sweeping out the underside of history also swept in its own underside. Death rates dropped so fast that within 40 years Planet Earth had doubled its people load. Grandparents who'd entered a steady-state world of 1.6 billion saw grandchildren join a runaway world of 4 billion. Indeed, in the 1960s Kenneth Boulding calculated that about 25 percent of all the human beings who'd ever lived were alive *at that moment*.

Moreover, the eminent economist and imaginative social thinker projected the figure would soon reach 50 percent. And this planetary overcrowding was arriving when Earth could barely carry its existing burden of human beings. Already, there'd been breakdowns in natural systems, energy resources and, above all, food supplies.

With the recognition of what came to be called the "Population Explosion" scholars manned their designated panic stations. The ship carrying humanity was steaming straight toward shoal waters. Indeed, that giant liner appeared headed for unavoidable catastrophe when South Asia's wheat crop failed in 1966 and then again 1967. The loss of a major staple two years in a row can cause any society to founder, and this region contained one out of every five persons alive.

Today the possibility of hundreds of millions starving to death seems unimaginable, but in the 1960s such a dreadful prospect was all too real. South Asia, after all, had always been hungry and just two decades earlier its northeastern corner had suffered what seemed like history's worst famine. In 1943, India's province of Bengal (including today's Bangladesh) devolved into a monstrous charnel house. Millions who were starving in the cities fled to the countryside, only to find the food producers starving too. With no sustenance for anyone, rural roadsides became littered with bodies and bones. Out amongst the farmsteads thousands of desperate souls could be seen in their last throes. Common too was the sight of dogs and vultures devouring the dead or nearly dead. Rather than see their offspring suffer, despairing, deserted or widowed mothers sold their older children and killed their babies. And, in what is probably standard form for famine-times, young women developed a special survival skill . . . plying their bodies for a bite to eat.

Amazingly, this is nowadays little known; the Bengal Famine seldom gets a mention despite a death toll 40 times that at Hiroshima two years later. The number who died approaches that of the Jews then perishing amidst Europe's five year Holocaust. In eastern India 4 million starved to death . . . in about a year.

Not surprisingly, when India achieved independence in 1947 the remembrances of mindless suffering beclouded the national outlook. Among its first acts, the new Indian government fashioned more farming areas and broke up existing farms on the false premise that more farmers would mean more food. But 20 years onward when the wheat crop failed India's food production had barely risen above its pre-independence level. Newspapers had by then given up reporting starvation deaths, which had become too numerous to be newsworthy.

Most worrisome of all, the population was surging at a rate sure to elicit disaster. By the 1960s there were an additional 100 million mouths to feed with a farm output stuck at 1947 levels.

Seen from afar, India was an undead society walking zombie-like toward the grave.

This is why the 1966 and 1967 crop collapses were so alarming. The ruthless mathematics of human increase and food decrease made the scholars' disaster scenarios inevitable. Specialists investigating the issue declared the beginnings of a famine beyond imagining. In 1968, for example, Paul Ehrlich published *The Population Bomb*, a sweeping indictment that soared up the bestseller lists and exploded in the Western mind. "The battle to feed humanity is over," the Stanford University biologist wrote. "In the 1970s, the world will undergo famine—hundreds of millions of people are going to starve to death in spite of any crash program embarked upon now."

Truth to tell, the horror behind these histrionics would have been long manifest had Americans been less generous. Thanks to technological transformations adopted during the 1920s and 1930s the U.S. was one of the few nations whose food production outstripped its baby production. Largely as a consequence, it was the only one prosperous enough to provide tens of millions of tons of food to impoverished countries without requiring proper payment. By the mid-1960s a vast American armada was annually hauling wheat, corn and sorghum over the seas to India and Pakistan—South Asia's barely surviving siblings that together contained more than half a billion hungry souls.

The sustenance in all those food-filled freighters was provided essentially free of charge, and some years India alone took 12 million tons. Yet that million-tons-a-month proved inadequate, and spawned what New Delhi's clueless communists derided as: "The annual pilgrimage to Washington to beg for more food."

Unhappily, New Delhi downplayed the gift that kept its millions from misery. Most Indians are unaware that U.S. farmers saved the lives of their parents and grandparents, thus making possible their own lives, not to mention those of their brothers, sisters and children.

Americans assumed that keeping nations from hunger was the perfect way to create lifelong friends, but India's leaders, by and large, placed their trust in the wonders of the Soviet system and openly belittled its super-power rival. Most regurgitated goodly measures of criticism of Westerners in general and Uncle Sam in particular. Then having declaimed American perfidy by day they dined on American provisions by night.

Perversely, the hunger was occurring in a fatherland of farmers. Almost 70 percent of the Indian populace grew food for a living. But theirs was an immense struggle: Soils were poor, overworked, baked hard by an unforgiving sun. Yields moved up or down with the mysteries of the monsoon, and never achieved exceptional levels even when the lifesaving downpours perfectly matched the crops' varying moisture needs during the growing season. Wheat, for example, averaged less than 750lbs an acre. Even the few farmers able to afford irrigation seldom surpassed 2000lbs an acre.

This—not politics, economics or social justice—was the fundamental flaw. A food supply is like an engine . . . its pistons and parts must act in perfect synchrony. Above all, though, it must be fueled by adequate and reliable field production.

Although Indian farmers held the key to salvation, Prime Minister Jawaharlal Nehru looked elsewhere. Bedazzled by Russia's transformation from a peasant society into an industrialized Soviet behemoth, he idealized central planning and instituted Stalinist five-year plans that elevated industrial development to the top of the national agenda. It has been said that for Nehru "industrial might was a bright bauble, nuclear power a golden dream, the army a necessity, foreign affairs an obsession." Local food production, by contrast, was left to tumble down the priority list.

Others in the leadership had no better grip on reality. Fifty agriculture colleges annually minted hundreds of agricultural scientists. Yet overall food output barely budged.

For that, there was a reason: the universities insisted on teaching the wrong lessons. Even the most idealistic students graduated ignorant of rural needs. Their minds were overstuffed with theory, including the maxim that India's peasants wanted nothing more than what their fathers and grandfathers had.

That dogma's truth certainly seemed self-evident; Indian farmers stuck by their ancient ways with cast-iron resolve. They were not only scornful of science but most were also illiterate, malnourished, sick, tired and miserable. Among them were the world's dirt-poorest creatures; roughly 270 million, so it was said, existed on 4 cents a day.

Thus the burden of India's suffering fell disproportionately on the only constituent capable of redeeming the situation—the skinny farmer and his ever-growing, ever-hungrier, ever-more-despairing kinfolk.

All in all, there seemed no possible way to counter the catastrophe to come.

Sadly, the scenes of privation were not restricted to this single society. In the 1960s the great mass of humanity began drifting toward the deadly shoals. Occupying neighboring berths on the Famine Boat's bottom deck were Pakistan, China, much of Latin America, most of Africa. In each, the scenes were achingly alike. Three continents were headed for disaster. Hunger had gone global.

With so many people in peril you might expect Western intellectuals to intervene, touting a wealth of wonderful answers. But the comfy cloisters at the campuses and think tanks issued only a collective chorus of discouraging words. For hungry humankind, the experts declared, there was no magic bullet, quick fix, shortcut or easy way out. In this conclusion they were unified and unanimous.

In truth the preachers of pessimism were intoxicated by the phenomena of bias-accumulation and self-propagandizing, which lie behind many of today's passionate activist causes. Accordingly, a long succession of pompous partisans leaped lemming-like into the sea of fallacy. One well-regarded Washington DC pundit published a learned tome demonstrating beyond all doubt that countries such as India "lacked the necessary pre-conditions for an agricultural take off."

This discouragement, defeatism, apathy and wooly-headed posturing compounded the danger and made the predictions self-fulfilling. Still, the soapbox scientists seemed unperturbed. Now they could watch from the shore as half humankind drifted toward disaster. Soon, the whole of South Asia would devolve into a house of horrors far surpassing that of '43. Roadsides would be littered with bones and bodies . . . dogs would devour the dead and nearly dead . . . mothers would sell children and kill newborns . . . and starving girls would peddle themselves . . . all on a scale beyond belief. Meanwhile those shoreline prognosticators would win respect and great honors for their prescience.

At this pivotal moment, with the planet in peril and the professionals in paralysis, a rank outsider whom neither politicians nor public had ever consulted or even heard of stepped up to try to turn the course of catastrophe. He was different from the rest: First, he was not an economist, political scientist or sociologist . . . he was an agriculturist. Second, he was a country boy of solid practicality, calm demeanor, deliberate mind and buoyant aggressiveness. Third, his specialty was applied science, the hard kind that aims to solve problems, not study them or propound policies for politicians. And fourth, he wielded his talents with audacious grace because, although a common man gifted with common sense, there beat in his breast the heart of an adventurer.

Approaching the hunger problem using the highly unorthodox notion of reason and reality, this maverick defied rather than deified the dogmas of his day. That was unusual for a researcher, but so too was his courage, character and chutzpah. And, weirdest of all—at least by modern standards—he ignored publicity, popularity and the public stage.

Perhaps it's hard to believe that so mad a scientist ever existed. But his separation from the pith of professionalism was even worse. With no axe to grind or thesis to prove, he never predicted, proselytized or pandered for money or political change. He functioned without particular plans, priorities or agenda. He did science "on-the-fly," allowing the unfolding of events to dictate each decision. And, although confronting arguably the greatest technical challenge of his age, he seldom sought his peers' advice. Instead, he let the real-world provide his instruction set and the results do his talking.

None of this was appreciated at the time, mainly because this loner who worked without script, scorecard, intellectual safety net or sounding board remained unknown. He hailed from an obscure facility lost to view in the depths of the Sonoran Desert. His technical support staff included a legion of farmer volunteers and a motley crew of Mexican boys, most of them scarcely literate. Yet from northern Mexico's boondocks 300 miles below Arizona this unlikely team—perhaps the strangest in scientific history—opened new passages to personal prosperity for struggling farmers in over 70 countries worldwide.

Their strategic conception was not temporary assistance but the mass amelioration of hunger, and their key creations were fast-maturing, high-yielding wheat varieties with amazing powers to resist disease and harsh conditions. Soon these powerful plants were shouldering food production increases hefty enough to lift hundreds of millions from Hunger's grasp. And they proved so alluring that getting them accepted required no coercion, financial inducement, fanfare or social reinforcement. Indeed, men of the soil would do anything, almost commit murder, to get these golden magnets that not only could feed their dependents but finance their ascent from destitution.

In this manner the novel seeds proved potent social elevators; their chromosomal capabilities enlivened impoverished lives. And the more that were sown, the more the rural regions prospered. These empowering gene gems thus spread welfare like a benediction, lifting both hunger and poverty from desperate families across the whole tapestry of South Asian society. Between 1964 and 1968, it has been said that India produced more wheat than in all the preceding 4000 years. Both it and Pakistan (including today's Bangladesh) thereby reshaped themselves into something new, different, happier, better.

For one thing, neither nation needed to beg for food; both halted America's sea-borne food convoys. In fact, their own farmers generated such an abundance of the fuel that runs society that both governments stashed away surpluses to meet future crises. And in the decades since that breakthrough, South Asian existence has been transformed. India's annual wheat harvest has soared six fold and its life expectancy has risen from 30 years (in 1947) to over 60 years.

Moreover, at some point Pakistan secretly gifted China a shipload of this man's fabulous Mexican seeds. Subsequently, the nation synonymous with famine since the depths of time has also put hunger behind. Indeed, nowadays China is the world's biggest grain producer; India is the second biggest. And both are budding super powers.

This book is the first in a series detailing the dramatic life of this scientist who helped the march of history avoid a major misstep. A wise person has declared that the joy of reading biographies is making new friends. Herein you'll stride out with perhaps the humblest yet most inspiring friend of our time . . . or any time. You'll meet the inner man previously hidden behind statistics and scientific jargon. You'll not only appreciate how he helped the hungry world feed itself, but also why he did it, where his abilities came from, and why so often he ignored his profession's dogma and operated beyond its customary limits.

This life's contours are wholly unlike those outsiders might anticipate from the field of food production. In truth, you might call this a "cereal thriller" because it includes the kind of outsized adventures heretofore reserved for beach-blanket suspense novels.

In applied science, as in life, context is everything. Thus, these pages also detail the social, scientific, geographic and historical landscapes through which he had to plow deep furrows to prepare the ground for his seeds. The back story is, in this special case, the real story.

Of course quietly steering the world around its worst calamity was not accomplished alone. In that sense, this is a group drama involving a cluster of cool collaborators who ignored hoopla and hype and got on with the job of making history. Their challenges were great and their achievements close-run, due not only to nature's obstacles but also to people who placed boulders in the path to a well-fed world. Indeed, our pages feature sinners who hindered progress, scoundrels who heisted seeds to plant in their pocketbooks, and supervisors who forever demanded this rebel conform to the proper professional way of doing things, despite the transparent rightness of his own approach.

The compassionate, nay sentimental, scientist at the heart of all this fury was of course trained in technical matters and propelled by facts, but fate took him into territories experimentalists normally dare not enter. Food, the real fabric of our lives, touches everything. So, to surmount hurdles inherent in feeding millions he sometimes ventured into the fiery crucibles of politics, history, technology and tradition, not to mention prejudice. A few times he found himself operating not just beyond the limits of research but also of reason.

In that regard, it's notable that his practices were more pragmatic than progressive. Rather than an Einstein-like intellectual committed to developing science he was an Edison-like inventor devoted to making science work for the common good. And in time his no-nonsense discoveries uncovered the deep-sea channel that allowed the famine boats bearing whole nations to float into a better-fed future.

Should you think all this reads like melodrama, there's good reason: *it is melodrama*. And after awarding the world an alternative to its fatal course he was made to suffer. The soapbox sophists whose reputations rested on proclamations of doom revenged themselves for having their reputations undermined. Hostility rose to such a fever pitch that he not only got denounced, derided and demonized but also dismissed from his job. His narrative thereby confirms the ironic old aphorism that no good deed goes unpunished.

Thus although outlining the highest of human ideals, this multi-volume narrative also exposes lesser sentiments, including some deliberately designed to further the interests of Death and Disaster.

Lest all this seem mere blather from a bygone era, we need note that this man was one of those born into that steady-state world of 1.6 billion people. During his lifetime, however, human numbers quadrupled while farmland increased by only about one tenth. He and his compatriots were the saviors who allowed the mass of mankind to keep eating when the number of mouths increased 300 percent and the quality farmland increased merely 10 percent.

This ultimate humanitarian achievement occurred because from the 1960s onward the breeders of rice, corn, and potato followed wheat's example, and refashioned those sister staples into fast-maturing, dwarf, disease-resisting, bin-busting varieties that performed prodigies under wildly different conditions and climates. As a result, the world's main food crops have shrunk; surrendering foliage but supporting more food. Most produce exceptional amounts regardless of season or latitude. Many mature fast enough to yield several harvests a year. And all are protected from their major diseases with rare genes painstakingly teased from their own species by natural plant-breeding practices.

Sadly, the hands-on hunger fighter who sparked all this remains lost to public view. His work sheltered perhaps a billion souls from starvation. He shaped modern life more than scholars have acknowledged, or even known. And he supported us too. You see, genes from the wheats he made for hungry nations are also in our own daily bread.

Today in fact, products stemming from his efforts feed most of humanity. And in the future his trailblazing and trendsetting will become even more important. The food supply is always under threat, and he and the other unsung crop doctors, all operating well below eyelevel, are the most basic supporters of human happiness. By keeping the sustenance growing, they raise lives incomparably more than the famous figures crowding the newspapers, textbooks and history tomes.

The following chapters begin this humble hero's story. Like other biographies they outline a chain of circumstance. In this special saga, however, some strange phenomenon—coincidence, chance, providence, destiny, fate, fortune, karma, kismet, cosmic necessity, lady luck . . . call it what you will—keeps sending strangers to rescue his career. These angels of deliverance tend to pop up just when the path forward is completely blocked. Could it be that some protective genius was motivating them to clear the way?

Considered in retrospect, too, the corrugations of the first 30 years—this volume's featured subject—look suspiciously like an apprenticeship for a long, hard, predestined calling. In fact the challenges that constantly swirl into his path seem choreographed to create the capacity for withstanding a lifetime of physical and mental shocks in distant and deprived lands.

Indeed, his formative experiences while growing up on a subsistence farm in Middle America provided all-too-intimate insights into the deprivation and depravity of the peasant existence. As a youth he endured pretty much the same hardships as the skinny destitutes far across the distant seas.

From the beginning he had to fight for food.

And that laid the foundation for all that would unfold.

BORLAUG

VOLUME 1

Right off the Farm, 1914 - 1944

PROLOGUE

That morning in December 1970 the former Iowa farm boy appeared distracted. Partly his distraction arose from the Klieg lights glaring down and the camera lenses staring up; partly it arose from the grandeur of the setting in the ancient auditorium; partly it arose from the fact of an orchestra at his back and the king of Norway by his side; partly it arose from the mass of people sitting silent and attentive before him, each clad in evening dress, despite the time: 10 AM.

Mostly, though, it arose from an overwhelming feeling of gratitude for coincidences that had saved his career, supporters who'd helped overcome insuperable difficulties and farmers of a dozen lands who, in the face of highbrow hostility, had awarded him their trust.

Compared to these unassuming thoughts, the words ringing around this bronzed loner with the looks of a movie star seemed incongruous. Madame Aase Lionaes, chairman of the Nobel Peace Prize Committee, declared: "Norman Borlaug is an indomitable man who fought rust and red tape . . . who, more than any other single man of our age, has provided bread for the hungry world."

This extravagant praise clashed with the hero's own humbleness. He'd begun life on a tiny impoverished farm 56 years before. Now, standing in that university chamber near Oslo he felt special affection for the contingent of Mexican farmers seated in the attentive throng. One had cashed out his life insurance so he and his wife could attend. "Normando," he explained, "has changed our lives and is our beloved friend."

Then the scientist's distracted mind circled back to a curious incident that had occurred two years earlier, following a five-year struggle to get a pair of perilously hungry countries to accept his bin-busting wheats. Despite the imminence of a famine predicted to take 200 million lives, senior scientists in both Pakistan and India blocked their farmers from sowing his seeds, even falsifying data to prove the seeds' inferiority.

Through dogged perseverance, however, he'd got his seeds accepted, and in 1968 had undertaken an inspection tour of the then-burgeoning farmlands. Despite the crop's apparent health and productivity, he'd suppressed all sense of celebration. Nature, he knew from first-hand experience, is the greatest proponent of the surprise attack.

The curious incident occurred when he'd arrived at Lahore at the end of the tour's final day. Having inspected wheat fields since dawn he was travel-stained, tired, hungry, and desperate for a relaxing bath, dinner and bed. Then the hotel clerk handed over a note. A local farmer was in trouble: "My wheat is sick," the note said. "The Doctor must come." Fearing this heralded Mother Nature's revenge the weary scientist clambered back into the van and headed back into the countryside accompanied by a sense of foreboding.

When he reached the seven-acre wheat field daylight was dying, but the smoking sun still touched the top of a magnificent crop of Mexipak 65, the dwarf variety he'd bred in Mexico and donated to Pakistan. Those pint-sized plants glowing in the honeyed light were so dense, uniform and sturdy an observer noted you could toss a notebook onto the flat surface of their plump heads, and it would stay. To the scientist this was clearly a 100-bushel-an-acre crop in a country where the average had seldom surpassed 10. "Where," he demanded, "are the sick plants?"

The nervous young farmer walked his guest alongside the irrigation ditch to the far corner. "There," he said, pointing to a cluster of stunted wheats obviously affected by too much salt in the soil.

Now the visitor knew his life's work had not fallen victim to nature's negativism. With rare petulance he told the man to drain that patch of soil, and strode back toward the van. By then, though, the front corner of the field had been transformed. Carpets covered what had been bare ground. Chairs and lanterns had appeared. Neighbors clustered around.

"Dr. Borlaug," the farmer said, peering at him with anxious stare, "we apologize for bringing you here under false pretenses. But we wanted to thank you for changing our lives. Your wheat will make it possible for me to marry that beautiful young woman there. We will build a house where you are standing. We knew no way to show our appreciation, so we asked the village ladies to help. They went to work and made this."

He turned, and two of the women held up a beautiful quilt. The separate squares had been sewn by families whose lives Mexipak 65 had uplifted. "Take this home to Mrs. Borlaug please," the reverent farmer said. "Keep it as a reminder that without your work the better life we see ahead would not have been possible."

Now, two years later, as he stood in the ancient Norse chamber with an orchestra at his back and a king by his side, Norman Borlaug remembered how the moon had risen over Pakistan that night and how a tear had rolled down a dusty cheek. Yes, he concluded, the epic journey had been worth it, and not really because he was here in Norway's capital to receive the Nobel Prize for Peace.

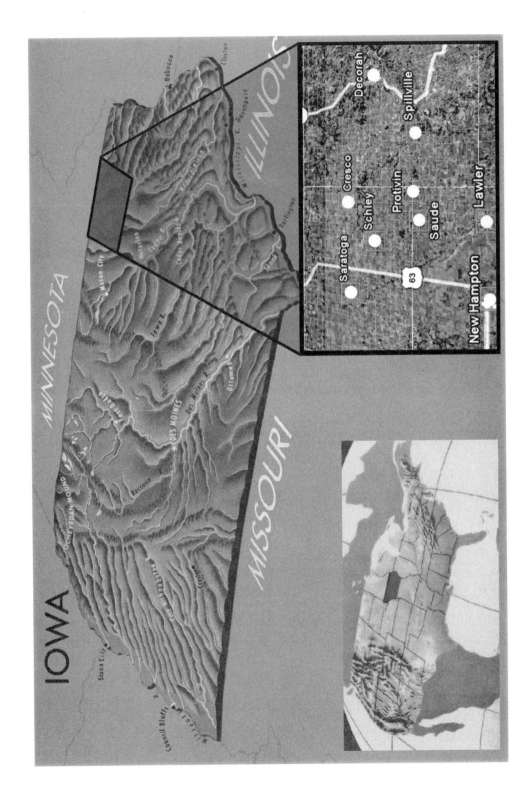

1914-1917

Hostage

N orman E. Borlaug—the middle name is Ernest and the pronunciation is BOR-LOG—was born into a country fearful for its food supply. Just three months after his entry into the world on March 25, 1914 an assassination in Central Europe triggered the Great War. Three years onward, when the federal government finally deigned to join that bizarre orgy of foreign self-destruction, Americans knew they might not have enough to eat. From coast to coast there was concern. Indeed, there was consternation. Before we could beat the Hun over there we clearly had to beat the hunger over here.

In this moment of crisis Woodrow Wilson knew exactly what to do: make every citizen eat less. No president had ever dared force the entire populace to diet, and to entice so supreme a sacrifice he proclaimed: "Food will win the war!" Then he swung the might of the federal bureaucracy behind the drive to cut consumption. From coast to coast children's groups were organized to sing the glories of the "delicious, nutritious, patriotic potato." And in thousands of cities and towns official posters blared:

Feed a fighter; Eat Only What You Need.
Waste Nothing, That [the soldier] and his Family May Have Enough.
Will you Eat Less—wheat, meat, fats and sugar—that we may still
    send food in ship loads.

To a surprising extent the belt-tightening was required because the wheat crop had failed. In the fall of 1916, millions of acres of the magnificent variety called Marquis sickened and died. From Missouri to Montana and even into the upper reaches of Manitoba the wheatland had turned wasteland.

Wheat was America's second-largest food and by the spring of 1917 the silos and general stores were running out of flour. Clearly, everyone would soon have to forego bread, cookies, crackers, cakes, pastries, pancakes, doughnuts, breakfast cereals, rolls, bagels and maybe very much more.

Making matters worse, the stellar variety named Marquis had succumbed to the foe farmers dreaded above all others: black stem rust.

Humanity's great nemesis, this malicious microbe is a force not only of darkness but of disorder. Each year it spews trillions of infective spores over the world's wheat crop, forever seeking a weak spot. Once inside a stalk, a spore replicates with abandon, imbibing so much inner juice that the plant falters and fails to set the seeds for people's needs.

Since at least Biblical times this fungal menace has spawned famines. Before the 20th Century it was unstoppable; even in our own 21st Century it remains nearly unstoppable. Only one practical antidote exists: a special wheat variety with the exquisitely rare, mysterious, almost mystical, ability to deny *every spore* access to its innermost tissues.

Finding a plant that survives the aerial assault, thrives in cultivation and meets the quirky concerns of commerce and consumers is nearly impossible. That's why Marquis had proved so magnificent. Since its creation in Canada in 1904 it had performed impeccably in the fields, not to mention grain mills, bakeries, bread shops and kitchens. But just twelve years onward the highly mutable microbe had broken Marquis's genetic code and its spores had turned thousands of square miles of food-producing fields into miasmas of putrefaction.

No wonder fear clung about the country. Food is society's most basic fuel, and the supply was now being squeezed in a death grip that could not be loosened. From here on, what 150 million North Americans ate would be determined by an invisible blob of genes and protoplasmic jelly that cared nothing for humankind or its hunger.

Thanks to that sinister self-centered rival, almost 200 million bushels of grain Americans anticipated eating in 1916 never eventuated. Canada's shortfall was 100 million bushels. In both countries that year the invisible invader denied every man, woman and child over 100 pounds of food. Many observers believed wheat itself was washed up.

For any nation food comes first, being the ultimate basis of trust as well as the fabric clothing the communal confidence that conjoins the citizenry. But faith in the food supply is also a fragile thing, prone to paranoia. This, however, proved North America's finest hour.

The specter of empty shelves stung all society's segments into embracing the president's directive to go on a diet. Compliance was beyond belief:

When, for example, the Wartime Prohibition Act banned alcoholic beverages to save on grain, Americans abandoned the saloon, not to mention the beer and cocktails they'd enjoyed privately in the parlor back home.

When forbidden to serve more than 2 ounces of bread, hotels and restaurants accepted it as a public duty.

When asked to adopt wheatless Mondays and Wednesdays, meatless Tuesdays, and porkless Thursdays and Saturdays, the public proved its patriotism.

When the "enormous waste of nearly 50,000 dozen eggs" was publicized, families forwent their Easter egg hunts.

When urged to plant Victory Gardens, millions of moms and dads grabbed a spade and dug up the backyard.

And when requested to bake Victory Bread—a shady concoction of oats and barley that stayed flat as a cracker—old-timers shudder at how gullible the average person really is.

Only when instructed to switch from beefsteak to whale meat did society fall short of the federal fiat. But after all, how many Americans could afford beefsteak?

For a freedom-loving people formerly cocksure about their daily bread, these strictures constituted an extreme food makeover. Beyond the horror of hunger, however, lay another powerful motivator: Herbert Hoover.

The federal government's Food Administrator, Hoover was the functionary actually issuing the blaring signs. The subsequent sacrifice came to be called "hooverizing." People touted the term with pleasure and pride. A 1918 Valentine card bespeaks the national sentiment:

I can hooverize on dinner,
and on lights and fuel too;
but I'll never learn to hooverize
when it comes to loving you.

Hooverizing attracted millions of adherents because the modest mining engineer behind the signs was a national icon. More than once in his young life he'd proved superhuman. His greatest feat—still springtime fresh in every mind—had begun less than three years before when he'd been asked to save a country from catastrophe. This country had 7 million people. And no food.

Though hardly known today, the tale was blockbuster news during Norman Borlaug's formative years. It began in August 1914 when German troops swept into Belgium and, among sundry brutalities, seized all cattle and crops. Britain responded with a coastal blockade. Sadly, however, its warships withholding supplies from the German foe also withheld them from Belgian friends. The result was famine. Even in peacetime Belgium imported four-fifths of what it ate; now it had nothing of its own and no way to get more.

Herbert Hoover took up the challenge of feeding the Belgians only with reluctance. That's understandable: How could any individual—least of all a Quaker—pull off so peaceable an enterprise amid the whirlwind of warriors waging World War?

But if anyone could succeed it was he. Neither dreamer nor ditherer, Hoover was a doer. Lacking precedent—no one having ever tried to feed a nation solely on relief supplies—he plunged ahead without worrying about anything so trivial as plans. The very first afternoon on the job he phoned the Chicago Commodity Exchange and ordered 10 million bushels of wheat. Then he worked 60 hours a week for almost three years, seeking ever more food and seeing it safely delivered to the Belgian people for free. To that end, he took no pay for his pains.

European authorities never made it easy for this jumped up pacifist from the naive neutral across the seas. Leaders on both sides of the battle went out of their way to stymie his efforts. Each insisted that by feeding Belgium he was assisting the enemy.

Regarding the man himself, both sets of belligerents betrayed total disdain. That's also understandable: Hoover hardly cut a swashbuckling presence. He was in fact quite charmless. From black hat and high collar to patent-leather shoes, he was as starched as a stuffed shirt can be. But the quarrelsome continentals saw only this shell and failed to spot the inner man who cared nothing for their feelings, their fight, their official forms or, above all, their political fancies. Results were all he wanted, not respect or rhetoric.

One local Pooh-Bah went so far as to call him "the most undiplomatic of diplomats," which actually showed a lot of insight. Hoover could be blunt beyond the point of rudeness. Often he was dictatorial. Once he cabled the governor of Kansas, demanding the state dispatch several shiploads of wheat *as a gift*. He also confronted Germany's Kaiser and Britain's prime minister, commanding they conform to his wishes.

Is it any wonder the European war capitals considered this gawky Yankee not only discourteous but downright impertinent? He paid no heed.

Hoover even ignored his own government, reporting neither to the State Department nor the War Department. Instead, he awarded his organization sovereign status, a unique conception that even today could be a model for dealing with international disasters. The Commission for Relief in Belgium displayed its own flag, drew up contracts and executed treaties with foreign powers that hated each other and were trying to destroy each other. It even demanded they provide special immunities and exemptions normally reserved unto nation states.

For this lone and little-known civilian, keeping everything going proved an immense challenge. Descending on Washington, London, Paris and Berlin, Hoover argued, exacted, exhorted, and pleaded for cash to succor the seven million innocents. When the British Prime Minister balked, the committed Quaker impaled him on the prongs of conscience. "Except for the breadstuffs imported by this Commission," he wrote David Lloyd George, "there is not one ounce of bread in Belgium today." That was enough. Hoover's rhetorical dart threatened to puncture the very ideals for which Britain was spilling its young blood in torrents. "You have made a good fight, and deserve to win out," the chastened Prime Minister replied, and thereupon threw in both support and sterling.

To overcome immediate financial disaster Hoover several times pledged personal responsibility for more money than he possessed. And he possessed a lot. Long before the ripe old age of 40 he'd made a fortune getting gold mines going in the waterless Australian desert. Not even he, however, could afford to feed millions of hungry humans.

Avoiding the war at sea proved more problematic. Despite huge signs shrieking "Belgian Relief Commission" the length of the hulls, more than a dozen of his ships were sunk in 1917, some with all hands. The majority fell victim to torpedoes, others to mines, and for a while most of the food got delivered direct to the Atlantic floor. Only after Spain and the Netherlands appealed to Berlin's better instincts were the U-boats ordered to permit Hoover's food-freighters safe passage.

It is hard to credit the scale on which the man approached his task. His goal was to provide *every adult in Belgium 1800 calories every day.*

Children would get even more. At noon each day, feeding stations in schools, churches, hospitals and other institutions provided 2.5 million kids a free lunch of stew, milk and crackers fortified with nutrients. And the results were a sight to see: "The troops of healthy cheerful chattering youngsters lining up for their portions," he later recalled, "were a gladdening lift from the drab life of an imprisoned people. And they did become healthy."

SAMARITAN

Herbert Hoover during World War I. In 1914 the 43-year-old engineer set out to feed Europeans who'd been overrun by the German Army and left to starve. Waiting for neither plans nor procedures, he organized his own shipping line and soon had freighters shuttling grain and other foodstuffs across the broad Atlantic.

Then, working behind the frontlines of the fiercest combat ever known, he distributed the free food with efficiency and dispatch and without bribery, bias or losses to petty pilfering or greedy German generals.

Later Hoover would join President Wilson's administration, but this venture was a personal enterprise staffed primarily by volunteers in at least six countries. Transcending professionals, politics, national interests, commerce and combat, these amateurs fed the hungry masses; above all, the children.

By wielding this weapon of peace amidst the chaos of all-consuming conflict Hoover touched his country's communal heart. Personifying America's highest ideal, he set the gold standard for kindness and caring. Before this moment, nation states ignored each other's problems; from here on, they felt duty-bound to succor the starving wherever they might be. Hoover's example thus established the notion of human rights.

SUPPLICANT

Belgian girl enjoys her daily bread, 1915. In two and half years, Hoover and his helpers solicited more than $200,000,000 in donations, acquired more than 2,500,000 tons of food, and shipped it through U-boat- and mine- infested waters to Rotterdam. From that Dutch port, they then moved the precious cargo by rail and canalboat to more than 4,700 communities in Belgium and German-occupied France. In total, they serviced nearly 20,000 square miles and 9,000,000 civilians, including this child.

Overall, more than 130,000 volunteers participated, including 40,000 distributing food in Belgium, 15,000 distributing food in occupied France, and 50,000 raising private donations in the U.S.

Writing to President Woodrow Wilson, Walter Hines Page (U.S. ambassador to Britain) summed up the man:

Life is worth more ... for knowing Hoover. But for him Belgium would now be starved, however generously people may have given food. He's gathering together and transporting and getting distributed $5,000,000 worth a month, with a perfect organization of volunteers, chiefly American. He has a fleet of 35 ships, flying the Commission's flag—the only flag that all belligerents have entered into an agreement to respect and to defend. He came to me the other day and said, "You must know the Commission is $600,000 in debt. But don't be uneasy. I've given my personal note for it." ... He's a simple, modest energetic little man who began his career in California and will end it in Heaven; and he doesn't want anybody's thanks.

For two years the relief ships carried flour, but after Marquis failed in 1916 Hoover crammed the holds with cornmeal. And from that arose a most peculiar problem: no Belgian would eat the stuff. Corn, they declared, was for animals. Undeterred, their persistent patron commandeered a Brussels skating rink and had his staff train all comers to cook corn bread. Housewives by the hundreds trooped through, and corn bread caught on.

Because Belgium lay behind enemy lines, Hoover's efforts almost defy belief. Yet he neither doubted the outcome nor the correctness of his course. "It is impossible," he observed in his memoirs, "for someone who has never seen real famine to picture it, the pallid faces, the unsmiling eyes, the thin, anemic, bloated children, the dead pall over towns where children no longer play in the streets, the empty shops, the dumb, listless movements and dumb grief of women; the sweep of contagious diseases and the processions of funerals."

By war's end none of this was anymore in evidence. Indeed, the populace was so well fed that more Belgian children were surviving than at any time in history. And whereas Europe's officials wished never to see the tenacious technocrat's bland visage again, thousands of Belgium's burghers had pinned his portrait to the parlor wall to admire throughout the day. And long after the war was over they continued enjoying that strange gritty yellow substance fashioned from the grain they'd formerly let only their animals enjoy.

On the home front this all-American story hit with force enough to move the moral outlook. The practical humanitarian demanding results rather than rhetoric or respect, created what later generations would call a role model. Thanks to Herbert Hoover, Americans of all ranks and ages came to appreciate that a lone individual with a can-do attitude could avert disaster in a hungry land. They also understood that countries with food must help countries without. For most, it was the first hint that the world was an extended human family and not just a jumble of self-absorbed sects and societies.

Among those delighting in the doughty engineer's deeds was young Norman Borlaug. The two were much alike. Both were Iowans—born a mere hundred miles apart. Both led similar boyhoods and developed similar outlooks. Both grew up penniless. But that's where the likeness ended. Orphaned at age 10, Hoover got packed off to relatives in Oregon, from whence he leaped first to fortune and then to fame. Borlaug, by contrast, was stuck at home with no hope of escaping the pigeonhole he'd been born to inhabit. For him, fame and fortune were foreclosed.

THE DAY THE OLD DIET DIED

As if World War hadn't provided enough death, the wheat crop also succumbed. In 1916 thousands of square miles of farmland mirrored this plot of dying wheat near St. Paul, Minnesota. In the absence of flour, life for Americans suddenly became fragile. The upper crust had to accept the cornbread and macaroni they'd forever disdained. Even beer and cocktails were abandoned. And bringing bread wheat back from the dead would prove one of the 20th Century's greatest scientific challenges.

During the war years the Borlaugs of course hooverized to beat the Hun. In reality, though, their lives went on pretty much as before. You see, they'd always supplied their own table and conserved every edible morsel. Despite residing in America since the late 1840s, the family still hadn't gotten past the immigrant's prime obsession: staying alive. Daily existence revolved around finding something to eat, an imperative so demanding they could never entertain wastage or culinary experimentation.

In 1917 and 1918, however, all Americans changed what they ate. With the wheat belt reddened to rustbelt, they had to switch to corn bread. Johnnycake, as Northerners called it, thereby became the staple of the Borlaugs as well as the Belgians.

Most Northerners considered eating foreign Southern food wholly unnatural. Norm recalls:

Before that time, we'd enjoyed pancakes for breakfast and homemade bread with every other meal. Now, those were gone. Granddad thought it was hell we couldn't get proper bread. I did too. Without a fresh loaf, living just didn't seem like living. Johnnycake was okay, but not all the time for god's sake!

This dietetic disruption heads his earliest recollections. Then a prototypical boy of the soil, he was renowned for three things: A cheerful whistle that within the family was a point of particular pleasure, even pride. A Nordic appearance—the outdoors life having blanched him into a sunshine towhead. And happy feet. From earliest days he ran everywhere: up the stairs, across the fields, through the woodlot, down the road. And he always jumped the stream. Constant motion endowed him a frame more sinewy than strong—a greyhound yes, but no German shepherd.

What this muscular dynamo's future held no one could say, but he sure wasn't cut out for life on the land; given such an active motor, he'd probably end up a track-and-field star.

That was a natural thought. Other than by capitalizing on exceptional brawn or exceptional brains country boys could never achieve anything in the hostile universe past the farm gate. Without uncommon talent for either sport or scholarship they were stuck in position.

But for "Norm Boy" Borlaug scholarship was hardly an option. While capable and quick-witted, he was not an ardent scholar. His sky-blue eyes were calm and reflective rather than gleaming with any sparkle for schoolwork. Thus, other than by way of athletics, he couldn't do more than what his father and grandfather did.

That is exactly what the world believed he should do . . . and wanted to do. No question, the Borlaug kid would be just like the others of his caste. He'd spend his life struggling to feed himself. Destiny decreed it.

Although Norm Boy's lifestyle differed from ours in ambition, it differed even more in ambience. Seen from the Space Age, country life in 1914 is as distant as its counterpart in Ancient Rome. Indeed, technologically speaking, rural Americans then lived more like Caesar's serfs than like us.

This was certainly so for the Borlaugs. For one thing, they were confined to their designated place. Around their farm and its contiguous community a disapproving world had erected solid walls.

In that outer perimeter of personal possibility there was just one small gap: Cresco, the county seat. The family, however, seldom got to visit that peephole in the social partition. Despite being a wondrous metropolis of 3500 souls, Cresco could seldom be enjoyed. You see, it was 14 miles away—a distance so enormous that a visit once or twice a year was all that could be spared.

Negotiating the intercontinental space between homestead and hometown was a true adventure in those days before distance died. The family used a sled in winter, a buggy in summer. Millions of Americans owned a buggy, a fancy wooden contrivance built on a light frame and four thin wheels that had to be very high to keep the riders above the mud. The Borlaug's, however, was pulled by two horses; it was a Cadillac of buggies.

Their sled was a two-horse model also. And it provided the better ride, traversing as it did a smooth surface. Regardless of mode, though, a visit to Cresco tied up a day. Even the rare road horses (as opposed to common plow horses) averaged less than 5 mph. A 28-mile round trip therefore absorbed close to six hours of travel time. Preparing the harnesses and animals subtracted an hour more. Cooling down, watering, feeding and resting the tired creatures misspent another hour of human exertion *after each leg*.

Squandering nine hours from a day threatened life itself. Time being the currency of survival and with existence already in doubt, the civilization 14 miles beyond the front gate had to remain *terra incognita*. For months on end, its exciting sights were merely the stuff of dreams.

At the Borlaug home that distant domain evidenced its presence only rarely, usually in the form of a singular sound that pierced the shroud of seclusion on a few very special occasions.

For the Borlaugs noise was a novelty. For years on end a soothing stillness clung about them like a quilt. Other than nature's melodies there were few sounds to tickle the eardrums, especially during winter, when their sanctuary was sated with silence.

When the Twentieth Century was still a teenager mechanical sounds were exotic enough to seem fantastic. The Borlaugs never heard a dishwasher, refrigerator, heating or cooling system, radio, television or power equipment—none of which existed. And the ring of a telephone never broke the stillness; only 1 in 20 American homes had a phone, and almost none happened to be in farm country.

Outside the house the soundscape was all-natural too. There was of course no hum of electrical wires, drone of aircraft, rumble of truck or clank of tractor. Sirens couldn't penetrate the complete quietude; police cruisers, fire trucks and motorized ambulances had yet to appear. The only thing to disturb the tranquility of the ribbon of dirt over the front fence was the Model T Ford that puttered past a few times a day.

The singular sound that on very special occasions shattered the solid shroud of seclusion was a train whistle. And even it remained beyond earshot except for a notable night every year or two when the temperature toyed with 25 below and the wind struggled to raise a whisper:

> On those utterly still nights we sat freezing on the porch just to enjoy the puffing of the steam locomotive and the hoot of the engineer's whistle as the 9-PM Milwaukee Road pulled out of Cresco. It was the one time we sensed we were part of a wider sphere. Those sound waves were our sole connection to the world.

In the fall of 1918, when the boy was four and a half, the outer realm penetrated rather more ominously. That morning he was outside "helping" his grandmother make soap. Twice a year she produced a dozen blocks of hard brown laundry soap by boiling a packet of lye with a slab of lard from a pig grudgingly and guiltily sacrificed to their own personal needs. Cleanliness, however, was critical.

As a hardscrabble farmwife Emma Borlaug was necessarily serious and unsentimental, but over her grandchild she cast a spirit of loving friendship that resonated warmth and wellbeing. The tallest member of the family—heightened even more by a roll of gray hair pinned up in the Gibson-Girl image of glamour and good taste—she cut an imposing figure. Of all her talents the greatest was patience. With the tiny tyke, she talked endlessly about this or that or nothing whatever.

Soapmaking always involved such chit-chatter while the lard and lye bubbled in a big black iron pot erected over the firepit behind the house. But this time when little Norm mentioned the strangely scary smoke he'd smelled all morning his grandmother made no response.

That departure from custom was perturbing; silence separated like never before. When he asked again, she merely grunted in her surprisingly tenor tones, "It's from Minnesota," and left the words hanging in the air, which was crackle-dry from weeks of drought.

To a toddler that made no sense. Minnesota was some galaxy far, far away. Only much later did he perceive that Emma was afraid. At the time, her deep voice, startling height and broad shoulders made her seem incapable of anxiety. The silence must have affected her too. "There's a fire up there," she finally snapped.

Looking back through the lens of a lifetime, he sees an old lady trying to avoid infecting fear on a four-year-old. And the situation was indeed fearful. The parched piney woods around Cloquet and Moose Lake caught fire on Saturday October 12. Next day they blew up like a box of matches. By Tuesday 1500 square miles of Minnesota and Wisconsin had been consumed, including 27 towns and 500 humans.

Cloquet and Moose Lake were nearly 250 miles to the north, yet Norm still senses the menacing mantle of odor and awe that enshrouded the Borlaug place. Conflagrations in Minnesota's "Big Woods" were known as Hinckley Fires, a term conjuring fear even during his boyhood—more than two decades after the one that loaned the rest its name.

Back then, on September 1, 1894, the air across the Big Woods had also been crackle-dry. No rain had fallen since April and an eerie yellow haze hung heavy. Suddenly, around 1 o'clock in the afternoon a satanic specter brighter than the sky loomed on the southern horizon. And then, hellfire itself rolled over Hinckley and its 1200 inhabitants.

Panicked, more than a hundred citizens dived into a damp depression beside the railroad tracks. "When the fire wave hit that swamp," an eyewitness reported, "there was one piercing cry of mortal anguish; then everything was still, except for the howling of the wind."

Next came one of history's great unsung acts of courage. Quite unaware of the danger ahead, a little train approached Hinckley from the north pulling a line of almost empty passenger cars. Suddenly, from the Duluth Limited's locomotive, engineer Jim Root spied a host of humanity running toward him up the track. Behind them gaped something like the Fiery Gates, opened wide enough to expose the Devil in person.

Thinking fast, Root yanked the brake lever, stepped down and hustled aboard what have been described as "women with singed hair, men lacking eyebrows and kids with fear-crazed eyes." All 300 or so.

Then, remembering a waterhole the locals called Skunk Lake six miles back the way he'd just come, Root clambered up into his cab, reversed the steam lever, and pulled the throttle wide open. By the time the Duluth Limited was reversing at full speed the sky-high curtain of fire had caught up. Flames were racing ahead along both sides. Below, the ties securing the rails were igniting in gouts of smoky submission.

Soon Root saw smoke billowing from the caboose—that being the front of the train, the wind of passage was acting as Beelzebub's bellows. Then the curtains of his cab caught; solder dripped from the lamp; flame pixies danced along the woodwork beside his head; the steam levers' wooden handles singed his hands. Suddenly a window exploded, scything glass shards into his neck and forehead.

HELL ON . . .

In 1894 the Duluth Limited delivered 300 people to Skunk Lake just as the Hinckley Firestorm swept overhead. During a similar firestorm in 1918 Norm saw his grandmother's fear and knew that the previous tragedy still haunted her memory.

. . . WHEELS

Norm was then 4 years old and life remained charged with the same danger and doubt Emma knew as a girl. He literally lived in the past, and neither he nor anyone else knew that unimaginable technologies were about to change everything.

Fireman Jack McGowan sprinkled water over the suffering engineer. Though in no great shape himself, he saved the day when Root tumbled to the floor in agony. Grabbing his limp partner by the collar, McGowan plunked him back on the driver's seat. Then he tossed a bucketful of water smack into the engineer's face. "Good," Jim Root said, "that's good."

Minutes later, the firestorm's smoky heart pressed all around, so no one could know where they were. But coal burning merrily in the tender cast a twinkling glow and, staring sideways, Root sensed its glare reflecting off something shiny. Praying that silvery gleam in the darkling void signified water, he released the steam valve and hauled on the brake handle.

As the Duluth Limited slid to a stop the passengers piled off, kicked barbed wire from a fence beside the tracks, and flung themselves forward into the abyss. Five months of drought had reduced Skunk Lake to a pit of slimy scum barely 18 inches deep. Squirming into the slop, the terrified throng tugged their mud-dampened shirts and blouses over their heads as a roof of fire enclosed the scene.

They were just in time. Within seconds the thundering flames had passed on to finer pastures. The train had passed on too. "In place of the elegant coaches," a participant recorded, "were bare trucks covered by a mass of iron work and debris."

But Engineer Root remained. And the men, women and children he'd hauled from Hinckley remained. All who'd kept their nerve and stayed aboard had survived.

This is just one among many incidents triggered by a conflagration that in just four hours engulfed more than 400 square miles, destroying six towns and perhaps 1000 people, including a whole Indian band. It is said that the pillar of flame towered upward four and a half miles and that terrified Iowans 200 miles away stared at the monstrous redness standing on their northern horizon, and quaked.

Being just 25 miles from the state line, Norm's grandparents were suitably situated. Likely, Nels and Emma saw that shaft of red radiance pierce the tranquil afternoon and mushroom to form an enormous roseate sky.

As far as Norm recalls this was never mentioned but, based on her attitude the morning in 1918 when they made soap over a backyard firepit, he's sure Emma Borlaug saw the 1894 Hinckley Firestorm when she was 30, and the sight sent a shiver of terror down the rest of her days.

1918-1919

Mortality

This old incident symbolizes the essence of the frontier drama: the horror, helplessness, courage, tragedy, and ultimate survival of the luckiest. Previous Borlaug generations experienced all those in goodly measure. Indeed, long after the frontier was foreclosed the boy's grandparents continued to exude the pioneer's rude attributes, most notably fortitude. Like their Viking forebears, Emma and Nels accepted whatever fate provided, and fashioned from it a family.

In this spirit of fate-based forbearance, those elders welcomed Norm and his parents into their home. All three generations lived together, grew together, worked the hundred-acres, and collectively cared for the humble two-bedroom farmhouse that half a century earlier had been a log cabin on the empty plain. This refuge was their rock.

To the little boy growing up in that ancient abode Nels Borlaug was more god than guy. To others, however, the grandfather hardly seemed blessed by supernatural heritage. Of average size and trim build, he had pinched-features, a weather-beaten face, graying close-cropped hair and a droopy white-flecked mustache. Everyone agreed, however, that his Nordic eyes set him apart; they were arctic-blue and intense enough to seem incandescent.

Nels was the youngest son of Ole and Solveig Borlaug, who in 1847 had abandoned a tiny plot beside a fjord in central Norway to sample Wisconsin and Dakota Territory and finally settle in the top right hand corner of Iowa, in an area most called Saude but some dubbed Little Norway.

Nels often entranced his little grandson with tales of life on the cutting edge. For almost 70 years on the plains the family members had cracked their hands and their heads working American land, while planting their blood along with the crops.

FOREBEARS RECALLED BY . . .

Probably taken in 1898, the photo shows Norm's grandparents Emma (34) and Nels (39) with their sons: Oscar (12), Henry (Norm's father, 9) and Ned (3). Thanks to them, Norm committed his life to helping hard working food producers. From birth, he understood that no one is smarter than those who have to feed themselves by their own sweat, strength and struggle—nor more deserving of respect, either.

. . . AN ADMIRING DESCENDANT

When baby Norm joined the family, the statuesque Emma lovingly tended him, but it was the self-confident Nels who set the boy's course in life:

Granddad Nels told me many lively stories, most of them in lilting Norwegian, which is probably why they had such an impact.

His tales were mostly drawn from his own youthful experience. Like millions of northern European immigrants, his parents reached the Midwest via the Great Lakes. Ole and Solveig initially farmed near Green Bay, Wisconsin, where he and two older brothers were born. While Nels was still a baby, however, they bought a covered wagon and moved to a larger farm at Norway Grove, Wisconsin. Later, they headed for Dakota Territory and settled on the banks of the Missouri, near today's Vermillion, South Dakota. They appeared to have found their promised land until rebellious Sioux began taking white scalps. Then, 23 immigrant families—all of them Norwegian—re-harnessed their oxen to the now very rickety prairie schooners and headed *eastwards*. Going the wrong way, they settled in Iowa at a spot they wryly called "New Oregon."

Northeastern Iowa was quite unlike Norway, and when I finally visited the tiny ancestral plot of land on the steep and stony banks of Sogne Fjord I knew Nels' parents, my great grandparents, had survived on potatoes. Moreover, I knew they'd fallen victim to the blight that devastated Europe's potato crop in the 1840s. Like millions of Irish, the Borlaugs had fled to America just for food.

I was born into that era when crop disease often forced people to flee. Despite almost seven decades trying to find enough to eat, my family had yet to escape famine's clutch. Even in 20th Century America fate, fungi, and finding daily bread controlled Borlaug lives.

Neither the passing of the pioneering age nor his own fluent English had rid Nels of the pleasure of speaking Norwegian. And in the boy's malleable mind its lilting rhythms endowed the old man's diverting discourses super strength. "It was Granddad," he says with a wry smile of recollection, "who most influenced my young life."

Although not big, tall, loud, forceful or assertive, Nels Borlaug constituted the demigod every subsistence farm required. Combining Norse fire and horse sense, he exuded natural leadership and earned the family's undying trust the hard way. You see, his frontier spirit, fortitude, and fine-tuned knowledge of the soil and weather in their tiny sliver of Mid-America was what kept them all alive.

Regardless of rapport, grandfather and grandson were far from buddies. The old man's eyes often alighted on the tiny towhead more with admonition than affection. As the oldest grandchild, Norm had to learn to lead the family onward when his turn came. But the standards to be met were not those dredged from mythical memories. No, the grandfather always stared forward. And somewhere out there, he'd spotted a finer future. Norm remembers the result:

> We saw no possible prospect of change. But if Granddad saw a better world ahead, we had to make ourselves worthy to meet it.

Surviving in faith-based farming demands such conviction. And because existence constituted a massive trust in the here-to-come the dinner talk often turned to education. None of them knew much about this mystery. Norm's parents had gotten to sixth grade. The grandparents had no formal learning, for in their day you had to pay to go to school. Yet Nels was the one who pushed education the hardest:

> Granddad grew up before school became compulsory, and was largely self-taught. But he was passionately devoted to learning, insisting that it was the only protection you could count on when times got tough. "Think for yourself, Norm Boy!" he'd bellow at me. "Fill your head now to fill your belly later!"

Such sentiments needed constant repetition since country kids could merely sample school. Most days they had to stay home and do chores. Boys fed horses, milked cows, churned butter, butchered chickens and picked corn. Girls separated milk, washed and ironed clothes, plucked chickens, cooked meals, and tended the vegetable garden.

Yet whilst farm kids could attend only part-time and few stayed past eighth grade, school was honored above all else. Even church! That suspect order of priority was actually sensible: Learning, after all, lifted present life and offered an escape from the horrors of here-and-now.

Naturally, each child walked to school and, because the law required that none hike more than two miles, rural elementary schools were scattered like confetti over the plains and prairies. Most were one-room boxes hardly more than highbrow hencoops. Typically each stood in solitary splendor in a farm field, unencumbered by surrounding structures. Other, that is, than two little outhouses.

The single classroom served every grade. Kids aged 5 through 17 learned their lessons side-by-side, absorbing as much from each other as from the gangly alien in their midst.

Norm smiles when he recalls the New Oregon Rural District School Number 8. Its lessons for living were what sustained him during the very long and very turbulent times to come. Here's how he sums it up:

Our learning often seemed more a civic duty than an academic duty. Each school day, for instance, opened with us shouting the Iowa Corn Song refrain:

> *We're from I-O-way, I-O-way.*
> *State of all the land*
> *Joy on ev-'ry hand.*
> *We're from I-O-way, I-O-way.*
> **That's** *where the tall corn grows.*

We were so proud we lived where the tall corn grew.

Though scholars may scoff at teaching sentiment to children, they're wrong to do so. Our elementary schooling was a preparation for life not for academic achievement. It succeeded largely by providing pride, poise and self-confidence as well as a code by which to measure ourselves.

Through its moral maxims we gained lifelong structural support because we knew where we stood, even though it was a very small spot. Overall, we gained what is, I think, the first requirement for a life of achievement: a solid place to step off from.

The mental osmosis that provided an intense pride in his special little place on earth would serve him well. But in time, sad to relate, he'd do much to turn that Iowa state song into nonsense verse.

Getting yourself to school contributed to the self-reliance so vital in a life of isolation. Each morning and afternoon little Norm trekked a mile-and-a-half through spring rains and fall mud and, yes, winter slush and snow. A ride was not possible even in winter: crank-starting a cold engine being so difficult that vehicles were dinosaurs during that half the calendar. Ice was actually welcomed on the roads to ease the passage of sleigh and sled.

During the winter of 1919, when he was in first grade and the only way to forecast the weather was to eye the sky, a bone-chilling wind suddenly whipped across the world. Within the schoolhouse the children shivered as frigid fingers pierced the flimsy walls. The biggest boy, Herbert Lee, tossed wood into the stove until its potbelly glowed as purple as a Bing cherry. Still they all shivered.

Early that afternoon the sky darkened, and with it the room. The teacher, Lena Halvorson, lit the oil lamps and cracked open the door to find a snow curtain obscuring the road, which was almost within spitting distance. Worse, the blizzard seemed to be intensifying; the wind rising in fury, the temperature tumbling; and the snow cascading like Niagara.

THE STEPPING-OFF PLACE

Borlaug is a proud product of a tuition tradition now deemed hopelessly outmoded: the one-room school. Here's his take:

When I entered the New Oregon Rural District School Number Eight in 1919 nothing had changed since its construction in 1865. The weather-worn, clapboard structure was set back from a dirt road on land loaned by a farmer. Except for two crude outhouses (boys on left; girls on right), it stood entirely alone, without a playground, fence or driveway.

Apart from a little foyer for wet coats and lunchboxes, the building was a single room, with high windows, bare floorboards and two rows of desks. Usually a dozen or so students attended, but when the fields were too frozen for farm work an additional half-dozen might come.

The desks were burnished by half a century of use and most had been secretly scored by the jackknives boys carried. I even noticed my father's initials, which added to a sense of continuity. He, my grandfather, an aunt, sundry uncles and cousins had all occupied those very same desks.

Sharing their lives was a comfort. They'd walked the same route to school, some from the same house I lived in; they'd suffered the same problems and surmounted them. That knowledge smoothed my progress; if they could do it, I could too.

Every school year included many days of below-zero weather. A potbelly stove provided our only heat. Each day an older child brought in firewood or coal from the pile outside. The rest of us aspired to that superhuman responsibility with all our little hearts. Still and all, frigid air seeped through cracks between the floorboards as well as through the thin, un-insulated walls. It sometimes seemed to inhabit our bones.

Other than the stove, the room's main fixture was a slate blackboard stretching across the front wall behind the teacher's desk. Above it, and in clear sight, rested a hickory stick about three feet long. (It was the disciplinary device of last resort, the ruler being much handier.) Near the blackboard, on a single tiny bookshelf, stood a single-volume encyclopedia, a Webster's Dictionary, about a dozen children's books and not much more of note. Down one side wall were white cards demonstrating the smooth swirling letters of someone's patented penmanship, which I must say never did me much good. There was also a big-lettered wall-chart listing the foods we should eat: MEAT, MILK, EGGS, FISH.

Progress in school was judged less by going from grade to grade than reader to reader. These books, which taught both English and moral fiber, came in five levels of difficulty. The last was remarkably advanced, taking us into Emerson, Whittier and Longfellow. By then, we'd covered a lot of literature in our short lives.

Graduating from one reader to the next was a big deal. Adults often asked which we were on, and if we were behind for our age we felt the sting of shame. Everybody knew exactly which reader you should be on; they'd been there too. In this way, those language guides provided an ever-present goad to conform to community expectations.

Each day the teacher led all eight grades through their separate lessons. During a single half-hour she might deal with five-year-olds to seventeen-year-olds. Most sessions were five-minute briefings; the learning was left to us. Seldom were there more than three students in a grade, and we'd be called to the front of the room, given instructions and handed an assignment. The work was done on our reserved section of the blackboard or on the slates we kept in our desks.

Many lessons involved recitation rather than writing. We read aloud, spelled aloud, and sung out grammar drills and multiplication tables at our little voice-box's highest volume settings. Spelling bees were held Fridays. There were also verbal vocabulary exercises, many of which involved reading poetry aloud. My favorites were Whittier's "Still Sits the Schoolhouse by the Road" and Longfellow's "Hiawatha."

Everyday the room echoed these torrents of purposeful noise, and it seems to me now that the younger kids absorbed a lot when the older ones were reciting multiplication tables, spelling and poems. We heard things "in deep background" for years before and after we got to them.

Also the older kids helped the younger ones, thereby helping both. That was the one-room school's ultimate strength: children learn fast from each other and build a lifetime bond.

Along with everything else, one-room school teachers—and nationally there were more than 100,000, many scarcely older or wiser than their pupils—faced life-or-death decisions with no one to call on. That afternoon of the blizzard, an anxious Lena Halvorson explained she'd walk six children home in the direction of Protivin, the Bohemian town to the east. Norm and the half-dozen others from Saude, the Norwegian community to the south, would have to make it home alone.

He recalls the sequel:

> There were about seven of us in the straggling line. As the smallest, I took my proper place in the middle. Children always moved Indian file through deep snow, the biggest boys breaking the trail while the biggest girls stayed in back watching over the little ones, who fitted themselves between.
>
> That order of march was never written down; it just came by instinct, like baby ducks waddling from the nest. And that day the journey was terrible. We trudged through the swirling whiteness, leaning on the wind, blinded by the sleet and struggling against the clinging waist-deep snow.
>
> I was miserable. Icy drafts slipped through my clothes and sliced the skin like a scalpel. It was hard to get a breath. Snow clung to my face, mittens, jacket. The melt inside my boots numbed my feet. I began stumbling. Soon it became too much to bear. Weariness pervaded every sense, including common sense. There was just one thing to do: I lay down to cry myself to sleep snuggled in the soft white shroud nature had so conveniently provided.
>
> Then a hand yanked my scarf away, grabbed my hair, and jerked my head up. Above me was a face tight-lipped with anger and fright. It was my cousin Sina. "Get up!" she screamed. "Get up!" She began slapping me over the ears. "Get up! Get up!"
>
> The other children were clustered round. There was fear in their voices. Some of the young ones were crying.
>
> Finally, Herbert Lee hoisted me onto my tired little legs. Sina took my hand and got me walking again. She was 12, sweet-tempered, and filled with self-assured authority.
>
> I was in tears when we entered the warm kitchen. I knew I'd let everyone down. But Grandmother Emma was as calm and goodhearted as ever. She'd just emptied her big wood-fired oven and the house smelled of yeast and hot bread.
>
> I've never forgotten that comforting fragrance. No food was ever so sweet as those loaves Grandmother baked the day when I was five and nearly died.

Death in those days was a presence. Every family bore private tragedies implanted like burrs beneath the breastbone. Indeed, grief and fear lurked just below the skin of society. Around the time of Borlaug's birth, American life expectancy was 46 years for men and 48 years for women.

Disease was the primary killer. Infections were everywhere . . . they were unstoppable . . . and they were monsters of every mind. From the expeditionary force President Wilson finally dispatched to the bizarre orgy of foreign self-destruction in France pneumonia alone claimed 40,000—a tally approaching the 54,000 ascribed to combat. And America attended what we now call World War I for a mere 19 months.

Mainly, though, premature mortality was due to the invisible enemies of childhood. Scarlet fever, diphtheria, measles (two types), mumps, whooping cough, croup, grippe, chickenpox, smallpox, tonsillitis, tuberculosis, infantile paralysis, and appendicitis were common enough to be considered normal—some said necessary—rites of early passage. Problem was, many a child failed to emerge on the far side. Out of every thousand American babies born in 1915, a hundred never enjoyed a single birthday.

To life's terrors was added the inability to avoid contagion's carriers. Insects were the worst. They were especially bad on farms, where flies remained omnipresent owing to the privy, the manure pile, and the cowpies littering the fields. Strangely, people liked having the barnyard, or at least the horse trough, near the house. No wonder typhoid, diarrhea, cholera and dysentery were widespread. Dysentery was familiar enough to be named "Summer Complaint," as if it were a seasonal feature of every year, which it was. Whenever temperatures soared, Summer Complaint reappeared like some disreputable relative who knew where a good church picnic could be found.

Beyond its prevalence, disease was paralyzing because there was no way to counter it. Whenever a child had a fever, a cut or a pain, everyone's eyes would glisten with dread. Tomorrow could open a void in the rest of existence.

What's more, a sick person endangered everyone. Officialdom therefore responded by locking the victim up with family and fate, tagging the house with a big yellow sign bearing commands such as: CONTAGION—KEEP OUT or QUARANTINE SCARLET FEVER or QUARANTINE—SMALLPOX.

Usually an official in suit and tie arrived from the sheriff's office or public health department and coldly and quickly hammered the terrifying manifesto beside your front door. The capitalized lettering was bold enough for every passerby to imbibe the subliminal message: BEWARE OF THESE PEOPLE.

HEARTBREAK . . .

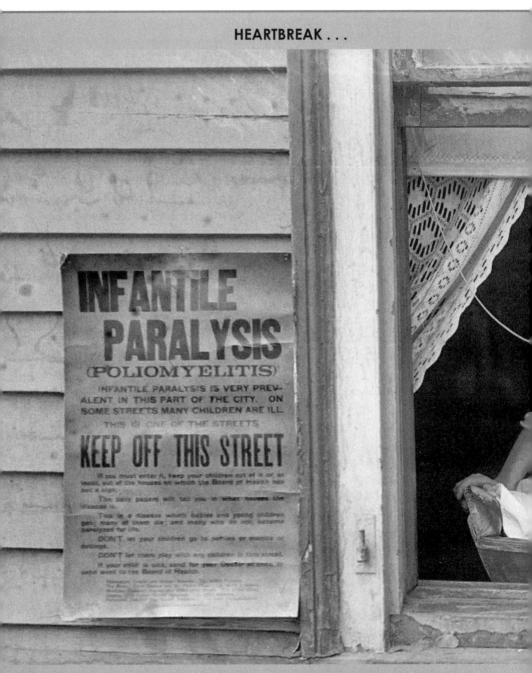

As the uncontested masters of human fate throughout the pre-modern era, contagions could turn a baby into a public enemy. Warnings instructing everyone to "KEEP OFF THIS STREET" were common. Some were to avoid a child—like this one.

. . . HOME

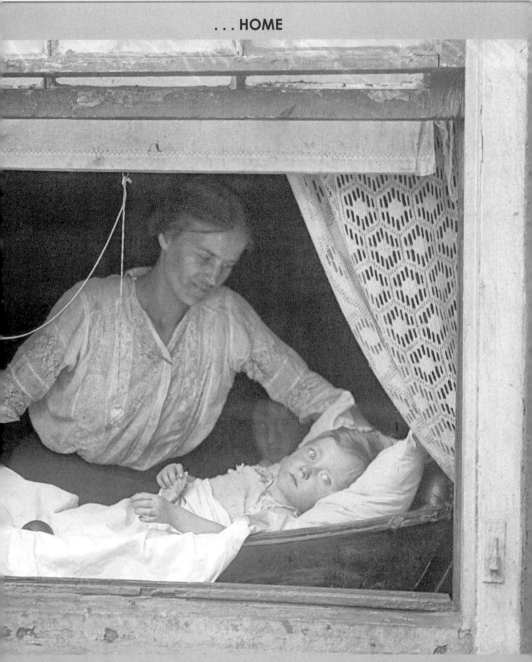

Thanks to science, poliomyelitis is nowadays nearly gone from the earth; almost no one faces the possibility of polio paralysis like this little girl. How far we've traveled during the span of Borlaug's lifetime. And how little we appreciate it.

All of this climaxed with the merciless microbe that liquefied lungs. Misnamed "Spanish Influenza," it apparently arose in an army camp in northeast Kansas in the spring of 1918. That was around the time Norm was celebrating his fourth birthday, just 300 miles to the northeast.

The Kansan contagion subsided quickly, and locals breathed a sigh of relief. But during the following months it quietly stowed away on the troopships and crossed the Atlantic with the conscripts.

Rested and reborn in France during August, this rogue raider seized the chance of a lifetime and raced through the packed camps and trenches. Its timing was terrible; freighters were then steaming from French ports toward every point of the compass. On board they carried the most heartbreaking cargo—and not just the youths who'd been gassed or shot or blown apart. Late in 1918, flu outbreaks sprang up simultaneously from Spitsbergen in the high Arctic to Southland, New Zealand, the last stop before the South Pole.

The U.S. was especially hard hit. By October, a fifth of all stateside soldiers were out of action. Some Army units had four out of five doughboys either in sickbed or deathbed. Camp Devens, for example, found its first case September 12. Within six days it had almost 7000. And a week later there were almost 13,000. The military brass in that infantry installation in Ayer, near Boston, had to order up special trains just to haul away bodies.

Civilians were equally at risk. Cities typically saw half their citizens fall victim, and many succumb. Massachusetts was especially hard hit: in about a year one Bostonian in ten had perished. At recess, local schoolgirls were jumping rope to an ironic new ditty:

I had a little bird
its name was Enza.
I opened the window
and in flew Enza.

That was about the sum of it; you breathed in some fresh air… and Destiny came along for the ride. Anyone could understand why Italian physicians in the Middle Ages had concluded such diseases descended by celestial "influence."

Soon the amorphous force descended on other eastern cities. The second week of October saw 2600 Philadelphians perish; the third week it was 4500. In seven days New York City lost 9000.

And the reality was worse than the numbers suggest. To the dismay of friends and relatives, the bodies were often purple or black. Death carts roamed the streets and families dumped their loved-one's repellent remains curbside, to be picked up like garbage.

Eventually corpses blocked the gutters . . . there were just not enough garbage men or gravediggers, let alone caskets. For a while in New York little boxes bearing dead babies and toddlers stretched several blocks, stacked 8 or 10 high.

Inevitably, doomsayers invoked visitations beyond human understanding. Their conclusion was hard to contest. Wasn't this the long anticipated Day of Reckoning? No natural event had killed so many American sinners, and it spread by means mysterious enough to be preternatural. Surely, He'd chosen this as the way to end the world.

On that score, few people had any doubt. The infection clearly had paranormal powers because all preventive efforts failed. It is reported that public drinking fountains were hourly sterilized with blowtorches, telephones were swabbed with alcohol, people wore muslin masks, and none dared shake hands.

Still the silent killer spread.

Panic then engulfed every other emotion, and families withdrew unto themselves. Orderly existence then began collapsing. Relatives refused to visit relatives; children were kept from friends; towns erected signs demanding strangers stay out.

With every state haunted by an invisible prowler, Americans retreated into hibernation: schools, libraries, playgrounds, churches, theaters, cinemas, stage shows, sporting events, stock markets, pool halls and other places of work and amusement padlocked their doors. The World War victory celebrations fixed for early 1919 fizzled because too few people turned out to cheer soldiers who marched with large white masks smothering their pride. Police and fire departments barely functioned. On the Surgeon General's advice, the District of Columbia declared "indoor public assemblages constitute a public menace at this time." Washington thereupon banned all meetings, its only *raison d'être*.

Because nothing brought relief, the suffering hordes ended up forlorn and forsaken. With the local hospitals overwhelmed, city fathers staked out areas beyond the town limits and erected tent facilities, and let them devolve into squalid exits from existence.

Though America had hardened its heart, the virus remained unfazed. Being vital and vigorous, it exercised the democratic prerogative: felling young and old, strong and weak, rich and poor, urban and rural—all without regard to race, color or creed.

HEALTHCARE...

St Louis, 1918. Red Cross workers pick up a body at the corner of Etzel and Page Avenues. During the half year in which 100,000 Americans died of flu *each month* brave people like these attended to the sick, the dying and the dead.

... HEROES

For performing their duty and putting themselves in harm's way, many such caregivers paid the ultimate price. Norman Borlaug was then 4 years old, and this was the reality of life in America and most of the world.

The horror hit home when you got a cough you couldn't control. Soon thereafter you'd begin gasping for breath as the virus hijacked your oxygen-transfer cells for its own procreation. Although most victims endured days of agonizing uncertainty, some felt a slight tickle in the morning, collapsed in the afternoon, breathed their last in the evening. The pain was mainly in the mind, as the lungs morphed to mucus and the bloodstream accumulated carbon dioxide until your skin darkened and you quietly suffocated in your own sputum.

Eventually, the Purple Death took to the rails and crossed half the continent to detrain in Northeast Iowa. Still vivid in Norm's memory is the dread pervading the air late in 1919 when the Thomas Borlaugs were stricken:

> That family had ten members, one of whom was my cousin Sina. They weren't allowed outside even to milk the cows or get food.
>
> Thus, each day for two weeks Grandmother Emma carried two big kettles of soup almost a mile to their farm. I went along, but we never dared enter the house. We placed the kettles on the porch and whisked away the empties. Although they'd already been scoured and scrubbed, Grandmother scalded them for an hour before refilling them with soup next day.
>
> What was it like for all my cousins, my great-aunt and my great-uncle trapped within that small house? That's troubling to think about. We never saw them. However, standing on the porch one day I noticed the curtains flutter.
>
> Sometimes I still wonder about that lost soul peering through the lace. How agonizing it must have been to see me so alive and so blessedly free.

Nationwide, this ghastly event killed more than the Great War, taking perhaps even as many lives as the Civil War—600,000. And behind its power and prevalence lay a deeply disturbing driving force: Undernourishment.

Of course, no American in 1918 realized that poor nutrition predisposed them to death and disease. How could they? Nutritional science was so rudimentary it could barely be called a science. The word "vitamin" had been around merely seven years, and remained a technical term. Even the few nutritionists had little appreciation for vitamins, most of which would hide from human understanding for years to come.

In April 1921 the consequences of nutritional ignorance struck the Borlaugs. Upon awakening one frosty morning the sleepy seven-year-old stumbled downstairs to find Granddad Nels' house a-bustle. Why were so many relatives visiting? Why were they in their Sunday best? What was happening?

No one explained. Then his father steered him away from the well-turned-out multitude and back up to the attic where the children slept. Quietly he announced there'd be no school that day; Little Norm was to stay upstairs and look after his two sisters, who were then 5 and 2. He had to keep them occupied *all day.*

Why?

Another baby had joined the family.

A baby brother?

No, a sister. Her name was Helen, and he could see her later.

On a mind so young and so impressionable the mystery surrounding his new sister left an indelible memory:

> Father didn't seem happy. Nor did Mother. That afternoon when I was ushered into their bedroom she lay still, eyes moist and reddened, and said not a word. Nearby in a little wooden cradle the baby also lay quiet and unmoving. The stillness and silence made the scene very scary.
>
> For three days the house hung with gloom; on the fourth, Father held my hand and walked me into the yard.
>
> Helen had gone back to heaven, he said.

After the burial in the church cemetery, Granddad Nels grabbed a couple of fishing poles and guided the bewildered boy to the stream behind the house.

As they sat together beside the gentle waters, he explained the situation: It was all part of life . . . nothing could be done . . . you just had to get over it.

Stoic endurance was then the foundation of sanity. Grieving for children was so commonplace it had to be accepted and put behind. You couldn't do more. It was God's plan. You just had to get over it.

Norm still isn't sure why his sister died. Probably, baby Helen was foredoomed because Mrs. Borlaug's pregnancy included the long winter months during which a balanced diet was beyond reach. It might have been a lack of folic acid (which wouldn't be named, let alone understood, for another 20 years). Or it could have been a deficiency in any number of other vitamins.

The death may even have been due to goiter. Shortly thereafter Clara Borlaug's throat swelled until it looked like a budding football. That indicator of extreme iodine deficiency was a common sight in the Upper Midwest, where Ice-Age glaciers had stripped the land of soil and its attendant minerals. Babies born to goitered mothers commonly died soon after birth.

A s we've said, these were routine experiences for every previous generation. Even during this boy's childhood—in other words, within living memory—no one was ever far from a half dozen modes of malnutrition. During winter months, fresh fruits were beyond reach, regardless of how rich or health conscious you might be and regardless also of any special need, such as pregnancy, sickness, blood loss or youthful growth spurt.

Little Norm got one orange a year—at the church Christmas Eve celebration. Every child in the village looked forward to that special treat from on high. Even now it is recalled with ineffable joy:

> That orange was something we dreamed about all year. Actually, though, a banana was the greater prize. However, if we ever got one of those during a year—and sometimes we didn't—it was usually half rotten.

One thing is clear: in those days this lively lad wasn't getting his vitamins. Fruits and vegetables were plentiful enough in season, but the season passed in a flash. Without cool stores and refrigerated transport no one could deliver perishables from warm climates, so, above all its other hazards, winter was a nutritional nightmare. A family that failed to stockpile its own vegetables or fruits went without for months. Indeed, from November to April most Americans were affected by deficiencies of vitamins A, C and D, not to mention minerals.

The Borlaugs kept vegetables in the "root cellar," a room much more common in rural houses than a bathroom. The carrots, turnips, cabbages, potatoes and onions hibernating in the tubs of sand below stairs were required to last all winter. They were the only foods that were fresh.

With warmth's return during springtime the family spent days jointly planting radishes, potatoes, sweet corn, tomatoes, carrots, peas, string beans, lettuce and maybe more. Only when the radishes matured did the daily diet recover some balance. Those spicy roots have fallen from favor, but back then their ability to mature within a month meant they filled a critical slot in the continuum of survival. During April and May millions ate radish, less for taste than for more time on earth.

With summer's arrival the family members began scavenging every morsel of edible plant material the property could disgorge. Throughout the warm season Norm and his sisters gathered blackberries, raspberries, chokecherries, currents and gooseberries in the woodlot behind the farm fields. In the fall, they picked apples, cherries and plums from the trees beside the house.

Most of that harvest got boiled in big pots and sealed into Mason jars. The procedure, strangely called "cold packing," absorbed many woman-months. To our modern eye the process may seem no big deal, but coming on top of hundred-degree summer heat, the boiling caldrons and blazing firebox turned the house into a living approximation of Hades' lowest circle.

That hothouse effect, however, had to be endured: getting the garden into glass was necessary to ensure existence.

A ctually, such things as root cellars, cold packing, and exiling the sick signified a giant leap from the way humans in the temperate zones eked out survival during all previous centuries. As recently as the 1400s median life expectancy had been 24 years. By the time of Borlaug's youth things had improved so much that, dietarily speaking, he could have been in the 1700s. Some seer has pointed out that people of his time ate the same foods in the same seasonal sequence as the Founding Fathers. No question, George Washington and Thomas Jefferson would feel quite at home dining with the Borlaugs in 1919.

For all its inherent value, however, cold packing could hardly be called adequate. Among other things, it failed to eliminate *Clostridium botulinum*, the bacterium producing perhaps the most powerful poison known. That toxin, now deified by the name "Botox," sometimes lofted whole families to the pearly gates at a single sitting.

Certainly, home processing was too unreliable for a national food supply. That became clear in 1917, when four of every ten draftees for Great War duty were declared unfit for service, due mostly to problems traceable to bad diet during babyhood. American men then averaged 5 foot 7 inches and 135 pounds.

The revelation that the most progressive of all nations harbored hidden hunger galvanized the politicos. But because nothing could be done directly, they had to fall back on making women work harder. Thus, after 1917 universities established nutrition departments and most states hammered into high-school girls' heads a newly sautéed subject called "Domestic Science" (later downgraded to "Home Economics").

These food-based fancies proved novel enough that few people could understand them. Or the need. Many resented them for breaking the divinely decreed boundary of elementary education: reading, writing and 'rithmetic. Yet nutrition and domestic science added a notable social good: they amounted to the first collective attempt anywhere on earth to properly feed a populace.

Despite allowing politicians to assume responsibilities God had awarded to the individual and family, these policies also saved lives, improved health, and lurched a developing nation toward a better future. Seen in retrospect, they made modern life possible. Though feeble, these social improvements would in time help Americans make the most of their capabilities. They were, at bottom, the first attempt to free society from Mother Nature's cruel clutch.

In the beginning, however, these newfangled fields of learning had little effect. The disease organisms were the ones needing behavior modification, and in 1919 that was beyond human recognition, let alone reach. Rampant infections, uncertain food production, and chronic malnutrition therefore continued unabated.

During Borlaug's boyhood such things were considered normal because people had yet to learn many perceptions of peril that nowadays seem instinctive. Most of that era's beliefs were time-honored superstitions. Falsity therefore fashioned existence itself, and even the Chosen of God living in the lap of freedom between the Atlantic and Pacific shores could never be really free. In a terrible sense they remained Hunger's hostages.

Find that hard to believe? You're not alone. Among the blessings of the modern era is the fact that most of these hazards have been so long forgotten that pundits refer to the past "The Good Old Days."

The wonderful "simpler time" of wistful nostalgia is, however, merely a foolish conceit derived from a mix of ignorance, forgetfulness and mushy sentiment. The "Good Old Days" never were. Life was then cluttered with concerns that could not be conquered. Providence ruled with cruel malice. The firewall between fate and fortune was narrow and nearby.

Death's omnipresence meant that heartbreaks were common and couldn't be avoided.

The greatest boogey monster—the monarch who ruled humans with and iron hand—was Mother Nature herself.

Obviously that was the celestial plan.

So you just had to get over it.

Even when burying a baby!

1920-1927

Awakening

A s the new decade emerged from its secret hideout in the future Americans discovered an altered world. The Twentieth Century had put adolescence behind, and the newly opened 1920s were proving a paragon of youthful energy, exuberance and idealism. With the end of the War to End All Wars—to say nothing of the wonder of women voters and the power of Prohibition—conflict had been confounded. Now there'd be peace, prosperity and never-ending pleasure. Hardship was history.

For the Republic of Borlaug, however, hardship remained a handmaiden. The inhabitants had no way to plumb the parallel universe otherwise known as United States. Their isolation was absolute.

This was not all bad. Looking back from today's lofty elevation, we can see a special upside: Seclusion lent a powerful sense of place and identity. Suspended in their separate sphere, all three generations floated comfortably around each other. Indeed, the ever-present challenges to existence enclosed them within a harmonious, mutually motivated partnership.

Within this communal cocoon, Norm's parents led by example. Both worked tirelessly, silently and with no complaint. Both possessed the unassertive homespun virtues expected of country yeomanry. And both provided the comity and character that produced a mellow, well-rounded, firmly grounded son.

Compact and barely over 5-feet, Clara Borlaug exemplified the amalgam of dignity and beauty commonly found in rural isolation. Even-tempered and kind, she bestowed warm smiles and soft eyes upon a happy humanity. Probably that warmth was often difficult to deliver, as each day she was required to play her appointed part in the age-old extended-family system—the complex combination of assertive mother, dutiful spouse *and submissive daughter-in-law.*

Henry Borlaug, on the other hand, was too tall for his times. Strangely, though, even at 6-foot-1—fully 6 inches above average—he blended with the crowd just like his wife. A private, soft-spoken, self-effacing farmer without envy or ambition, he remained a force within the family. Although a smile was rare, he cast a spell of solidity that strengthened the son more than rank cheerfulness ever could.

Family relations underwent their first existential test in 1921. That's when their little republic faced a population crisis: the ancient pile had only two bedrooms, and could no longer service three generations. Not only was Norm growing up but so too were his sisters: Palma had arrived in 1916; Charlotte in 1919. The girls now needed the attic for themselves.

Following deep discussions the parents decided there was only one answer: Norm Boy had to leave.

That edict was less horrifying than it might seem:

> Strangely, it wasn't hard being sent away at age seven. The Borlaugs formed a sort of clan; the different branches operated in mutual togetherness. My father's younger brother Ned and his wife Nettie lived about a mile away and then had no children. They made wonderful surrogate parents and treated me like a son right up until they died in the 1970s.

Perhaps he'd have been more upset had banishment from the family hearth been extended. After about a year, however, his parents withdrew their lifesavings from the Cresco Bank and purchased 56 acres next to the ancestral homestead. And on that new island of hope Henry Borlaug spent the better part of 1922 erecting a simple six-room farmhouse as well as the requisite accompaniment of outbuildings.

Then arrived the moment a child would remember forever:

> October 20, 1922 . . . that's when my family left Granddad's house. The day was cold and clear, but once we were settled inside our new home everything was cozy and comforting and fragrant with fresh-cut pinewood and new paint.
>
> For me, the feeling was special; I'd been taken back into the fold. For the first time my parents, my sisters and I were *together and by ourselves.* Our circle was complete; the world seemed right.

In appearance the new farm mimics the pastoral plowlands beloved by primitive artists. Miraculously spurned, or at least neglected, by the Ice Ages, the land remains textured with low hills and shallow valleys. There's even a tiny stream that pierces the timbered hollow behind the house as it hurries southeastward to spill into the Little Turkey River and, after a 70-mile waltz with the willows, donate its crystal trickle to the muddy Mississippi.

Assume it is late July 1925. Anyone venturing along the dusty corrugations called "The County Road" finds complete contentment in the aura surrounding the Borlaug acreage. Exuding stability and security, it is the kind of bucolic spread over which citified sentimentalists rhapsodize. Everything appears trim, serene, stable, orderly and above all white.

Let's paint that farmscape as the passerby sees it.

After daubing in the gray gravel road and proud white picket fence at the very front of the canvas, we turn to the house looming behind. Less American Gothic than frontier blockhouse, it has two stories, with a verandah across the front and an attic window peeping on high. Square and severely symmetrical, it bears two windows upstairs, two downstairs, and a narrow door dead center.

Bordering the steps leading to the front stoop is a neatly clipped hedge of spirea too brilliant even for titanium white. And in the space beside the hedge we struggle to depict Clara Borlaug's sole excess: a bed of peonies—their warm, fleshy, red-and-pink highlights also proving beyond the power of our palette (to say nothing of our talent).

Down the right side of the house, we brush in something that looks like an inverted exclamation point: the gravel driveway that ends where a ring of concrete projects from the soil. That gray circlet encloses a well that operates by the kind of hand pump now used only in fairy tales.

Beyond, and properly veiled by the house, we must sketch a small boxy structure barely bigger than an upright coffin. Like other families across rural America the Borlaugs have no indoor toilet, and they've never seen anything that flushes.

Looking to the right of our canvass, 50 yards out from the driveway, lies the livestock area. Here, the main feature is a long squat barn designed to help three horses, ten beef cattle and twelve milk cows endure the hazards of an Iowa winter. Beside that, sprawls a slat-sided structure, part granary for oats and part crib for corn on the cob. Nearby are three smaller outliers: a rough coop for the chickens, a boxy shed where bacon and ham get smoked, and an exact counterpart where twice a day the cream is separated from the milk. Their purposes may vary, but all are neat, rectangular and a proper shade of whitewash.

In the whole sharp and shiny farmyard scene the sole jarring note is a heap of ratty-looking brown oat straw all shot through with holes like Swiss cheese. Last fall the dozen pigs burrowed cozy caves into the huge

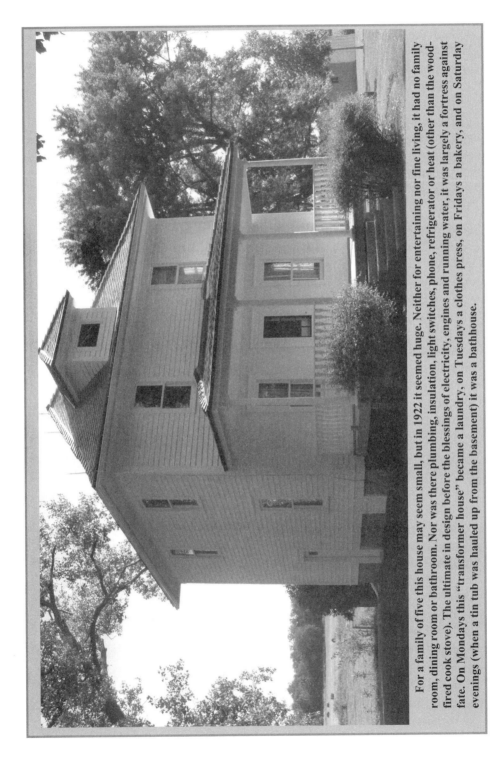

For a family of five this house may seem small, but in 1922 it seemed huge. Neither for entertaining nor fine living, it had no family room, dining room or bathroom. Nor was there plumbing, insulation, light switches, phone, refrigerator or heat (other than the wood-fired cook stove). The ultimate in design before the blessings of electricity, engines and running water, it was largely a fortress against fate. On Mondays this "transformer house" became a laundry, on Tuesdays a clothes press, on Fridays a bakery, and on Saturday evenings (when a tin tub was hauled up from the basement) it was a bathhouse.

straw-stack; nine months onward the unfeeling cattle have surpassed the Big Bad Wolf and *eaten* the pigs out of house and home.

To complete the property's east side, just to the left of the house, we slash broad jade brushstrokes to highlight the U-shaped line of white pines Norm and his dad had planted when construction began three years back. Surprisingly, the trees have already merged into a green wall capable of keeping Arctic blasts from knifing into the Borlaug's thin-skinned shelter nestled behind.

On the blank spot beyond that windbreak's nethermost arm, we must portray the kitchen garden. This being July, its manure-leavened black earth is lined out with rows of various vegetables: olive green, earthy green, even cobalt green for the potatoes that form the family life insurance; should all else fail they'll keep the Borlaugs from starving.

Next to that, dabbing boldly, we brush in the grove of seven apple trees, a cherry and two plums—the fruits are already peering shyly through the foliage. There's also the ragged remains of a Mount Everest of firewood Norm Boy piled up last November, when he was all of ten.

Now we lift our gaze to the picture's middle ground. Stretching border to border directly behind the garden, the house and the farm structures are the open fields. This being high summer, the corn is tasseling. Cadmium Green. The oat grain is ripening. Cobalt Yellow. And the stream rippling through the back right-hand corner is heliographing digitized messages too chaotic for the brush to decode. Its far bank anchors the permanent pasture, complete with ten yearlings and twelve milk cows absorbed in bluegrass delights. Brown Ochre on Emerald Green.

To complete our canvas we finally brush in the backdrop—a tree-filled woodlot and a hayfield primed for mowing. From deep within the straw-colored timothy grass, sassy clover blossoms create a reddish shimmer, like shot-silk in the sun.

The product of our artistry is something glorious—a portrait of a pastoral paradise.

However, you'd only call it that if you didn't live there. For the inhabitants, that farmstead is more akin to pastoral purgatory. The mix of facilities and landscapes takes them at least halfway to hell. Even though farming a single organism is dicey enough, the Borlaugs must master five forms of animal husbandry (horses, pigs, poultry, dairy cows and beef cattle), four types of crop husbandry (corn, oats, hay and permanent pasture) and a couple of hazardous horticultural ventures (vegetables and fruit trees). In each of those eleven taxing intellectual pursuits they must be expert . . . their nutritional well-being, nay their existence, depends thereon.

Regardless of its complexity, clutter and mélange of mischiefs, this busy cosmos typifies the American farm. Spreads of similar form and plan could be seen coast to coast. First and foremost they're designed for survival, not for servicing society. Few produce much for anyone else to eat. Some produce not enough for their owners.

All, however, keep their puppet-masters in perpetual motion.

I magine again you're standing on the road before the Borlaug farm in July 1925, and this time you physically enter its postcard-perfection by striding up the driveway. Taking the stairs beside the spirea hedge and peonies you step through the front door and into another complex, cluttered and quite distinct cosmos. The home turns out to be less a shelter than a factory, laundry, bakery, cannery, and packinghouse.

It had to be all those—cash being too scarce to share with shopkeepers. For the occupants the year's main income is earned on two great occasions. The first is the winter day when Henry Borlaug hitches his horse team to a large sled with wooden sides and hauls a dozen or so hogs along the icy roadbed to Lawler, the nearest railhead. And the second is the sultry summer day when he marches 5 or 10 cattle the same 10-miles to that train depot just across the county line. Both hogs and cattle end up in the Chicago stockyards, from whence, in the fullness of time, some anonymous paymaster sends a few dollars in compensation.

There is, however, a separate source of income: Twice a week, Henry Borlaug dispatches six milk-cans of cream to the nearby village of Saude (population about 20). Those Monday and Friday contributions, hand-separated from the output of the dozen cows, end up producing a few pounds of butter (also destined for Chicago dinner tables) as well as a few more of the paymaster's priceless pittances.

Together the cattle, hogs and cans of cream keep the family a step above poverty. Just a baby-step, though: The *annual* spoil for all that toil is barely $1000.

Despite their small means, they are the first Borlaugs to make money or contribute anything toward feeding others. This became clear when Norm was eight and his grandfather put his math skills to the test. Pulling out the family account book, the old man selected the page for 1895 and demanded the boy tote up the figures. Norm recalls that the cash income that year came to $128. He's thought about it a lot since; Emma, Nels and their three sons, working with nary a day off, earned in aggregate $2.50 a week. Of necessity, spending went for bare essentials. One month's store bill was: salt, 2 cents; pepper, 2 cents; vinegar, 5 cents; cotton and needles, 5 cents; four yards of red flannel, $1; and a can of oil, 20 cents.

Although by the 1920s the family had bootstrapped itself out of such iron parsimony, poverty still breathes icy drafts down every neck. In economists' parlance, they are subsistence farmers—their purpose, their profession and their ambition is solely to eat. Success for them does not extend to financial satisfaction, let alone any kind of fun. Food on the table is the ultimate fulfillment.

To succeed at feeding your clan from your own land requires a special mindset. Basically, every essence must be devoted to producing what you eat. Such a life is neither for the farsighted nor the frail, and it's certainly not for the faint of heart.

The three children and two adults on the Borlaug place know all that only too well. Their success is subject to strictures and perils beyond their control. Floods, droughts, tornadoes, hail-storms, windstorms, ill-timed downpours, or crop diseases can drop in without warning. Worse than any cat burglar, nature's thieves leave behind nothing to fatten a person, let alone a purse.

With Mother Nature so mean, so fickle and yet so immune to bribery, Borlaug survival demands absolute self-reliance. Everything must be grown at home and prepared at home. Subsistence life is thus little more than self-imposed slavery. No family member gets a vacation, receives wages, or can follow the call of wanderlust, whim or schooling. Their hands are forever full. Just growing food.

With money too rare to be missed, the Borlaugs measure their wealth only in family values. And of course there's no falling back on government services. Absent a tax base, governments have nothing with which to weave social safety nets.

Living is thus a high-wire act. Not even the roads are maintained. Borlaug's region, for example, has no transportation department and the dirt traces that serve the family are forever forgetting their purpose. Following heavy rains, and especially during the spring thaw, they soften to soups capable of consuming buggies, wagons, carts and even Model Ts. A traveler's most important accessories thus are planks and shovels. And the millions of miles of rural arteries needed to sustain half of all Americans are forever clotted with mud.

Actually things would have been a lot worse had not farmers serviced their own roads. Typically, they'd harness a team to a wagon and, under

MUD MATTERS

Mud ruled Borlaug's youth. Rural regions had few paved roads, and rain created quagmires deep enough to deny travelers the chance to move. Until the sun dried the streets you had to stay put. Residents like the Borlaugs often couldn't get out for a week. Other states advised their automobile owners to avoid Iowa altogether.

Only a horse could extricate hapless drivers like this one. Many farmers managed to pay all their household bills by selling their horse's services (at the outrageous rate of $1.00 a tow) to the clueless modernists who considered wheels superior to hooves.

the township supervisor's direction, spend a day hauling gravel or sand to fill the neighborhood's most voracious "stuckholes."

In return for road-care, the town grants a tax break, commonly excusing participants from paying to vote. Despite what history books say, the Poll Tax was also a northern custom; even in Borlaug's boyhood the privilege of casting a ballot cost Iowans a dollar. "We never worried about it," Norm explains. "We spent a day a year fixing the roads."

Given all its challenges, farming was then not a word . . . it was a sentence. Beyond climate and roads, farm families were shackled to seeds, soil, seasons, weeds, animal care and, above all, the clock. "We never felt free," notes another Hawkeye State survivor. "Morning and evening we had to feed all the animals and milk each cow. Social calls and family celebrations had to be brief. 'We must get home,' we said wistfully, and even resentfully, as we edged out the door."

Throughout Middle America a farmer was a cross between an authority figure and an ant. That was a fact of life, but subsistence farms were seductive enough to attract a never-ending flow of new suckers. Farming for food could be started with almost nothing. It required only a hard-working couple with children (the more the better). This easy-entry lifestyle also provided spiritual compensations: By working and raising their kids in concert, and by collectively clambering onto the bottom rung of the ladder of opportunity the family achieved independence.

Many people considered this the very essence of Americanism, which it was. But it came with a catch: the ladder of opportunity had only one rung. Subsistence farmers had to function full throttle just to eat. They had neither time nor money to climb any higher.

In this peculiar form of self-imposed slavery, boys were required for their strength, and were educated before girls (who, everyone agreed, were best kept in ignorance of higher things). Indeed, from about age 11 the oldest son had to prepare himself *to head the family*, a farmer's death being all too common. Across the countryside, formal education thus ended with the elementary grades. Farm country had few high schools. Or desire for them.

Keeping things that way was customary. City dwellers were entitled to cheap food. It was their birthright. Pshaw, country folk always had been poor: obviously, rural poverty was predestined; fate itself closed that horizon. "Farmers have never made much money," President Coolidge declared. "I don't think there's anything anyone can do about that."

Given the urban class's ordained supremacy, even farm families accepted such patronizing. Thus throughout the "progressive" 1920s rural yeomen were victimized by the premeditated sin of suppressed food prices. Rather than protest, they swallowed their pride, suppressed their anger, and continued providing cheap bread to the upper crust. As was their age-old obligation.

S till and all, change was a-coming. And among its harbingers was a phenomenon too close to heaven for human comprehension. You see, during this miraculous decade the outer world dreamed up a form of sound vibes possessing the mind-bending power to penetrate the void. Norm recalls the disbelief everyone felt when they learned that something truly weird now inhabited the air across the countryside:

One winter evening, when we'd been in the new house about a year, Granddad walked into the kitchen carrying a strange-looking contraption about the size of a cigar box. "Just wanted to show you this," he said. "Got it from a feller in Cresco today. Come on outside."

We went out into the crisp darkness and frosty quiet behind the house and he clapped "cups" over his ears and fiddled with a metal alligator clip. Then he transferred the cups to my ears, and in my head arose sounds. They were clearly human, but were coming from some unknown world by a means beyond comprehension. People were there, yet I couldn't see or touch them. How could that be? Songs without singers and music without instruments was altogether too fantastic to be factual.

I've since learned that Granddad's device consisted basically of a crystal diode, which was the simplest kind of vacuum tube, and a tuning coil, which was nothing more than a little copper wire wound around a cardboard tube, not unlike those in toilet-paper rolls. There was also the alligator clip and, as I recall, a real cat's whisker.

The whole device could be made for a few cents, and it worked by magic, having neither battery nor any other power supply. By hooking the clip to the right spot on the wire coil you could intercept messages from a celestial place called KDKA.

The beings populating that planet with the unpronounceable name on the far side of the ether communicated at night, and their civilization was so advanced they could throw their music and messages right into your mind.

Nothing like that had ever been dreamed of before.

Even its name rang with mystery: radio!

In time, this otherworldly companion would capture the hearts of those who'd been forever shrouded from the American spectacle. The first technological phenomenon to jolt the rural regions, radio subverted the age-old separation between society and its food suppliers. Unlike the train whistle that entertained only on crystalline nights every year or two, the new sounds filled the lonely dark *every night*. And they elicited strange and wholly new sensations: *fun and fascination*.

Besides being a farmer's personal friend, this factual science fiction mutated the rural mindset. Farm folk had previously accepted their sheltered existence as inevitable, but during the mid-1920s corrosive doubt infected the minds of all who tilled the soil. Having stripped the scales from their eyes, radio provided envy along with entertainment.

The result was Midwest malaise. Daniel Boorstin has summarized the result: "Many farmers lacked access to adequate education for their children, to proper medical facilities, to recreational or cultural activities, to virtually anything that might give them a sense of being valued members of a community. Older farmers felt the sting of watching their children leave the farm for the city. They felt the humiliation of being ridiculed as 'hayseeds' by the new urban culture that was coming to dominate American life. There was, in short, a general feeling of obsolescence, of being left behind by a society that no longer placed much value on the virtues of rural life."

The latter half of the decade saw this bitterness darken as a second miraculous medium proved even better at faking out unsophisticated farm folk. Despite an absence of color and sound, movies mesmerized the millions who'd grown up in blissful blindness of the realm beyond their sight. By opening eyes to life behind the lost horizon Hollywood enflamed the rural masses with a burning desire.

Though they enjoyed the mystique of movies and radio, the Borlaugs could seldom experience the outer world's mind-bending magic tricks. With cash so rare, their own indulgences had to revolve around the few cents generated by Clara Borlaug's eggs.

This ritual reliance on eggs was a rural reality. Most country folk kept a few chickens, and all allowed their womenfolk to dispose of the eggs exactly as they pleased:

> I usually fed the hens and gathered the eggs, but it was understood that Mother was the real owner. Each week she took her eggs to the general store in Saude. She never got paid in cash. The storekeeper [her cousin, Greg Vaala] made out a Due Bill identifying how much credit she'd earned against future purchases. It was almost nothing because all the other women were bartering eggs too. Yet it was almost everything. Over time, those eggs got us the necessities we couldn't produce for ourselves: sugar, flour, salt, oatmeal, coffee beans, thread, yarn and, very rarely, a little cloth. These luxuries were the highlights of our lives.

Bartering for meager necessities seems to modern eyes like something found only in outlandish foreign backwaters, but in the 1920s what option did rural Americans have? Surplus cash being something only city folks possessed, sugar, flour, salt, oatmeal, coffee beans, thread, yarn and, very rarely, a little cloth were the greatest of treasures.

Farmers even had to supply their own fuel for cooking, heating, and field operations. As late as 1932, not one farm in ten was electrified. The reason was simple: the power companies refused to hook up more. Noting the distances between country houses as well as the dismal farm

IT TOOK A VILLAGE IN AMERICA, TOO

Norm Boy Borlaug grew up within a support system unlike any we know.

Our village was named for a town in Norway's Telemark province from which most of our ancestors hailed. Saude was a family friendly place of shared lives, shared heritage and shared counties: Chickasaw and Howard. There, we felt an almost tribal sense of belonging: Loyalties were local; decisions were collective; and ideals were shared. Individualism was suppressed, but we felt a sort of glory in being part of a whole that was larger than ourselves.

Apart from two Lutheran churches, Saude had a general store that for a while also served as our post office. Next door was a blacksmith who shoed horses, bent ironwork, mended broken implements and even fixed the newfangled Model T's. Across the side street was a feed mill for grinding oats for pigs and poultry. And beside that stood the Farmers' Cooperative Creamery that churned our cream into butter. Local farmers delivered their cans of cream by buggy, wagon, sled or Model T. In summer cream soured so fast we had to keep it cool and deliver it every other day; in winter we had to warm it to keep it from freezing. The butter was put in big tubs and sent by train to dealers in Chicago.

There being no electricity, the creamery's huge churns were powered by coal-fired steam boilers. To keep the butter hard we carried long saws out onto the frozen Saude Creek and cut out blocks of ice as big as mattresses. Teams of horses hauled those on sleds to the creamery, where they were stacked in the cellar and covered in sawdust. The process was amazingly effective. Even in the hundred-degree days of August, enough ice remained to keep the butter solid. Thank god for that: no one would buy liquid butter.

Hauling the tubs of butter was easiest in winter. Trucks could barely move on frozen roads, but sleds slipped easily across them. There were no snowplows and salting was both unknown and unwanted. Until the coming out of the automobile, snow on the road was our friend.

The country store held most of its merchandise in bags, barrels, bolts, baskets, bins or jute sacks. The clerk, dressed in white apron, would forbid you to touch anything. He measured out the requisite amount of flour, honey, candies, cloth, oil or whatever. This convenience came with at least three concerns: One, the merchandise was open and easily contaminated by flies or dust. Two, there was no way to tell how fresh the contents were. And three, the clerk could shave a penny's worth from the proper amount, and you'd never know.

I was a teenager when packaged products first showed up and eliminated those concerns. Packaging was another 1920s innovation that eased our lives.

LITTLE NORWAY

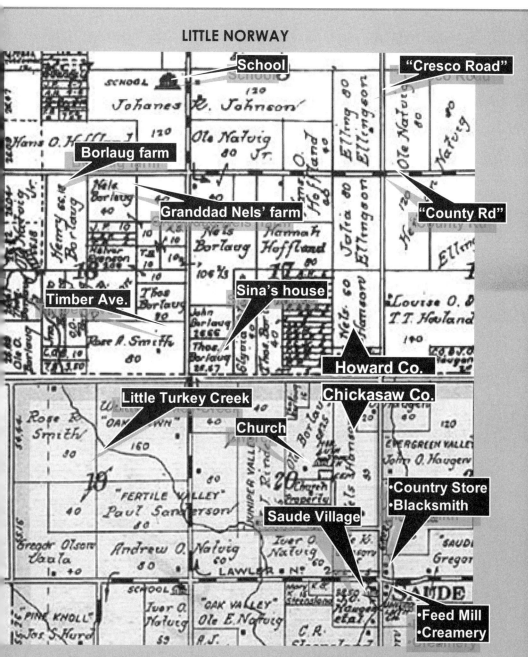

This combines the 1915 plat maps of New Oregon Township (Howard County) and Utica Township (Chickasaw County). The roads are a mile apart. "Cresco Road" is now Unity Ave (Union Ave. in Chickasaw County). "County Road" is now 200th St. Sina's house is where influenza struck; the church is where Baby Helen is buried.

incomes, corporate executives shook their heads in mock horror. Clearly, supplying precious electricity to farming folk would *never* be in the stockholders' interest.

That rebuff conferred mountains of manual misery on those trapped within their personal principalities. Everything that required cooking, heating, cooling, lighting, lifting, pumping, chopping, vacuuming, spreading, ironing, washing, or drying had to be done by the force of muscles—the family's or the horses'.

Among other things, this explains why tiny tykes maintained mountains of firewood. Building those oaken alps was a bane of youth. The Borlaug's stove gobbled billets at a rate to break an eight-year-old's spirit. What was universally called the "range" occupied a quarter of the kitchen, and keeping it running required infinite care. Beyond satisfying its wood appetite you had to constantly adjust the chimney damper and close the draft vent to keep the fire drawing perfectly. And perfection was paramount. Regardless of human desires, the metal box reigned supreme. Without its blessings, no one could eat.

Actually, that metal manservant did more than make food edible. For one thing, a copper-lined reservoir at its right-hand end produced hot water. Seldom more than lukewarm, it was scooped out with pitcher to wash the dishes, the hands, or the body.

For another, the stove exuded warmth. On winter mornings Norm's mother stuffed the firebox until the whole cast-iron contraption glowed. Then like some giant artificial heart it brought the homestead throbbing to life. "Getting out of bed in twenty-below temperatures was torture almost beyond endurance," he explains; "the range made it possible."

Even after day was done, that blessed cube remained a boon companion. During evening hours all winter long they lowered the oven door and settled around the nearby table with their books, newspapers or homework. There was comradeship under the flickery golden lamplight in that kitchen, which was the biggest room and was properly arranged for primetime pleasure. The choicest spot for a kid to sit was on the open oven door; where the heat of glowing embers warmed the back deep enough to linger a lifetime.

Obviously, Borlaug was born into what today we belittle by the euphemism "Third World." And, as in all primitive lands, rural America relied on child labor. Indeed, the gap between kids and the grownup world was wafer thin. Girls and boys in those good old days couldn't avoid the drudgery now reserved strictly for adulthood.

WILLING WORKFORCE

Bright-eyed Norm Boy, age 8. He and his older cousin Vilmar Borlaug are clad in their standard attire. Farm boys lived in work cap, overalls and boots. With chores dominating their days, precious little time remained for play, let alone pals.

For a boy as young as eight the chores were far from easy. Except for a few midsummer weeks when the sun awoke early he began in the dark, hauling in the wood and water and driving the cows to the milking shed.

At age eleven his sinewy frame was laden with even more dawntime duties: feeding the chickens, separating the cream, hauling skim milk to the pigs and lighting the stove (big-time responsibility). After school, he also trimmed lamp wicks, gathered new-dug potatoes, hauled hay, turned the grindstone, cut kindling and piled firewood. He didn't (and doesn't) complain: chores were not impositions; they were imperatives.

Assume yet again that we're present on that late-July day of 1925. The heavy work begins after breakfast when Norm's father hitches two horses to a cultivator and proceeds to one of his four ten-acre cornfields. Up and down each line of plants he goes, guiding the high-wheeled contraption so that the two gangs of small shovels suspended underneath scrape out the weeds.

By mid-morning the sun is a branding iron on the back, the shadows are short and sharp, the humidity has hit horrendous. In the depths of the eight-foot-high plant canyons there's no possibility of a breeze. Henry Borlaug and his team constitute a continuum of human- and horse-flesh: straining together, suffering together, sweating together.

At mid-morning, there's a two-minute rest to swig the water jug and mop the brow. Then it's back to waging ferocious weed warfare.

Norm is nearby. He laughs sideways at the recollection:

> Being on 'holiday,' I cannot escape. Sadly the hoe is in the same damn place I left it the day before. I've got to fight thistles for the rest of the day.

Of all the banes of existence weeds are the worst; they constantly press a family toward peril. Many present a triple threat—economic, moral and legal. You see, weeds rob crops of life; they betray that worst of all sinners, a slovenly farmer; and certain ones are banned by law.

The loathing of Canadian thistles springs mainly from legal liability: State law requires that *every* thistle be destroyed before the fall winds can waft its seeds around the neighborhood.

This is why a boy's contribution is vital. And in a sense his duty is more grueling than his dad's because it demands hand-to-hand combat. Peering down through the bluegrass and clover he seeks the spiny green guerillas. Thwap! Thwap! Thwap! Ten thousand Thwaps!

To clear the whole estate, the insurgents in olive-drab must be exterminated in proper sequence: first the oat fields and pastures, then the spaces between the corn plants where the cultivator shovels can't reach, next the hayfield, and finally the roadside in front of the white picket fence. The child's responsibility is immense:

> Our reputation as upright citizens weighed on my shoulders and arm muscles. The weight is still there. I hate that hoe even now!

That hate was as old as history, but it was as futile as the rest. Thistles are too canny for humankind. Even as their tops are struck off, their bottoms are sprouting rhizomes. Those underground stems are hardly hindered by hoeing, so the fall breezes waft thistledown around the neighborhood regardless of a kid's summer of slavery. Every knock at the door then pierces the conscience: Surely this time the county agent has come to indict the closet criminals.

While the males are tied to their tasks, mother and daughters work the washboard, the wind-powered clothes dryer (aka clothesline) and pull weeds in the vegetable garden. Though female duties are especially onerous, no complaint emerges. The sense of shared burden is the tie binding this survival squad.

By noon the morning rituals have subtracted seven hours from each of five lives. Of course, before quitting for dinner father and son must unhitch, water, and feed the horses. And the womenfolk must face a grueling session over the broiling oven.

That midday meal is the main one, which is why it's dinner. On most summer days there's fried chicken, boiled potatoes, fresh peas, lettuce, and radishes. Leftovers are saved for supper, which is always a reprise, since food can neither be wasted nor stored.

Following dinner, the women wash the dishes and start their afternoon chores. Norm Boy trudges back to his hated hoe. His father re-hitches the horses and within half an hour is again scouring the sun-blanched rows, scooping out more of the green, grasping, greedy invaders who aim to overrun his tiny portion of paradise.

Returning to the barn around six, Norm rubs down the four-footed fellow workers, goops salve on their scratches, and hauls in fresh water and oats for their supper. With weeds proliferating in three more ten-acre fields, the power supply must be maintained in tip-top running order.

Finally, the family members are required to wring one last measure of work from the daylight. Man and boy repeat the dawn chores: milking, separating and carrying the skimmed milk to the hogs. And the womenfolk suffer another sweat session over the cruel cook stove.

As they all gather round the supper table at 8 o'clock they are together in spirit. Even the sun shares their exhaustion, and can no longer prevent dusk from launching its assault forces.

Triumphant at last, night crawls over the scene the painters and passersby consider so picturesque and so pleasing.

As a full-fledged member of the muscular work force, Norm Boy naturally finds his friends among the animals. Their bond is based as much on empathy as on equality.

For one thing, he's proud of his family's advanced power source. We may find that attitude hard to understand. However, before leaving Norway to come to America, Norm's great-grandfather, Ole Borlaug, had been as productive as most farmers in history. Having to rely on his own muscle, he'd tilled a whole acre *with a hoe*. Yet in northeastern Iowa just 70 years later his grandson, Henry, tills more than 100 acres— 56 of his own and 60 more rented from Ole's own son Nels. Together with three powerful, thousand-pound plow horses Henry and great-grandson Norman produce an amazing 40 acres of corn and even feed a few of the new homeland's citizens!

Humanity's association with draft animals has been long and intimate. Norm appreciates that age-old inter-species dependence: Horse power was the vital motor of his youth. Should the animals fail, the family fails. Without equine strength and sinew the Borlaugs would be more than out of power, they'd be out of prospects.

These days countries that rely on work animals are considered hopelessly backward, but the U.S. grew up on creatures' backs too. Cattle led the way, and for centuries Americans valued cows more for muscle than for meat or milk. Indeed, oxen powered farms worldwide until the 19th Century when Yankee ingenuity devised contraptions for connecting to a horse collar.

With the coming of the cultivator, planter and other incredible inventions, small farmers switched prime movers. Rural productivity then soared so high that the change from ox to horse boosted civilization as much as steam power would half a century later. By the time of Norm's birth steam-powered farm machines existed, but four-footed horsepower still furnished the food. In 1915, for instance, the 6.5 million American farmers owned more than 21 million horses and mules.

America's plow horses are mere runts compared to the proud Clydesdales touting beer on today's TV screens. Nonetheless, they work hard, laboring eight hours a day for almost nine months at a stretch.

And those undersized helpmates move much more than the plow, planter and cultivator: Harnessed in pairs, they draw disks and harrows that prepare the seedbeds for oats, clover and corn. They power the corn binder that cuts green corn plants and ties them into bundles, and later they shift the sun-dried bundles to the silo on a "bundle wagon." From time to time they tow the mower and haul the resulting hay into the barn on a hay wagon. And they pull the binder that cuts and bundles oat plants, as well as the dray that in due course delivers those bundles to the steam-powered thrashing machine a group of neighbors has hired. Late in the season, they tug the grain wagon that totes the resulting grains to the granary. After that, they spread manure with a smelly machine everyone detests. And they plow cornfields in the fall (if winter allows) or in the spring (if it doesn't).

But only when snow is more than knee-deep do the horses carry people. Usually that means Norm Boy and Bob plod more than a mile down the county road to the junction with the Cresco Road where the community mailboxes stand lined up for duty. He always rides bareback; the old saddle hanging on the barn wall remains on its hook even when its time to face the snow and haul the mail home.

Youngest of the three plow horses, Bob was big, brawny, reddish-brown and very mettlesome. He and Norm comprise a Borlaug sub-family. Born the very same day, they grew up learning the strange ways of the world. From birth there was telepathy between the species . . . so much so they're near to brothers:

> Our friendship was mutual; with a swoop of his nose Bob would nudge me like some co-conspirator hell bent on mischief. He didn't do that with anyone else, and how could I resist? We enjoyed many adventures together. We'd take excursions into the woods, to the fishing hole on the Little Turkey River, and we often took off together to see the relatives down the road.

However not everything was play. His best pal was also his business partner. Boy and bay are responsible for cultivating certain cornfields, and their special closeness lingers:

> Bob had an uncanny understanding of when midday was coming up. If I tried to squeeze in an extra pass within half an hour of noon, he'd stamp down a few corn plants as we round the far end of the row.

The boy's best buddy had a rebellious personality, a built in alarm clock, and limited loyalty when it came to lunchtime!

BEST OF . . .

Without playmates or playtime, farm boys back in Borlaug's day lacked companions. Other than at school and church on Sunday mornings (or maybe Saturday night because, unlike God, farmers often couldn't afford a day of rest) they seldom played free and unfettered with their peers. For many, therefore, the horse became their best friend.

. . . BUDDIES

This brotherhood was not all bad: boys cared for their big buddy and that equine equal taught them loyalty and congeniality. This tolerance and concern for their fellows helped create the Midwest's legendary character traits. Borlaug certainly knows what great teachers horses are; his big bay buddy Bob taught him togetherness.

For all their power and performance, horses also held up lives in the negative sense. The Borlaugs forfeited hours a day to feeding, watering, currying, and anointing sores with oil. And whenever the barn was occupied—which was every night of the year—the stalls had to be cleaned and fresh straw dragged in for bedding, regardless of weather or whatever pleasure might be in prospect.

Preparing for a season of work stole most of early spring. Being out of shape from standing in the barn all winter, horses needed weeks of pre-season training. And, like all star athletes, they had to be treated with care. Necks required special attention; any chafing where the collar presses the flesh would fester once fieldwork began. In fact, a chafed neck usually necessitated a stint on injured reserve. Thus, every week Norm and his father must clean the collars and salve the big soft shoulders as if their future depends on them. As it does.

Above all, though, horses stole land. At least half the farm's acreage produced the hay for three horses and a score of cattle and calves. That's why a 100 acre farm grew merely 40 acres of corn.

The bounty of that farm-within-a-farm determines the Borlaug's existence. And of all the natural barriers corn's productivity was the most inflexible. The ceiling over their success was 25 bushels per acre. Of course other families were more blessed: In a good season some neighbor always bragged of getting 30. None, though, ever surpassed that. Clearly, 30 bushels an acre was the limit imposed by God.

Actually, getting those ears of corn from the fields involved the year's worst anguish. Not even Yankee ingenuity had produced a horse-drawn corn-harvester; the entire crop was harvested by hand. Fathers and sons started in October with the goal of gathering everything by Thanksgiving. Sometimes the task stretched out through half the winter because each ear had to be pulled off its plant while simultaneously stripping away the husk, thereby leaving clean cobs and kernels.

Day after day, corn pickers walked the rows while down the row to the right horses drew a wagon fitted with a "bang board"—a barrier not unlike a sheet of plywood standing up along the far side. On his left hand the harvester wore a husking glove with a short hook attached to the palm. Grabbing an ear of corn with the right hand he swung the left over, gouging the hook downward at just the right depth to slice open the husk. Then with a twist of the left wrist he broke the ear free of its shank, wrenched it from the surrounding husk, and flung it with the exact trajectory to clear the top of the stalk towering overhead and hit the bang board one row over. Even before it had rebounded into the wagon he addressed the next plant and clicked his tongue to urge the horses forward and keep the wagon in line.

As the picker proceeded, an observer would see something like a human windmill, arms waving and corn flying out in a steady stream as the horses plodded forward and the wagon filled, ear by agonizing ear.

All corn was gathered this way, constituting a burden beyond belief. Across the Corn Belt, an average acre contained 12,000 plants and farms like Borlaug's averaged 40 acres of corn, so an average father/son lineup had to pick almost half a million ears. Norm shudders to recall:

> That was true hell. Although we wore cotton gloves and covered our forearms with sleeves torn from old sweaters, the husks still managed to cut and scrape until our hands and arms were raw and bleeding.

Despite the inhuman demands of this torture, the Borlaugs handled an infinitesimal fraction of the national harvest. The number of ears hand-harvested across Iowa is almost unimaginable—at least a hundred billion (a modern count has put today's statewide harvest at 420 billion ears). A dozen other states produced corn in quantity also. Is it any wonder that in farm country three-quarters of those nowadays honored by the name "teenager" never got an education? For them, high school was a luxury beyond the wildest dream. They had to pick corn.

Moreover, relentless nature took malicious pleasure in probing the outer limits of male endurance. Not uncommonly, for instance, thunderstorms blew the fields flat. Then, hundreds of thousands of soggy plants had to be lifted one-by-one to locate the ears that always seemed to prefer the underside. On such occasions a boy's back ached almost more than a any body could bear.

Considering how they cursed corn picking, people of the Plains were aghast when a young Iowa State graduate turned it into a game. Henry Agard Wallace has since been labeled "American Dreamer," which certainly seems apt: the contest he conceived was utterly crazy. Neither for gold nor glory, it sought to find not only the fastest, but the finest corn picker. There was a formal scoring system and gimlet-eyed judges who deducted points for ears left in the field, husk fragments left on an ear or kernels pierced by the hook-in-the-hand.

The competition began in Iowa's capital, Des Moines, and to everyone's amazement soared in popularity. County, state, and regional eliminations soon were underway. Then Illinois, Indiana, Nebraska,

THE WORLD SERIES . . .

Each fall during much of Borlaug's youth, rural folks convened by the thousands in some carefully prepared corn patch to watch young men compete against the plant, themselves and their peers. The one harvesting the most corn in an 80-minute period won the contest. Champions could pick almost 4000 ears—or more than one a second!

. . . OF CORN

In corn husking contests the fans mingled with their favorite as he charged along, yanking ear after ear from plant after plant for an hour and twenty minutes. Here admirers trail at least 16 contestants. The resulting image presents a sort of bar graph indicating each contestant's popularity and pace along his designated row.

Kansas, Minnesota and Wisconsin started parallel contests. Eventually there arose the granddaddy of them all: The National Corn Husking Championship.

Corn huskers, it has been said, were more than athletes; they were artists who turned the farmer's terrible task into a ballet of beauty. Having reduced the process to three or four smooth moves, they pulled off feats of athleticism breathtaking to behold:

> A champion could handle 40 bushels in less than two hours, hitting the bang board with an ear of corn about sixty times a minute. To me, that was impossible. I've spent all day harvesting 40 bushels, and been utterly done in.

It is not hard to fathom why competitive corn picking piqued interest across at least seven states. Rural America had no live sporting events, and Plains people endured days of such similarity that these contests exuded excitement way beyond modern understanding.

Indeed, they grew into huge spectacles: It was not unknown for 150,000 fans to show up in some cornfield to walk the rows behind their favorites, enjoying the national finals from the very heart of the action.

On that great occasion the Corn Belt seethed with game-day sensations, not to mention side-bets. The thrill of victory and the agony of defeat were carried far and wide through local newspapers and play-by-play radio. The Goodyear Blimp sometimes hovered overhead. It was the nation's largest athletic event; a sort of rustic World Series.

The rewards, however, fell a little short. The National Corn husking Champion received a gold medal, $50, and a bib-overall donated by OshKosh B'Gosh!

Borlaug remembers all this with a not altogether regretful sigh:

> With the coming of the combine harvester in the 1940s, corn husking contests lost meaning and popular interest. But, thinking back, I'm sure thousands of fathers were infinitely grateful to Henry Wallace for turning the year's worst chore into something boys would train for in the family corn patch.
>
> It sure helped me get through each acre. Day after day for almost two months I'd be bringing in the corn but also honing my technique, strengthening my muscles, timing my performance, and seeing myself crowned the next National Corn Husking Champion of the United States!

1928-1929

Dreamy Days

Whatever fool ambition young Borlaug might entertain there was nothing he could do about it. Farm boys in the 1920s existed within a circumscribed boundary, like an electron in a quantum shell . . . or maybe a mouse.

Just getting past grade school required a miracle. Country kids who failed to do farm work undermined the family. And when life itself is the bottom line even a free education is too expensive. Thus Norm Boy had no way to escape the fate of his forefathers.

The fact that he did decamp the cloister and make his way in the world is due to the interventions of kindly outsiders. And the first of those was his cool-headed cousin. Since surviving the Spanish Flu nine years before, Sina Borlaug had risen to replace Lena Halvorson as the local teacher. The sweet-tempered self-assured authority figure who'd once saved an exhausted five-year-old from the seductive snow now oversaw his daily progress at New Oregon Rural District School Number 8.

Wise beyond her 21 years, Sina had chivvied Norm through seventh grade and rewarded his hard-won triumph with a souvenir plaque whose words left a lifetime imprint:

Advance in learning as you advance in life.
Good instruction is better than riches.
Kindness is the noblest weapon to conquer with.

However, Sina's grandest contribution occurred one Saturday in the spring of 1928 when Norm was completing what everyone assumed was his final year of schooling.

That morning she appeared at the farmhouse, unannounced. Because eighth-grade math had the boy baffled, the teacher's sudden presence

CAREER SAVER #1

Fate's first facilitator, Sina Borlaug started Norm on what nowadays seems like a predestined career course. As the local school teacher, Cousin Sina spotted the bright promise in her pupil's ice-blue eyes. Her dilemma was that he was in eighth-grade and like other country boys was required to quit school and run the farm the rest of his days. She decided to get her bright-eyed pupil sent to high school, and that became the first step on the long path toward feeding a billion hungry souls.

caused concern. But Sina hadn't come to scold. Gathering the family round the kitchen table, she declared in ringing tones: "Norman should go to high school. As a scholar he's no great shakes, but he's got grit!"

To us, advocating a 14-year-old attend high school seems normal and natural, but Sina's suggestion caused more heartache than any math score. You see, school buses were unknown in 1928 and, although the horse-and-buggy era had passed on, 14 miles was still too far to commute, especially during the winter months. Norm Boy would thus have to board in town. Though his parents were high on education, Sina's proposal meant they'd have to pay rent and sacrifice *half* their field force *five days out of every seven.*

This dilemma roiled all of farm country. Yes, autos were now muscle machines capable of 25mph, but rotten roads still kept farm folk caged.

The shackles came off thanks to a government agency you might not expect: the U.S. Postal Service. Its Rural Free Delivery not only established road standards for the nation but also sponsored the first good roads to get out to farming communities.

Whereas the Postal Service was intent on helping its mail carriers, the Congress in 1916 handed the Secretary of Agriculture an enormous sum—$374 million—for new roads linking farmers to their fellow citizens. President Woodrow Wilson declared that the money would "promote a fuller and more attractive rural life." Possibly, he also saw it producing more of the food he'd promised would win the war.

State governments later took up the cause. In the 1920s, for instance, Pennsylvania Governor Gifford Pinchot—the noted forester, friend of Theodore Roosevelt, and former volunteer delivering Herbert Hoover's food in German-occupied France—made his state a leader in building farm-to-market roads.

By then, cars had real roofs and motorists were willing to venture out when the sun didn't shine. The resulting clamor for all-weather roads quickly catalyzed a campaign supported by farmer *and* manufacturer. Both understood that roads were veins as well as arteries, and that goods flowing freely both ways would benefit the whole body.

In the making of America, this put the melt in the melting pot. Previously, millions lived in isolation and remained loyal to their village, which provided all they'd ever needed or wanted. But as reliable roads penetrated the backwoods farm folk began participating in something very grand: the American pageant.

Norm sums up:

> Paved roads not only took us to the world, they reshaped rural existence by allowing farm folks to leave home once in a while.
> The possibility of being able to go places changed our whole perspective. It made possible marvels as strange as "shopping." By then Granddad had a Model T and sometimes we'd motor to town just to wander up and down admiring the delights displayed in Cresco's shop windows.
> A few times Granddad even treated us to a moving picture show. The film of course lacked sound and color, but it provided the year's most memorable moments.
> Moreover, all-weather roads meant that fresh produce could reach us. Fruits and vegetables began appearing during the months they'd never before been seen. That made our lives not only more interesting, but also more healthy; for the first time we could balance our diet during the dead of winter.

And pavement precipitated yet another potent phenomenon. Before this point, railroads and a few Model T's had moved farm products; now the truck began muscling in. Though still primitive and puny, trucks were cheap enough for locals to own, and they filled two missing links: One, they carried small loads from farm to market. Two, they provided a fast service for perishables such as vegetables and dairy products.

Then in 1925 a truly fabulous vision emerged: concrete strips connecting the states. By approving a federal identification system the Department of Agriculture again led the way. East-west strips were assigned even numbers; north-south strips got odd numbers; transcontinental concrete connections were numerated in multiples of ten and were designated "Routes." All were also adorned with shields bearing the state's name across the top and the federal number below. It's perhaps no surprise that the shield looks an awful lot like the Department of Agriculture's own logo.

Rural folks at first considered this mere Washington meddling. To the millions who throughout a lifetime dealt with only one or two traces of nameless dirt and gravel, assigning roads numbers seemed utterly absurd. However, in time long-distance highways solidified the national character; even the ethnic super-patriots soon became American.

The first pavement to penetrate Norm's corner of Iowa was being constructed when he went to high school in 1928. Highway 63, running from the Minnesota line to New Hampton, passed within nine miles of the farm. The thrill of seeing construction crews laying that concrete ribbon drew crowds of sightseers from far and wide:

Several times we went over to admire this marvel. By today's standards it was narrow, primitive and unsafe at any speed, but we'd never seen a surface so smooth or solid or safe. Now we could drive worry-free whatever the season. We'd never considered such a possibility; driving had forever been fraught with the fear of plunging into bottomless mud right around the next bend.

This narrow band of concrete had huge social consequences. Beyond mobility and better food, it endowed us a kind of nobility. This is where we first sensed the concept of the open road, and that expanded vision had an electrifying effect. The horizon that had always been close by was gone. Now we were part of the big wide world where all the action occurred.

Also electrifying was the Sears Roebuck catalog. With the Rural Free Delivery and reliable all-weather roads, businesses in far away cities could access every corner of the land. Firms like Sears and Montgomery-Ward could now reach customers in remote farmsteads. For us and the other rural inhabitants their catalogs became both a wonder and an insight into things that set our imaginations alight.

Highway 63 did nothing to ease the family's dilemma over whether Norm Boy could attend high school. As we've said, by lodging in Cresco he'd be unavailable for farm chores and would thereby jeopardize his family's survival.

Still and all, in that hopelessly old-fashioned era teachers were trusted, so Sina's pronouncement proved sufficient. Henry Borlaug agreed to shoulder the full weight of work throughout the week, thereby releasing his strapping son to the realm of the dark side and its host of unholy influences.

That immense change of life occurred one morning in September 1928 when Norm crossed his First Great Divide—the one separating him from the planet past the front fence. Living with town folk enlarged his world beyond a farm boy's traditional boundary. He seemed to have crawled from a cocoon and come into a shiny new continent.

His timing was perfect. The '20s had been hard on farmers but 1928 was a year of euphoria; rural society was on the rise and its flowering lent the Plains a happy aspect. Satisfaction is a state of mind, and feelings in the countryside flew as high as flagpoles. Living was not only easy, it was about to get easier because the presidential election was in full swing and Republican candidate Herbert Hoover was promising to secure more food. His campaign slogan said it all: "A Chicken for Every Pot and two cars in every garage. Progress is changing from the full dinner pail to the full garage."

This was the heartland's headiest moment. Who could doubt the Great

Engineer? He'd fed the Belgians hadn't he? Put him in charge and everyone would eat chicken and keep two cars in garages—an amazing thought because families had never had one car . . . let alone a garage.

In November 1928 more Americans voted than in any previous election. Hope drew them to the polls, and Hoover's electoral victory loosed a wave of rural rapture. Yes, there was now no doubt about it, food producers would be in the forefront of progress and they'd soon reap satisfaction and success. Just like the city slickers always had.

For Cresco High's freshman class, however, all the jawing about future prosperity jarred with everyday reality. At the time, reading, writing and "figuring" dominated the curriculum. Rural youths who could read a local newspaper, write a reasonable letter and add simple sums were considered educated above their station. Farmers, after all, required only weak minds and strong backs. Everyone on high was absolutely sure of that. They were sure, too, that farm boys lacked ambition and yearned for nothing more than the life of their fathers.

Like many falsehoods, this one projected an aura of believability. Farmers certainly seemed to know their place. They stayed close to home and distrusted book learning as well as every suggestion emanating from professors or the printed page. To the country mind, intellectuals were best resisted, or at least ridiculed for their ignorance of the real world.

Yet despite universal agreement over the food producers' preset status, the searing shame of wheatless days and johnnycake breakfasts had shaken even the Eastern establishment's confidence in the soil and its servants. And no wonder: When the food supply wobbles nothing stays stable, least of all confidence in politicians and proclamations.

As far back as 1917, right after Marquis' collapse, Congress had enacted the Smith-Hughes Vocational Agriculture Program, a federal subsidy aimed mainly at training boys to run farms. With one in three citizens then living on the land this was not some sideshow in the American carnival; for a full third of the citizenry it was survival central.

In our modern enlightened age, planners and professionals surely would scoff at public schools expounding farm training. But the Smith-Hughes program created a scholastic tsunami that lifted at least one little boat. It exposed Norm to the way plants grow, the nature of soils, and the true wonders of corn. Seen in retrospect, Cresco High's Vo-Ag class set him sailing down the long tidal reach away from food production based on faith and toward the far better one based on fact.

However, not until 1929, in his sophomore high-school year, would he actually experience any fact-based farming. That September a new Vo-Ag instructor arrived. Fresh from Iowa State College, Harry Shroder was a devotee of something few people had heard of. Exuding all the zeal of a convert to a cult, he preached the exalted powers of science's newest revelation. Fertilizer.

Shroder's students didn't take to the new creed. Having never experienced this mysterious mixture of elemental plant foods, they reflected all the cynicism of their forefathers. Thus when the teacher proposed a planting trial they responded with the reluctance of hostile heretics.

Shroder cared nothing for that: he was one of the self-confident rarities who help others teach themselves. On a farm about a mile along the main road running through Cresco (on the site where today's high school stands) he had the class prepare small plots of soil, all identical. Some were then left untouched while others received differing combinations of nitrogen, phosphorus and potassium salts. Then the boys planted corn evenly across the whole area.

By season's end they could but gawk at what they'd wrought. A few pounds of powdered plant food in a hundred tons of soil lifted corn production into the stratosphere. This seemed quite surreal: Norm's family had sacrificed everything to achieve 25 bushels an acre. With almost no effort these student skeptics delivered the equivalent of 50!

For them this was a defining moment. Like Columbus running into the New World it might seem wrong but it clearly was real. The soil upon which Howard County farmers depended was malnourished, and that fundamental fact had gone unseen until a few high-school kids ran this simple test. Obviously the ceiling over farm life had nothing to do with God and everything to do with the ground.

That revelation impacted more than just plants and people; it dethroned Mother Nature. With fertilizer, the merest commoner could actually compel the absolute monarch to behave better!

In Norm's case this fling with fertilizer sparked a flame that would flare into an obsession with agricultural advancement. But that bonfire was for the future—a future that nearly didn't arrive because, according to the 1917 Act of Congress, anyone taking Vo-Ag courses had to abandon hope of higher learning and hurry home to help the folks. This was their responsibility, and most certainly it would have happened here. What carried young Borlaug past the high-school terminus was an educational conveyance with a distinctly different set of wheels.

Sport was big in Cresco—big enough to define this wayside whistle-stop. Despite a student body only 300 strong, Cresco High basked in statewide fame. The year before Norm arrived it had captured the state high-school football championship. A major contributor had been a quicksilver running back named George Champlin, who'd become team captain and town hero.

Naturally, Norm gravitated to football. Notwithstanding modest size (140 pounds, including boots, leather helmet and sopping locks on drizzly days), he played guard. As a junior he made the varsity squad and the following year got elevated to captain. As keeper of the town renown, however, he let everyone down. Cresco High's record under Borlaug leadership was 2 and 8—its worst ever showing. Although three key players had been lost to injury, he still feels the shame.

That happened in 1932, so we're getting ahead of our story. The point is that football was NOT what bore him right off the farm. The real vehicle ran on quite a different track.

Back in his freshman year, almost by accident, he'd gone out for wrestling. Farm work fashioned strength, sinew and a sturdy body, but the only appeal of grappling with others was that it helped sustain fitness during the snowy season when he lived in town and could find a few free hours. Sadly, not even that worked out; his very first meet delivered the wrestler's curse: boils.

In that era before washing machines, wrestling-mats were too big for frequent laundering. Consequently, they accumulated residues of sweat and skin that cultured colonies of staphylococcus. After slamming into one of those a knee, neck, backside, elbow or some even worse spot often erupted into a pus-packed, pulsating pile of bacterial depravity. Norm shudders at the recollection:

> During my first couple of years I suffered boil trouble. It hurt like hell but nothing could be done. Anyone with a boil was barred from competing until nature had run its course. Unfortunately nature had no appreciation for the significance of sport . . . I was out for the season.

For the moment, then, it seemed as if sport would get him nowhere. But he wasn't discouraged; his eyes were actually fixed on the baseball diamond. Like millions of country boys, he knew with Biblical certitude that the Big Leagues would take him to the top.

This universal boyhood belief resulted from radio's power to o'er-leap the cultural divide. By then, there existed a fabulous 50 kilowatt station that could reach across Middle America *during daytime* when baseball was played. Previously, a several-days-old journalist's description was the closest country kids could come to the action. Following the action live thus had a stunning effect. Play-by-play commentary created something close to mass addiction:

> Shortly after radio arrived through Granddad's crystal set we graduated to a battery powered Atwater Kent. This was our first true 20th Century technology. The batteries were bottles filled with liquid. They were kept charged through a wire that ran up the wall and out through a window to a little windmill on the roof. That whirling fan provided the only electricity in the whole house. It was our single concession to modernity and it powered our radio.
>
> An Atwater Kent's main selling point was the loudspeaker. This new invention allowed us to sit together and enjoy the entertainers who now commanded the night air that had previously been silent.
>
> Then, during the latter part of the 1920s a handful of high-power stations put out signals you could actually hear during the day. That added yet more excitement to life. Every Iowa farm boy loved WGN, which broadcast the Chicago Cubs on summer afternoons. What a joy! After unloading a wagonload of hay I'd dash inside for a drink of water and a chance to catch the score. The Cubs then became a major part of my being. Deep down, I knew that one day I'd be their second base.

Given that celestial plan, Cresco High's signature failing was its inability to understand baseball's importance. How could he make the Cubbies without the training and experience to develop the necessary skills? Any school that disregarded baseball was downright un-American!

To counter this pedagogical irresponsibility he started his own league.

Although the greater Saude community already had a baseball team, high-school students were barred from participating. Thus, while still a sophomore, he organized a parallel competition for teenagers. Getting that going wasn't so hard. In Saude and the surrounding communities—Protovin, Spillville, Jerico, Schley—he found teens interested in playing. They worked out a roster of games for the 1929 season; then each went out and recruited friends and neighbors to form a team representing their village. That in turn meant that the players represented their ethnic heritage and embodied Old World cultural loyalties.

When recalling how this bush-league for boys brought together teams representing different national identities even Norm evokes surprise at the outcome:

We were just squads of farm kids aged fifteen to eighteen. The Saude players were Norwegians except for the three Seery brothers, who were Irish and came from Schley. Other teams were Bohemian [Czech], German and Irish.

The facilities were very poor. The Saude home ground was a cow pasture with no dirt diamond and grass that grew too long. Bases were sand-filled sacks. Bats and gloves and balls were all well worn.

Yet we soon began attracting spectators, even cheering sections. By season's end fans were coming from miles around, and our Saturday exploits were the talk of the neighborhood.

Looking back, I can see that this was a surprisingly tough and talented group. With the unreality of youth, most of us dreamed of competing in college. Consequently, we dared not collect money for better facilities or equipment.

Back in those days colleges opposed commercialism as if it were a capital crime. A member of the Faculty Athletic Committee grilled each student who tried out for competitive sports. The first question was: "Did you play during the summer?" If you answered in the affirmative, the follow up question was: "Did you ever play a game where a collection was taken or a charge made at the gate?" Had you done that *even once* you could never play college sport. Ever!

Although we never took money, we were several times delighted to find that new balls or bats had mysteriously appeared in the cow pasture overnight.

I didn't realize it at the time but these clashes on the baseball diamond helped unite northeast Iowa's immigrant communities, which were so isolated their phone companies served only themselves. Villagers used their own languages and seldom needed to talk with outsiders. However, all took a keen interest in their baseball team's prowess against the rival villages.

Saude's biggest rivals were the Bohemians down in Spillville. We played them regularly and during my senior year our game was incorporated into Spillville's Fourth-of-July Celebration and was played at Dvorak Riverside Park, beside the Turkey River.

Though the afternoon proved to be hot as the devil, no one in the crowd of several hundred seemed to mind. Indeed, the conviviality between the Bohemians and Norwegians made that my most memorable Independence Day. Sadly we lost in extra innings, however the action proved so thrilling that someone later said it was as good as the fireworks.

Best of all, by day's end we all felt part of *America*.

Norm not only played second base, he captained the Saude squad. With eyes focused firmly on Wrigley Field, he led from the front. Bush baseball was his last chance of breaking out from the locked-down life; it would get him to Chicago. The great future that lay in waiting depended on his skills at batting, base-running and fielding.

During this grace period before the 1930s got their awful grip on wayward America, the Borlaugs were among many families looking toward the future. Indeed, across the Midwest people were peering past the horizon because the selfsame visionary who'd concocted corn husking contests had now dreamed a new dream.

Henry Wallace's latest moonlight madness involved a corn so special no one—not even in farm country—had imagined its like. His revelation derived from corn's prudence in positioning the male flowers at the top of the stem, while keeping the female flowers several feet below. Separating the sexes, however, exposes corn to molestation because the female flower can be shielded from natural pollination by enshrouding it in something as simple as a paper bag. When the time for fertilization arrives one merely removes the covering and shakes the pollen of a particular male flower over the virgin stigmas to create something unusual in the promiscuous plant world: seed whose parents are precisely known.

Charles Darwin first spotted the significance of this, and explored it to uncover truths relating to evolution. Starting in 1871, the great naturalist forced corn plants to pollinate themselves generation upon generation, only to discover that inbreeding in corn—as in royal families of his day—led to genetic weakness. His inbred plants were stunted and their ears were pocked with holes where infertility had prevented pollination.

No wonder Darwin abandoned this sorry line of investigation—what possible use could there be in making a crop *stunted and sterile*?

Three decades later, the issue was revisited by a gentle bearded biologist working at the Carnegie Institution on Long Island, New York. After five generations of inbreeding, George Harrison Shull had corns that reproduced true to type. He had, in other words, turned mongrels into purebreds—like English Setters, say.

Botanical incest made his purebreds as puny as Darwin's, but Shull then did something utterly silly: he took pollen from one degenerate and shook it on the female flower of another degenerate. Subsequently, the seeds were collected and the next season he planted them to see just how bad doubly degenerate corn would be.

Instead, he got to experience one of science's rare Eureka Moments. Far from producing the ultimate runt, matings between genetically challenged corn produced what he described as "an extraordinarily powerful hybrid . . . more vigorous than any of the inbred races."

It was a discovery to amaze an age, the Vegetable Kingdom's version of 90-pound weaklings breeding Hercules. And the offspring were certainly Herculean, having stiff stalks and massively productive ears jam-packed with plump kernels.

Shull termed this magical natural power "hybrid vigor."

Henry Wallace linked this magic to mankind's needs. From his teenage years he made inbred corns and crossbred them to see what would transpire. Unlike those hard-nosed graspers glorified as industry titans, this young man was diffident and even unworldly. His motivation was altruism rather than commercialism. Quite right, too: this strange sideline in abstract biology seemed too far-out to furnish anything functional.

Regardless of the lunacy behind his quest, this dream-weaver continued experimenting year after fateful year in fields just off the main street of Des Moines. Then when one of his plants proved robust enough to yield more than any previously known corn he rather tentatively set up a small business on his wife's family farm in the nearby hamlet of Johnston.

Reluctant to move beyond research, he had to be propelled into promoting the seeds for sale to the public. In 1926, however, his one-person Pioneer Hi-Bred Corn Company advertised the availability of Copper Cross. Soon word got about that Copper Cross yielded 25 to 100 more bushels of grain than a bushel of seed had ever given before.

In a world of sameness and steadiness this change was so colossal you'd expect every cornpone to clamor for Copper Cross. Instead, the super seed sowed resistance, doubt, even hostility. Across thousands of dinner tables, not to mention the counters of general stores, the wrangling developed into high-decibel discord.

The resistance arose not just from the conventional fear of change. No, the main concern was that to grow the new-fangled corn *you had to buy new seed every year!*

That requirement went beyond reason . . . it was the undoing of self-dependence and jeopardized the centuries-old source of survival—subsistence farming. Heavens to Betsy, hybrids needed cash.

Most farmers considered this more than an affront to their purse; it was an affront to their pride. The consensus around those dinner tables and general stores was that seeds that must be bought couldn't be worth the cost. That was certainly the Borlaugs' belief:

> In the late twenties Dad, Granddad and my very voluble Uncle Oscar got highly exercised over the issue of whether to buy hybrid corn seed. It was the first time I'd heard any family members yell at

each other. And it was disturbing.

Only Oscar was for trying hybrids. The others declared we should stay with Reid's Yellow Dent. Its seed was free . . . we collected it from our own fields. How could you possibly do better than that?

Norm's Uncle Oscar, a lifelong bachelor who by then managed Granddad Nels's farm, had been rebellious since conception. A free thinker, he tended to support anything modern. However, even the most progressive agricultural authorities dithered over this decision. "No one should make a complete change in one year," *Successful Farming* magazine warned its readers in April 1932. "Start with a small acreage now and find out the possibilities of hybrid corn."

Such cautions are easy to understand. The tradition of Middle America was tradition; farmers were conformists, not to mention custodians of the proper way. Why should they relinquish the pillars of the past to risk the fates of the future? Just for a seed.

Given these cultural canons few farmers would even test the new corn. As late as 1935 barely one acre in a hundred across the Corn Belt was sown to hybrids. Nonetheless, the adventursome loners who bought the sky-eyed experimenter's corn spawn reaped a fine reward, typically doubling their former take. Moreover, the stalks were so stiff that not even the pushy winds of fall could knock them over. The crop could, in other words, be harvested without testing the outer limits of male stamina. For the first time.

American Heritage magazine relates how an Illinois skeptic underwent his epiphany: "In 1936 a dreadful drought and heat wave— over one-hundred-degree days for two weeks—hung over the corn belt," wrote Joseph Kastner. "An Illinois farmer named Walter Meers, dreaming of growing 100 bushels per acre, had taken a chance on a field of hybrids. He watched in despair as all his corn wilted and dried in the heat. When rain came, it was too late to help his corn—except that field of hybrids which straightened up, greened out, and for all the traumatic heat, produced a miraculous one hundred and twenty bushels per acre."

That seems an exaggeration, but millions of growers did experience personal revelations. Hybrid corn thus touched the tipping point. And the door to a food-production revolution swung wide open.

For Henry Wallace success brought new setbacks. The "Hercules Effect" was peculiar in that it lasted but a single generation. Thus he had to create new seed every year, and the process proved very complex and very time consuming. Indeed, as farmer excitement outran his ability to furnish seed Pioneer Hi-Bred teetered toward financial failure.

A KID'S DREAM . . .

In 1913 Henry Wallace gives his grandfather a glimpse of hybrid corn seed. The revered elder (also named Henry Wallace) favored corns yielding the most handsome ears and kernels. His anointed masterpiece, the stunning Reid's Yellow Dent, was the Corn Belt's gold standard. However, his 25-year-old grandson in the sporty modern cap cared nothing for appearances: "What's looks to a hog?" he said. For him, bushels-per-acre was the only concern, and in time his high-yielding hybrids would send the national food supply rising like an escalator. From this point onward, seeds based on measured information would trump those based on mystical intuition.

. . . WORKS OUT

In time, young Wallace's seeds will build a billion dollar company and a trillion dollar industry. Corn being America's top crop, high-test hybrids will lift the national food supply. At the same time millions of farmers will become masters of their own fate. Those seeds certainly helped the Borlaugs slip into a comfortable lifestyle. And they taught Norm Boy Borlaug that high-performing seeds bestow on farm communities *and whole nations* the greatest of all blessings.

Then his wife stepped in: Knowing nothing about hybrid corn but everything about Henry, Ilo Browne Wallace donated her inheritance, thereby launching one of history's most successful family enterprises. Thanks to that trusting spirit, her husband who cared nothing for prosperity prospered mightily. She made the diffident dreamer a titan of industry despite himself.

No wonder the unworldly couple conquered the world of commerce. Though Iowa's corn harvests had never topped the divinely decreed 30 bushels an acre, the statewide "yieldscape" soon began lift off. In a decade or so hybrids and fertilizer together rocketed the state average to the unimaginable altitude of 75 bushels an acre.

Those may seem like mere numbers, and they are. But they're also indices of human aspiration. Thus as America's biggest crop scaled the heights of its inherent capabilities, so did farm life. On the back of hybrid corn millions of poverty-stricken farm families quickly clambered into the middle class. The ladder of opportunity's second rung had finally appeared: it was this super seed.

Here's where Borlaug himself came to appreciate a seed's power for public good. Securely locked in his subconscious was the understanding that a highly productive seed spreads blessings throughout society. Henry Wallace had spent 15 years developing Copper Cross; in time, Borlaug would more than match that record and produce seeds so productive that, like Archimedes' lever, they could lift the world.

Moreover, this was not the end of the astonishments to hit the heartland in the 1920s. Hard on the heels of hybrid corn and fertilizer came the mechanical horse to recast life yet again.

Around the time of Norm's birth Henry Ford perfected his Model T assembly line, and three years later, in 1917, the cranky crusader started another assembly line to mass-produce a tractor.

A farmer's son, Ford knew what he was doing. His Fordson lacked the storied Model T's persona or pizzazz, but it impacted human affairs even more. That little gray gadget broke the power barrier restraining food production since the first seeds were sown 10,000 years before. It could far exceed 5 mph, pull loads horses couldn't budge, motor on from dawn through sunset or, if asked politely, through the dark of night.

For all that, country folk resisted: Why on God's green earth should a family admit a metal monster into its midst? A horse was friendly, alive, a known quantity. The tractor was an intruder.

Coming on top of all the other rural revolutions this one might have lingered in obscurity longer had not President Wilson's made his big push for food to win the Great War. By the time the guns fell silent in France in 1918, federally subsidized machines were turning American sod. And from that point forward the tinny trespasser kept propagating, evolving and spreading. Within two decades, its pumped-up progeny were revitalizing ranches and farms coast to coast. In what amounts to a blinding flash in the course of human events, the horse became history and the age of muscle morphed into the age of machine.

Like hybrid corn and inorganic fertilizer, the tractor boosted food production beyond all expectations. For one thing, the 75 million acres required to feed 21 million horses and mules were immediately released to feed humans. Without breaking a single acre of virgin soil the tractor doubled America's food-grain production.

By the time the Borlaugs bought their steel-wheeled Fordson in the spring of '29 farm tractors were common. Norm's father and grandfather shared this hand-cranked helpmate that imbibed kerosene and insisted on taking every winter off. Luckily, during that frigid half of the year there wasn't much to do. Between October and April, it mostly drove the circular saw that "buzzed" tree limbs into billets that fed the range for purposes of cooking, cleaning and keeping away the cold.

Using tractors as portable power sources was then routine, and for good reason: In proper regard for their venerated stockholders the electric companies still refused to wire up rural America. Thus the tractor took on electricity's designated duties. Power take-offs turned water pumps, corn grinders, mills that ground oats into animal feed, augers that filled granaries and choppers that sliced corn plants for silage.

The rural robot thereby turned personal redeemer, as millions allowed the miracle of the machine age into their life. Among those was Norm:

> That little gray tractor produced no manure, so flies were no longer a bother and we could keep it near the house. It worked without a feed of oats morning, noon and night. Greatest of all, it seldom needed salve or soothing and never got a rub down, so we were freed from tending animals every day of our lives.
>
> In time, inspired engineers devised a corn-picking mechanism that could be fastened to a tractor's power take-off. What a godsend! The two-month horror of harvesting, husking, and heaving hundreds of thousands of corn ears was no more. Tractor-powered devices gathered the crop and elevated the cobs into the crib so easily young men like me forgot the shooting pains that had burdened sleep during every previous harvest season. With a tractor shouldering the brutal burdens corn picking seemed almost a lark.

Henry Ford's greatest invention. Before this, farmers needed sun, soil, seeds and strong muscles; but with a tractor they no longer needed their children as field hands. Norm experienced this huge humanitarian impact. When he was 15 the family bought an early steel-wheeled Fordson like this one. The fact that it didn't need constant feeding and attention lifted the main restriction on their lives and made possible such luxuries as a day off or a visit to town.

None of us had ever considered work to be anything like that. But relief from endless drudgery equated to emancipation from servitude. Country kids like me finally could follow our heart's desire. And that amounted to the ultimate freedom.

One thing Norm couldn't know is that his time spent with the touchy old tractor would serve him well. In a later life, in a hungry country, he'd pilot an old Farmall for days on end plowing, harrowing, weeding and preparing plots and fields in a remote desert where, thanks to his boss' disapproval, he works entirely alone and without equipment other than the small device provided by a considerate neighbor.

A s the decade of the '20s crept toward its demise the spirit of enterprise was reborn; around the farms you heard a new kinda talk. Three distinctly different technologies—fertilizer, hybrid corn and the tractor—were acting like ratchets, raising harvests, horizons and hopes. Within those ten years they'd uplifted the countryside three times over. So the new talk was happy talk.

Country folk were uplifted too. Across Middle America the tempo of existence quickened and broadened. The locked-down life came unlatched and out marched the modern era in double time. By decade's end Midwesterners had leapt from exemplars of conformity to exemplars of change. As 1929 got underway millions of country folk were welcoming newness not just with open minds but with open hearts.

So it was that the age-old rules of the rural universe got overthrown. In just ten years the never-ending fight for subsistence and survival had passed into history. The house that had forever been a surrogate factory, laundry, bakery, cannery, and packinghouse was no longer any of those. With money to share with shopkeepers, the farmers finally had a home, not to mention a fate of their own choosing.

The sudden switch from survival farming to surplus farming also refashioned the face of the countryside. With the unwieldy mix of crops and creatures now unnecessary, families jettisoned them with glee. Norm's father, for instance, sold off all but two of his cows (*paying* for milk being quite unthinkable). He retired Bob and the other horses under what modern advertising hypes as "assisted living" (spoiled rotten in this case). Although the need to barter eggs had disappeared, he still kept a few chickens to provide fried eggs for breakfast and fried chicken for dinner. There was, however, no more scavenging for food in the woodlot. Even the vegetable plot was abandoned. Potatoes were no longer the only policy for life insurance.

Henry Borlaug's sole specialties now were corn and hogs. Freed from the need to feed horse teams, he tore down fences and cultivated the entire hundred acres. He sowed Wallace's seeds. He applied fertilizer. He fired up the tractor to fight the weeds. And he harvested 52 bushels an acre; more than twice the family's previous best.

Because this doubling of yield was accomplished over twice the former acreage, the land on which the family had struggled to survive for 80 years suddenly produced four times the bounty. And the human toil had tumbled to a tad of its former torment.

This coalescing of efficiencies provided blessings across the countryside. Millions of farm families stared at the last page of their single-entry ledger, and discovered a miracle. The awe in their eyes was almost as impressive as the wads in their wallets. "Wonder of wonders, Ma. We got money!"

The collective joy, arising phoenix-like from the death of a primitive age, yielded the greatest wealth any rural region had ever accumulated. American consumers benefited too. Farm productivity is the spark plug of the food supply, which is of course the engine of the nation.

Now selling grain by the ton, the Borlaugs helped hundreds of fellow citizens not only with food but cheaper food. They and millions like them strengthened and steadied the platform that underpins society.

To the farmers themselves, the greatest uplift was liberation from looking after animals. With no cows to coddle or horses to handle, they could pursue outside interests—a trip to town, say, or a big-band concert across the county line—free of worry . . . or guilt. They could finally accept the sacred gift of mobility the all-weather roads made possible. Norm sums up the feeling of freedom:

> Only those who experienced it can appreciate the blend of excitement and satisfaction in having your life's prospects made over. Farm families had seen their frontier expand but now, with no animals to care for, they could go out and explore it. Suddenly we could shape our own fate without the old restrictions. We could get an education; maybe even a profession. The possibilities seemed endless. That sudden perception was so overwhelming it amounted to a change in consciousness.
>
> For the Borlaugs this amounted to a dream come true. Previously, the prospect of better times had been merely a family faith, one that most likely would never eventuate in our lifetimes. Now, however, it was clear that Granddad had been right all along. His fabled future had arrived. And it was even more fabulous than anything we'd dared wish for. The solid wall around rural life had

virtually vanished in the mists; the larger world was ours for the taking!

The amazing thing was that this unbounded existence had been opened by people none of us knew and inventions none of us had ever foreseen. Harry Shroder, Henry Wallace and Henry Ford and their improbable creations came out of nowhere to put us on the highway to happiness.

All in all, the decade delivered so many technological triumphs that the 1920s can be said to have made modern America. Food is, after all, a fuel more basic than anything produced by industry. And this decade secured the supply that set up the nation.

That extreme farm makeover was not, however, an unmitigated blessing: On the positive side, millions of the traditionally dispossessed leaped up the ladder of prosperity, to say nothing of freedom, fulfillment and self respect. And the age-old poverty-driven, survival-based, hierarchical, extended family system gave way to the free nuclear family.

On the negative side, the slow life sped up, villages began dying, local loyalties loosened, farms expanded, and the separation of family members tore apart the cocoon of community. In time, villages by the thousands lost their purpose, and disappeared into the ether. Even Saude vanished, leaving only a name on the map and the memory, slowly fading like the Cheshire cat's smile. The 1920s thus stole much of farm country's storied "pastoral innocence." Which was certainly sad.

Sad too was Nels Borlaug's fate. His future served as his past. Inventions were revered now, and the new horsepower appealed most vividly to youthful and uninhibited minds. A chasm thus opened between the generations, and old-timers found themselves left on the farther side. Their knowledge of soil and weather in their tiny sliver of America might be unsurpassed, but it had been rendered obsolete. With nothing to offer, they were put out to pasture. Just like the horses.

And there was another thing nearly as troubling: Unemployment descended on farm youths like a flannel blanket. No longer needed as a household workforce, they had to stay in school all the way to eighth grade . . . or even beyond. They had to endure endless classroom tedium. Heavens above, a few were forced to suffer leisure.

That was so far from God's plan it seemed immoral!

That January they reached the greatest of all years: 1929. It opened as the epitome of progress. And the months ahead promised even greater prospects. That May, Herbert Hoover entered the White

House and as the balmy summer drew to a close, everyone was excited. Indeed, the air breathed across mid-America seemed oxygenated.

The hit song of the moment captured that mood:

> *Blue skies are smiling at me;*
> *Blue skies are all I see.*

But late in October something both mean and mysterious supervened: Millions of prudent hard-working Midwesterners suddenly fell pell-mell back into poverty and home detention. An evil force they'd never heard of and couldn't combat knocked the smiles from their faces. With its inexplicable thousand-mile reach, Wall Street reached out and ravaged the rural regions that hardly knew what Wall Street was. Plunging stocks even pulled the sapphire smiles from the skies.

Thus, as the '20s ground to a halt the heartland suffered a grievous body wound not of its own making. The inhabitants underwent a mood swing; the bubble-of-high-hopes burst, and loosed a torrent of hopeless gloom that ran across the region like a river. Millions recoiled into what remained of their communal carapace. The sociological scenery regained its somber shade. And the unbearable burden of bleakness fell right back on the bent and battered rural shoulders. The ascendant life had gone so quickly it surely must have been a fraud.

This psychic subsidence was very hard to take. The year of the yo-yo ended as the saddest of years. Having first raised hopes beyond reason, 1929 finally ravished the wondrous new order between food producers and food consumers.

Thus, the decade that had opened promising peace, prosperity and never-ending pleasure passed into history leaving nothing but ill will and anguish. Once more, farmers could only press their noses against the window of the world. They'd been cast out and stuffed back in their parallel planet just as in the days of yore.

Such was the social scene when young Borlaug began his sophomore year. Life was disoriented. More than that, it was dissolving. The underdog dreams had died. Only one thing now sprang eternal: despair.

That's how he felt. For him, there was no longer any possibility of a future beyond high school. He could never be a professional.

His great escape had ended at the prison gate.

Now back in shackles and chains, he had only one option: to spend the rest of his days struggling to grow food for his family.

Just as a son of the soil was supposed to do.

1930-1933

Nightmares

I n September 1930, his junior year began with a surprise: During the summer break the school board had hired a feisty new principal.

An intense, dark-haired "Dutchman," David C. Bartelma also coached wrestling. Short and scarcely 135 pounds, he seemed a giant to the students, having been chosen an alternate on the U.S. squad selected for the 1924 Olympic Games in Paris. In little Cresco this star seemed to have descended not from Iowa Falls but from the outermost fringes of the known universe!

One of those rare educators with the knack for inducing life-changing attitudes, Bartelma broke with tradition and treated his charges more like brother than boss. A master of mind games, he not only chided, he challenged the wrestlers to attempt the impossible. And to that end he promoted a five-point strategy:

Give your best . . .
Believe you can succeed . . .
Face adversity squarely . . .
Be confident you'll find the answers when problems arise.
Then go out and win some bouts!

Better than Freud at his finest, Coach Bartelma exploited peer pressure and personal persuasion for psychological impact. Also his teaching encompassed more than mere athletics. By insisting they give their utmost both on the playing field *and* in the classroom, he imbued Cresco High with the power of positive thinking. "Give the best God gave you," he'd scream, "or don't bother competing!"

Under this man's barrage of taunting and tutelage Norm plumbed his own personal depths, becoming fast, agile, tricky, strong, and star of the

CAREER SAVER #2

Fate's second facilitator, David Bartelma. Cresco's high-school principal, he taught Norm wrestling as well as the mentality for making a good life. His goading resonated with the boy's own grit and solidified the rock-like dedication that would support the long, chaotic and often very insecure career to come.

PROBLEM-SOLVING TRAINEE

Borlaug's lucky charm proved to be high school wrestling. The sport drew out his inherent dedication, ignited his latent smarts, and allowed him to taste the sweetness of accomplishment. In time those traits would triangulate his professional prowess. More importantly, though, wrestling provided an escape hatch. It got him right off the farm.

takedown. Out on the wrestling mat, with nowhere to hide and no one to help, the answers had to come from within. Success, therefore, took more than muscle . . . it took mental aptitude. When trapped in tight circumstances, he had to devise a move. Any move. Instantly. And then devise another.

Mental quickness also begat mental strength. Wrestlers mostly fight themselves; given the myriad ways to squirm out of trouble, they lose mainly by surrendering to pessimism. Surmounting the standoff between a body wanting to quit and a brain wanting to continue boosts willpower. Success means neither giving in nor giving up, no matter what the torture.

Pedagogs may deny it, but wrestling provides as many life lessons as reading, and here's where the skinny introvert, a newcomer to intellectual interests, morphed into a fine-tuned thinker capable of facing whatever fate or circumstance might toss in his path. He explains:

> Wrestling made me mentally tough. Given my small size and small hands I had to focus very hard . . . if my thoughts wavered I got humiliated fast. Thus I learned to never give up whatever the odds.

This, then, is how he got the first taste of talent, and it was terrific. It was also the beginning of wisdom. Now he knew he could succeed beyond the farm gate. He'd imbibed the Coach's five-point strategy for better living. And he'd employ those positive powers the rest of his days.

Seen in retrospect, the wrestling coach steered this young life more than all the other educators combined. Bartelma made a callow youth muscular in mind as well as motor. From here on, Borlaug exudes an air of confidence that seems unshakable, no matter how adverse the situation. Ultimately, his unflappability will prove more valuable than anything imparted by books or blackboards. And he'll win many bouts.

Throughout 1930 kids in the Corn State's northeastern niche knew little of the terrible goings on in the creepy world of commerce. The nation's emerging economic infection appeared to have overlooked or avoided them. Norm saw no breadlines, soup kitchens, or ragged men swarming for a job that paid a few cents an hour. Nonetheless as the year progressed, more and more Howard County farmers licked their lips and tasted the dread of dispossession.

Then in 1931 the dollar disease emerged full blown when two of Cresco's three banks padlocked their doors, sealing forever the depositors' hard-won cash. Victims included some utterly bewildered Borlaug neighbors who'd scrupulously followed the age-old policy of prudence by maintaining a healthy balance in the savings account. Every week for a lifetime they'd deposited every surplus penny. Now that deed of solid citizenship had left them destitute.

The Borlaugs' small cash reserve went too, and with it their new-found dreams. That summer, Norm's hope of joining the workforce evaporated. He couldn't even work at home—the farm being too small and too unprofitable to gainfully employ both father *and* son.

In September 1931 he returned to Cresco High for his final fling with formal learning. And with sport too. During that winter of his senior year he won the District Meet, which included high-school wrestlers from several northeastern counties. By now he was among Iowa's best, and later that semester he reached the finals of the State High School Tournament held in Des Moines.

Also earning distinction in the capital city was a fellow team member. Ervin Upton competed in the next weight-class down (135lb), and he too reached the finals. The fact that both these small-town boys had triumphed in the big city was cause for celebration. Indeed, they subsequently became training partners as well as best pals. And as our story unfolds that bond will prove beneficial.

Other than that, though, his final year of high school offered little worth celebrating. Members of the Class of '32 dared not discuss the future. They'd soon be dumped into a society that was adrift and wholly lacking in opportunities. They knew that work was the key to success, but along with everything else work had died. Thus they'd never be able to open the door to satisfaction. There was no handle!

After the commencement ceremony in May 1932 most Cresco High graduates slunk off to individualized despair.

They'd earned a rite of passage to nowhere.

Not even home.

An incident that graduation day emphasized the depths to which good folks had sunk. Following the ceremony Norm and Erv Upton remained in town and spent the night with their pal Bob Smylie. All three played on the football team. As left tackle, Bob lined up beside Norm, so for a couple of hours a week the two shared brainwaves.

Bob was not from a local farm; he'd arrived in Cresco just the year before. His father had been Superintendent of Schools for a central-Iowa town. However, collapsing tax revenues had forced the councilors to abolish the superintendent's position. Hoping to uncover some means of sustaining themselves, the Smylies headed off and after 200 miles ended up in remote Cresco, where they operated a one-pump gas station at the corner of Highway 9 and today's Schroder Drive.

Desperate for every single cent, the family adopted a then-unique business strategy: 24 hour service. Bob drew the graveyard shift. After dossing down in the station's tiny loft, he'd wake up whenever he heard a vehicle pull in downstairs. At, say, two in the morning he'd roll off his camp cot, scamper down a ladder, crank a heavy handle, pump a few gallons of gas, and climb back to the bed above his head.

On typical nights a couple of trucks might stop by (the geriatric cars of 1932 tended to be nyctophobic). Likely, he sold 20 gallons—maybe $4 worth. The resulting 20 cents profit, though, was more than enough to keep a growing boy from his bed rest.

Even today, Norm is haunted by that garret over the gas station:

> It was almost bare. Bob had unfolded a couple of camp cots, but could offer us nothing more. He was burdened by appalling poverty. When Erv and I returned to our homes next day, we left our friend living in that crummy little loft. He had nothing to look forward to except being woken up all through the night. I felt a deep sadness. From such utter deprivation Bob Smylie had no chance of amounting to *anything*.

Of course few of the high-school class of 1932 could amount to much. With the economy in the tank, the likelihood of going to college was indeed remote. Scholarships and fellowships were not even the stuff of dreams. Norm's grades had been good—he'd been listed among the school's outstanding students and had won the American Legion Citizenship Award as well as the Athletic Coaches' Medal of Honor. But there was no prospect of financial help, and that meant no possibility of higher education. College took cash. And none of that could be conjured up.

Actually, that moneyless summer of '32 is of fearful recollection. Farm prices plunged to levels so ruinous that even the prudent became prone to panic. Indeed, the low-grade fever warming millions of rural minds melted the social contract between town and country, and erupted in the worst form of social boil: a farmers' strike!

During that summer, the rural masses decided to teach the city folk a lesson in the importance of food, to say nothing of supply and demand. Thousands of farmers withheld their produce; some even burned their fields. In ten days, so they declared, the national reserves would run out; food would become scarce; bellies would rumble; prices would soar. And to this glorious end they bellowed:

Let's call a farmers' holiday
A holiday let's hold.
We'll eat our wheat and ham and eggs
And let them eat their gold.

Across the Corn Belt activists brewed up protests they swore would be "worse than the Boston Tea Party." In a dozen states roads were strewn with nails, baling wire, logs or spiked telegraph poles to stop food from getting to the cities. In August, for example, 1500 irate farmers blocked every highway into Sioux City. All farm trucks were strip-searched. Those headed for hospitals were allowed to pass; the rest had their loads—milk, meat, cheese, eggs, vegetables, fruits and so forth—dumped into the ditches.

Like today's failing nations in Africa, America in 1932 was entwined in civil conflict whose technical, social and economic coils were complex enough to camouflage common sense. With their hands on the aorta of national life, the farmers let heady thoughts so overheat their minds that the Midwest seemed poised for the ultimate conflagration. "Unless something is done for the American farmer," Edward A. O'Neal III, president of the American Farm Bureau Federation, told Congress, "we'll have revolution in the countryside in less than twelve months."

This possibility of rural revolt panicked the politicians. None had imagined a challenge to democracy coming from this quarter. Yes, the jobless in the unionized industrial cities, like Detroit and Pittsburgh, might rebel. But the lovers of freedom out on the peaceful plains and prairies where common decency and tolerance prevailed? Never!

Still and all, country folk were getting mighty angry. Many regarded America with contempt. Some saw Soviet Russia as a utopian ideal: weren't its people happy? And working? And eating?

New Russia's Primer, a book comparing the smooth simplicity of Communism with the chaos of Capitalism, became a bestseller and Book-of-the-Month Club selection. And for reporting the wonders of Soviet organization a New York Times reporter earned the 1933 Pulitzer Prize.

Such rabid rhetoric further undermined domestic tranquility. Indeed, even the coolest heads soon flared into firebrands. Norm recalls:

OUTLAWS IN OVERALLS

Sioux City, Iowa, 1932. Between 1930 and 1933, when Borlaug was 16 to 19, America's food producers rebelled. No longer willing to accept enforced poverty, farmer groups like the one shown here stopped food shipments to the cities. Hunger, they hoped, would force the city slickers to recognize and relieve the heartland's hurt.

It sure was scary. But the cause was clear. Farming no longer paid! Thanks to Dad's natural prudence our finances were fairly secure, but several neighbors were fighting foreclosure. Some had mortgaged their properties; others had merely taken out a loan for a tractor or maybe a car. Now they were losing everything.

Many such victims merely abandoned their properties. The populace that venerated permanence suddenly embraced wanderlust. Almost overnight millions turned transient, heading west in search of a new American Dream. Throughout the Great Plains, roads filled with jalopies wobbly-wheeling westward.

As these millions took off toward the setting sun whole counties emptied out. Commerce then ground to a halt and banks began collapsing. Even back in '31, before the economic tremors registered on the rural Richter scale, 1075 small-town banks failed. Their customers were worse than destitute . . . they were in California!

All this was of national consequence. As a writer of the time put it: "In the fact that farmers were less and less able to buy the things that the people in the cities were making, lies the explanation of how one surplus caused another, until farmers were burning wheat while bread lines lengthened in the cities, until the fantastic spectacle of poverty in the midst of plenty traversed America like a dance of death."

Given the ripeness for rural revolt, that tragic tarantella would have spawned manic destruction were it not for a surprising innovation: the "penny sale." This unique departure from legality, perhaps even from integrity, quickly took hold across God's good country.

Penny sales were a perversion of the public foreclosure auctions in which a gang of locals calmly surrounded legitimate bidders and not so gently escorted them from the premises. Should any misbegotten gold-digger resist, a popular expedient was to whip off his trousers, which invariably sent him whizzing for his wheels. Then, with all opposition swept aside, a designated local stepped forward and cast the only bids: 5 cents for a plow, say, or 2 bits for a team of mules. Finally, they bought the property for a few dollars and gifted the whole thing back to its former owners.

This was one of the few times when persons of felonious intent embodied the finest of values. Not since the Revolution had so many civilians united in collective criminality as the farmers in the early 1930s. Their sin was to save families by the thousands from the shame of eviction and the loss of their equity. It was, in a way, a moment in which the power of common sense trumped that of the Constitution.

And the mass resistance was hardly limited to meatheads. One Minnesota sheriff decided to sneak in a foreclosure sale while his town's militants were off attending what they called a "unity meeting." When word of his snap auction leaked out, 60 farm wives stormed the police station and incarcerated both sheriff and deputy inside their own jail cells.

Norm experienced this ingenious illegality only tangentially when he attended a penny sale outside the tiny community of Saratoga. That raucous scene in the summer of '32 seemed surreal because everyone, including the sheriff, knew they were fostering a felony. As an Iowan's cradle-to-grave responsibility was to display probity and rectitude, the fevered scene—for all its moral magnificence—amounted to dalliance with the devil.

Even to young Borlaug the sham transactions were deeply troubling. This was his first (but far from last) brush with the ambiguity lurking in the rear of revolutions. And its impact was lasting. From here on he'd never be disturbed by the specter of illegality when he found it loitering with moral intent.

Having exactly paralleled the president's term of office, Norm's high school career climaxed with Herbert Hoover's 1932 run for reelection. His senior year began amid September's campaign smoke. And this time the Great Engineer was in deep trouble: He'd been at the helm during the country's worst economic collapse. Moreover, he seemed uncomfortable on the stump and no longer resonated with the public. Americans now considered him a hopeless stuffed shirt. Just like the European Pooh-Bahs had.

This was no longer the doer who launched himself full tilt into tasks, who demanded results not rhetoric, and who had no patience for red tape. Now a purely political body, Hoover avoided decisions and favored being a facilitator who brought disputants together, encouraged partnerships, and delegated the decisions to the specialists. He had, in other words, become thoroughly modern.

By contrast, his opponent was such a man of action that the general public had no clue he was actually immobile. Self-confident and supremely optimistic, Franklin Delano Roosevelt radiated a strange mix of charm and haughty self-assurance. His big smile and obvious relish for the campaign trail made people feel he cared for them individually.

His message was one of pure hope with a dash of hokum. It was fashioned from a simple philosophical premise: "the nation was in trouble and the government would do something." In reality, FDR had become the Hoover of old—eager to launch himself full tilt into tasks, demanding results not rhetoric, immune to the fear of failure, indifferent to red tape, and free of worry about anything so trivial as plans.

That November more Americans voted than in 1928, powered this time by poverty. And Roosevelt won in a landslide: 472 Electoral College votes to 59.

Four months later, on the cold dank morning of March 4, 1933, his last day in the White House, Hoover awoke to a final humiliation: overnight, the banking system had collapsed. "We are at the end of our string," the Chief Executive sighed, "there is nothing more we can do."

So there it was. Herbert Hoover could not after all repeat what he'd done for Belgium. The world's greatest food administrator had let his own countrymen starve and had let the financial crisis run its course like an un-dammed river. Since 1929 about 10,000 banks had failed, and he'd accepted the fact. Why not? Wasn't the Great Depression was an act of God? Clearly even a Quaker was outmatched.

Later that morning as he exited through the Front Portico the nation appeared to be falling off a cliff. To him, it must also have seemed like he was falling from the White House into a personal abyss.

In hopelessness Hoover was far from alone: the country was scared to its inner core, bereft of ideas, at the end of its string. Even the iron-willed Eleanor Roosevelt wondered whether anyone could "do anything to save America now."

On that particular March morning destiny awakened her husband, who had every right to feel as forlorn as his forerunner. Just a month earlier, at a public gathering in Miami, death had come within a foot of his forehead. The bullet, fired by an unemployed bricklayer down on his luck, had struck the mayor of Chicago, who was standing behind FDR. Fatally stricken, Anton Cermak was rushed to hospital in the Roosevelt limousine, cradled in the president-elect's bloodied arms and sprawled across the metal rods encasing the unfeeling legs.

Through all the danger and distress of that moment FDR remained unfazed. He is said to have slept well that night and apparently never mentioned the incident again.

A month later, having just taken the oath of office, the 32nd president confronted a crowd that included a contingent of World War veterans furious at being cheated of the prosperity for which they'd imperiled their lives just 15 years before. Some 10,000 ex-soldiers had built makeshift camps within the District of Columbia. Although unarmed and accompanied by wives, children and family pets, they were agitated enough to seem like warriors on active service. Indeed, for several months the Federal City had felt besieged from within.

Regardless of reality, the Feds considered this a threat to national survival and rushed in more troops than Washington had had there since Grant and Sherman's day, when national survival truly was on the line.

This would not, however, be the Army's finest campaign. The foemen it faced were destitute comrades who as eager youths had staked their lives for duty, honor, country. Many were highly decorated for bravery in the face of the Hun. Now, though, the Army considered them depraved vermin to be mown down in the streets. Tanks milled

CAPITAL . . .

In 1932 and 1933 America resembled those chaotic backward countries we now call failed states. Washington D.C., for example, was besieged by veterans seeking early disbursement of a promised bonus for their service in World War I. In response . . .

. . . CHAOS

. . . the Army donned its gas masks, fixed bayonets, and turned Independence Avenue into a war zone. Borlaug was 18 when anarchy reigned in the capital of the free world. America seemed to be in a death spiral. And there was no hope for anyone, least of all him.

around the Capitol. Federal buildings along Pennsylvania Avenue had echoed the drumming hoof beats of an honest-to-god cavalry charge. And the shacks sheltering the old soldiers had been burned, during which travesty a little boy ran into the flames to rescue his pet rabbit and got shot for disobeying a federal order.

The mood had turned so ugly that the inauguration parade was placed in the hands of doughty Douglas MacArthur. The hardheaded hero of the frontlines in France knew exactly what was needed: machine-gun nests at strategic points along the President's motorcade route from the Capitol to the White House.

On the new president none of this made any mark. Seemingly unaware of any danger lurking within the human sea washing up the Capitol Steps, FDR repeated the oath of office in the rain, turned stiffly to the podium and, ignoring both public applause and possible assassination, stood erect on his steel braces. At that moment the skies cleared and the sun burst through the parting clouds like a celestial benediction.

Then pulling from his pocket some notes he'd scribbled a few days earlier the new president blared his famous sing-song phrases:

Let me first assert my firm belief
that the only thing we have to fear...
is fear itself.

Next he identified America's most fundamental affliction: the "name-less, unreasoning, unjustified terror which paralyzes needed efforts to convert retreat into advance."

Basically, this was bluster; for the moment Roosevelt's sole asset was a buoyant boom. All he could do was capitalize on his larynx's powers of persuasion. Yet he remained supremely confident. The overachiever who 12 years earlier had surrendered his spinal cord to nature's invisible hand knew bright dreams could light the path that rose from the depths of despair.

The old recordings render FDR's voice reedy, but by some quirk those scratchy sounds hosted hope. Millions glued to their radios in one of the first ever coast-to-coast hookups felt their hearts stir. The sincerity coloring those aerial vibrations, caused millions of heads to nod approval as he declared: "This nation asks for action, and action now." He would, he said, ask Congress for power "as great as the power that would be given to me if we were in fact invaded by a foreign foe."

These empty phrases filled the public spirit almost to overflowing.

Pessimism reversed itself, accelerating past remission to flirt with exhilaration.

More than any other presidential election this one tipped the national mood. His wife found the swing to sanguinity ". . . a little terrifying. You felt that they would do anything—if only someone would tell them what to do." Despite knowing that the finger on the national pulse was her husband's, Eleanor Roosevelt remained fearful. The new administration was, she declared, "going it blindly. We are in a tremendous stream and none of us knows where we are going to land."

FDR felt no such fears. He was putting on a tutorial in how to turn things around when they've reached the end of the string. Psychology is then more vital than technology; positive thinking more powerful than practicality; morale more important than money or method.

It was a lesson Borlaug and his peers absorbed into their souls, and it helps explain why in time they'd be called The Greatest Generation. They never got discouraged. Even when at the end of their string.

Great words may have been vital, but the problems were both deaf and ill-disposed to concede defeat. So next morning, the president rolled into the Oval Office, spent a moment communing alone, yelled for his aides, and turned his little wooden wheelchair toward the future. This was the time for great works.

Rowdiness in the rural heartland was the most pressing problem. Having learned that poverty was not preordained, the newly enfranchised citizenry of the soil now loathed slaving for subsistence. They wanted money. Sure, the taste had been short-lived but the sweetness lingered long.

For starters, then, the new broom in the White House needed to sweep out rural unrest, and fast. Trouble was, nothing suggested itself. There was no way to repel, let alone quell, angry farmers. Nor was there time for learned reviews, academic analyses, even proper planning. In military terms, the moment demanded a bold offensive. "We've got to do *something*," he said; "try anything."

This exposed FDR's most basic talent: the readiness to lead the multitude along new and untrodden paths where there were no guide-posts and every step might prove a misstep. Exuding the force of affirmative, he demanded Congress assemble in special session. Then during the next 100 days, perhaps the wildest three months in peacetime political history, he delivered a flurry of bills targeting federal largess on those trapped below the bottom of the economic pile. In an off-hand remark he dubbed his cocktail of crude offensives "a new deal for the

American people."

This hasty jumble of "do *something*, try anything" concepts transformed the relation between the government and the governed. And not everyone approved . . . not by a long shot. To many, the new president was a raving lunatic; his program a sell-out to communism, sovietism, socialism, revolution, dictatorship or totalitarianism. It was definitely un-American. Critics declared him a diseased tyrant out to end private property, the Constitution, the American Way and even Western Civilization. Some expressed undying preference for Hitler. Venomous stories of the president's disability, ancestry, and marital relations were passed around as gospel truths. FDR (mostly) laughed, and went on dreaming and scheming and pushing progress ahead of him like a ball down a dark corridor.

T his was the uncivil state of American civics when the 18-year-old Borlaug boy finished high school. He graduated into what Eleanor Roosevelt later called "The Lost Generation." The honor was hardly great, and the first lady's concerns were genuine. "I have moments of real terror." she explained, "when I think we may be losing this generation."

That fear was well founded. Already 2 million citizens were national nomads, roaming aimlessly, living out of boxcars, jumping freights, hitch-hiking, panhandling . . . ever hopeful of a job or a meal, often finding neither. More than a quarter-million of them had yet to reach their majority. They were "riding the rods" to nowhere.

Although life for most young souls had lost all meaning, Norm Boy managed to stay home, stay active and stay upbeat. It was never easy. From June 1932 he worked around the farm for his food and keep. For cash he toiled for the neighbors, who paid him a dollar a day to thrash oats or fill silos with chopped green corn plants (done the old hard way, using horse- and human muscle). During winter he felled their dead trees, split the trunks into fence posts and firewood, and got rewarded with 75 cents for each long, hard, frozen-fingered day.

Although laborious, all this was also something of a lark. The work kept this former wrestler in great physical shape and the meager compensation failed to crush the effervescence that had buoyed him since birth. Indeed, the bedlam and bleakness were strangely stimulating for a restive 18-year-old occupying the limbo between poverty and possibility.

Adding to the fizz was the knowledge that he had things easy. You see, his family was not in debt and was eating. Nevertheless, adjusting to hopelessness was hard, despite the weather's best efforts at helping. The summer of '32 delivered far too many hundred-degree days; then gave way to a winter that delivered far too many 30-below-zero days.

During those frigid weeks of January'33, he was overjoyed to learn that the Midwest Amateur Athletic University Wrestling Tournament would be held in tiny Cresco late in February. The competition was for college students, but to his surprise the sponsors created for him a special category: "Unattached to Any Institution."

Powered by latent bitterness, he wrestled his heart out, and his toil-tempered body proved almost unbeatable. He out-pinned, out-pointed and out-escaped all comers until the final bout, where he faced a star from Iowa State Teacher's College.

Norm had never clapped eyes on a campus, while his opponent was a senior who a week earlier had won the All State College Tournament. Despite the seeming mismatch, the struggle proved torrid enough that the third period ended tied. Then during overtime—on a close, even disputable call—the referee awarded the other youth an escape.

Whereas Norm found that frustrating, fortune found it fitting. That this unheralded high school kid could walk in off the farm and compete with college champions had impressed the opponent's coach: "If you'd like to come to Teacher's College next fall," he whispered as the dejected youngster trailed off the mat, "I'll try to find you a job."

Those words changed everything. This single, seductive, very vague sentence was enough to convince the man-child his months of struggle had paid off. Right there, standing in his cotton shorts and sweaty singlet before the excited crowd with cheers echoing around the Cresco High gym, his number had come up. Indeed, the prospect of a fine future instantly blossomed into rosy brilliance before his disbelieving eyes.

In seven more months he'd go to Teacher's College!

L ater the reality of his condition hit home, precipitating a frantic fight for funds. For one thing, as the world warmed and the snow melted he explored a new route to financial success by running lines of traps through the woods behind the house, and managed to catch a number of weasel, muskrat and skunk. The pelts he dispatched by parcel post to a rough-and-tumble Kansas City dealer who sent back small thin envelopes enclosing a dollar bill or two.

Dreams of the big one are perhaps the only pleasure open to anyone plumb out of cash, and each evening he secured a trap deep in the stream behind the house. It seemed merely a silly obsession until one morning that snare contained a mink. The thrill is still experienced in flashback. The pelt brought $10! It was not unlike hitting the lottery when you reckoned you'd hit rock bottom.

When 1933 finally managed to right its weather in March—about the time when FDR was inaugurated—Norm again approached the neighbors, only to find they were down to paying just 50 cents for a hard day's toil.

Nonetheless, through that summer he beat himself up performing their chores. What did he have to lose? This would be the last farm work he'd ever do. Never again would he labor in the fields. He had a profession!

Then in June a letter from Cedar Falls arrived. His application was accepted and a job would be found to help him meet personal expenses.

He replied, expressing deepest gratitude and confirmed he'd report on time in mid-September. Of that there was no doubt: This was his one chance for a good life. He couldn't afford to miss it!

By now he'd hoarded $50 from the pelts and the neighbors' pennies, and the scent of success, a fragrance more heady in 1933 than perhaps any other year in American history, became hard to suppress. Of the quarter-million souls in his gone-to-hell generation he was among the handful to cop a break.

Opportunity never knocked twice in those dark days, so his career was absolutely beyond doubt. Contemplating the decades ahead was a treat to be savored: He was going to end up a science teacher and athletics coach at a high school somewhere in the great Hawkeye State.

This was a calling beyond any previous Borlaug's expectation. It was truly incredible: From the depths of despair he'd reached a plateau inaccessible to almost every farm boy in America. No longer would he be tied to the life of his fathers. Let others squander their days raising food . . . he was going to be a man of the big wide wonderful outer sphere!

On the Saturday afternoon about a week before he needed to report to Cedar Falls, George Champlin's brown Model A roadster rattled up the driveway.

This was a puzzlement . . . the quicksilver running back of the famous football squad graduated the year before Norm enrolled at Cresco High. They'd never crossed paths, but Norm knew that Champlin played for one of the greatest college teams of all time, the University of Minnesota Golden Gophers. That was a point of pride throughout Howard County.

So why had the hometown hero driven all the way out to the humble Borlaug home on a September Saturday?

CAREER SAVER #3

Fate's third facilitator, George Champlin. This All-American football star gulled Borlaug into going to the University of Minnesota, regardless of the fact that Norm had no money, no job, nowhere to live and had not even applied for admission. Champlin's bolt from the blue turned the boy away from the teaching profession to which he was pledged, and put him on the proper path.

The newcomer quickly made his point. "Norm," he blurted, "I've just been talking with Dave Bartelma, and he says you're a good lineman. Tomorrow I'm leaving for Minneapolis . . . early football practice. I've been asked to find players for the freshman squad. Come with me and I'll get you a try out."

This was all so sudden and so preposterous the 19-year-old teacher-to-be could only stammer: ". . . B-B-But I'm going to Teacher's College . . . I'm leaving next Friday!"

The words slipped out with difficulty through the damnable catch in his throat resulting from the breathtaking possibility of attending *a real university*. On the other hand, the thought of dropping the glittering jewel in his hand was altogether too absurd to contemplate.

Patiently he explained exactly why he couldn't possibly go to Minnesota. Champlin, however, countered with canny answers to every line of reasoning rooted in sense and sensibility:

Money. George explained that, compared to Cedar Falls, Minneapolis offered many more chances for finding work.

Academic requirements. No problem; Bartelma says that with grades like yours you'll be accepted . . . you won't even need to take the entrance exam.

Accommodation. George had a room near the campus. Norm could stay there. It was real expensive—$20 a month—but there were two double beds, so the rent could be shared among four.

Commitment to the Teacher's College. Again George had a slick response: "Drive up with me and see for yourself," he said, "If you don't like it, you can hitchhike home."

Then the gridiron star tossed his long bomb: "Erv Upton's coming."

It proved a game-winner: The flustered and severely shaken youth mutely nodded acceptance. If his friend Erv could make the Gophers, why couldn't he?

Champlin barked at him to start packing . . . he'd be back tomorrow.

Understandably, a townie's flippant disruption of long-settled plans worried the family as much as Norm himself.

Yet not every member was put out. Sunday afternoon, an obviously thrilled Nels Borlaug linked arms and marched his grandson out the gate to where George Champlin stood beside his fancy Ford.

Then from a pocket the family patriarch hauled a frayed leather pouch and spilled its entire contents into his grandson's hand. "You'll make more use of 'em than I will, Norm Boy," he said.

There were eleven silver dollars.

1933-34
Hunger Pains

Now he had $61 with which to start university. It seemed ridiculous: the first quarter's out-of-state tuition would take $25. Beyond that he needed food, books, board, and cash for the second quarter. Gamecock Champlin, however, fizzed with self-faith. "You'll have no trouble," he gushed. "Just you wait and see."

Soon they'd collected Erv Upton from his farm east of Cresco and were heading north. Although the Minnesota border was just 10 miles past the town, Norm had never left his home state, so this ride was a special thrill. As the Model A Roadster was a two-seater, George's passengers took turns sitting in the cramped rumble seat that opened out of the sloping back where God had meant a trunk to reside.

Highway travel was then so rare that this journey constituted Norm and Erv's ultimate liberation. This was their "coming out," and they gleefully embraced the imposing vision of Rochester, where famous people retreated for miraculous Mayo Clinic cures. Then both scanned the looming landscape as the enormous distance to the Twin Cities flew by—160 miles!

Both neophytes were in a sort of ecstasy. The afternoon was brilliant, the sky cloudless, the sunshine glorious and, despite deep uncertainties, Norm Boy Borlaug somehow knew he was headed right. He was crossing his Second Great Divide: the one that only yesterday separated him from the possibility of a college degree. Mile by mile, his world was expanding beyond the boundary farm boys could rightfully entertain. He was going places!

The final stretch brought the adventure to a climax. Minneapolis sported streetcars, sidewalks and shop windows a block long . . . astonishments he'd seen only in books. The size, noise, confusion, and bustle were such as to overwhelm a lifetime resident of the state of stillness. There was even that most mind-boggling of all edifices: a skyscraper. The shiny 32-story Foshay Tower was the brainchild of a self-promoting tycoon who'd borrowed $6000 and whipped up this concrete pillar as a tribute to his own soaring genius. His self-proclaimed "Washington Monument of the Midwest" was only four years old, and the stirring sounds of the late lamented John Phillip Sousa and his 75-piece band still marched in the memory of those who'd attended the dedication.

At ground level, however, things were less than inspiring. Compared with the clean countryside, the grand metropolis proved dowdy, dingy, dirty. Indeed, in that fall of 1933 it was dismal. On all sides, poverty displayed its wares: broken windows, faded signs, boarded shopfronts, peeling paint. In the depths of shop doorways bodies, including tiny ones, huddled like sacks of grain. Pavement was their pillow. How, he wondered, could they survive the upcoming winter?

Many buildings were empty shells. Even Foshay's splendid spire had few tenants. Wilbur himself was in Kansas . . . occupying a cell in Leavenworth Prison, following a federal conviction for fraud.

Like other cities this one sported garbage-ghettos wherein thousands of squatter families hashed together habitations out of packing crates, cardboard and rusty sheet-metal. People still relished slapping the Great Engineer's name on things, and these suburbs of squalor—usually located near the town dump for easy access to food and building supplies—were universally known as "hoovervilles." In Minneapolis thousands of the dispossessed crowded into the Gateway District hooverville; out of luck, out of work, out of rent, out of hope, and mostly out of any bread for the mouth.

Hunger was certainly not too embarrassed to show its face in public. Beggars patrolled the precincts seeking scraps rather than cents. Just the year before, a University of Minnesota graduate student had dressed in rags and lived with a gang of young hobos. He recorded that everywhere he saw "signs of malnutrition—prominent ribs, concave abdomens, arms and legs on which the skin was loose and baggy, hungry eyes, and nervous mannerisms."

The frightening reality was that many Americans couldn't afford to eat. Money in 1933 was a mythical substance and food was rare enough that breadlines stretched for blocks and any crust was critical.

The reason was plain. Since 1929, industrial output had fallen by half; payroll jobs by a quarter. Unemployment, by contrast, had soared from 3 percent to 25 percent and at least 13 million could find no work. Even the lucky ones with a paying job remained hard up: blue-collar wages had sunk 60 percent, white-collar salaries 40 percent.

Collectively, the heartbreaks and hopelessness shattered even America's shock-resistant social structure. Middleclass families scavenged for leftovers in the trash bins behind restaurants, sold treasured heirlooms, and forfeited their homes—moving in with relatives or taking to the roads and rails seeking relief or maybe rainbows. In 1933, orphanages overflowed, the suicide rate tripled, and the marriage rate tumbled, as did (surprisingly and tellingly) the birth rate.

On this particular Sunday afternoon, though, Norm was beyond contemplating calamity; Champlin was hurtling him onto his personal cloud nine. Four blocks from campus—near the railroad yards and in a village-like enclave called University Dinkytown—George swung the brown roadster, now seemingly dipped in dust, into 15th Avenue SE and pulled up before number 505. A complex of three three-story, red brick buildings, the Kearsarge Apartments proved plain but pleasant. The corner unit's second floor housed Champlin's room. Apart from the two beds, there was a small wooden table, four not-too-sturdy chairs . . . and nothing more.

Having dumped their bags and peeked at their afterlife's astounding setting Norm and Erv found themselves rushed back downstairs. "We must get to the coffee shop," their electrically charged friend declared, "before the other kids take all the jobs."

Located nearby and just a block from campus, the University Coffee Shop seated 75 customers and boasted three U-shaped counters and a row of booths down one wall. That night the manager was too busy to break in raw recruits. "Come back tomorrow morning at seven," Spencer Holle barked: "Work an hour, get a meal."

That final phrase sure came as a relief. The two Iowa rubes weren't after money. Food, you see, bought life itself.

On their return to the apartment Champlin exuded his usual optimism: "Well, you've got a place to sleep and a place to eat," he said. "In a few days you'll report for football practice, pay your fees, and enroll. Then you'll be A-okay."

Wow, the world was sunny side up! Norm found the limitless prospects hard to grasp. Only the previous day he'd been but a farm lad.

At six on Monday morning Erv and Norm tumbled from bed and hustled off to their new calling. The experience proved daunting beyond their imaginings. Spencer Holle, a former hammer thrower on the university and U.S. Olympic teams, was barrel-chested, muscle bound and

The real depression. To victims such as these unemployed in Gateway Park, Minneapolis the word meant more than an economic disease. Formerly productive workers spent years in endless, pointless contemplation of their plight. In 1933, hard times and helplessness ruled jointly. To Norm, this sight demonstrated the downside of living high and relying on others for food.

very demanding. His intimidating presence neither helped Norm's nerves nor his grip on the crockery. Bustling in and out of the kitchen with platters of fried eggs and buttermilk pancakes the anxious rookie who'd never labored at anything less dainty than farm chores mixed up his orders.

The evening stint brought no improvement. As the dinner hour wound down, George Champlin arrived to check on his protégés, and Norm overheard Holle say in slow and terrifying tones: "Either I'll make a waiter out of Borlaug or I'll kill him!"

Suddenly the new recruit forgot his fright, found his focus, and discovered within himself a waiter with brain to match the brawn.

By Wednesday, George had wangled him a second job: parking cars in the garage beneath the Adult Education Center. Whenever a symphony concert, a lecture, an art exhibit or other function was held next door in the Northrop Auditorium Norm got a chance to earn tips.

His twice-weekly take—roughly 50 cents—meant everything: A month's accumulation paid the rent.

He'd now been fast-tracked to a land of undreamed possibilities, and had attained another inaccessible plateau. Not without a stab of guilt, he mailed a polite apology to the Iowa State Teacher's College. Sorry, but he wouldn't be coming to Cedar Falls.

Then a few days later muddle, like Lazarus, arose again. After perusing his out-of-state transcript, the university authorities declared him ineligible.

Actually, the problem was a mere technicality. For purposes of admittance, Minnesota excluded ninth grade records. In ninth grade Norm had aced both math and science, but that now counted for nothing. In the university's view he was missing a year of science and a year of math. No way could he be approved. Rules were rules!

The discrepancy was of course just on paper. He was told to relax . . . those in his predicament could take a special exam. So on Saturday he trudged to campus for the test of a lifetime. He was a bundle of fears. And rightly so: The math and science questions proved familiar, but the long months cutting cordwood and catching critters had softened the synapses and allowed the answers to escape the confines of the brain.

He flunked.

That did it. The psychologist in charge of testing and matriculation declared the University of Minnesota couldn't possibly accept him. To Dean E. Williamson this Iowa oaf had proven doubly unfit. Indeed, Norm himself found the decision unsurprising:

At that moment I considered myself a complete flop.

Now he prepared to hitchhike home in disgrace. How he regretted turning down the Teacher's College, the only school he was good enough for. The outer world's layers had closed around him like an onion. He'd been squeezed back into his proper place. The family farm.

That retreat would have happened and history would have gone awry had not George Champlin again become fate's facilitator. Frog-marching Borlaug into the Assistant Dean's office, the 22-year-old gridiron gamecock declared with passion charging his words: "Something's wrong with your testing up here in Minnesota. Give this guy another chance. He's not as dumb as you think!"

Norm could've died, but this was the exception proving the power of audacity. That very year the university had instituted a program to provide deprived youngsters with two years of remedial study. Eventually, the University of Minnesota Junior College would spawn the national J.C. system; in 1933, though, it was merely a band-aid for the hurts of hard times.

The university had entrusted the experimental initiative to one of its brightest stars: Frederick Hovde, a chemical engineer, Rhodes Scholar, and all-American quarterback of the glorious 1928 Golden Gophers. Having been charged with helping the under-prepared and underprivileged, Dean Hovde needed bumpkins, not to mention corn-fed bumpkins. Young Borlaug was the recruit of the dean's dreams.

Such, however, could not be said for the football coach's dreams. True to his word, Champlin arranged a try out. It was a dismal failure. The legendary figure of big, bruising Bronko Nagurski dominated the Minnesota mindset and the hard-nosed coach, Bernie Bierman, emphasized power running behind a mammoth offensive line. The team had recently swept the Big Ten, and was about to win three straight National Championships.

For the first and last time Norm found himself intimidated by his fellow man. One glance, told him he needed to find something safer to life and limb. Accordingly, both he and Erv Upton enrolled for wrestling, and were quickly disabused of any high hopes on that front. Indeed, they were appalled. In Minnesota their sport counted for nothing. The coach was a lawyer who donated a few hours a couple of afternoons a week. He was certainly sincere, but even by Iowa's high-school standards, woefully deficient in skill and insight.

CAREER SAVER #4

Fate's fourth facilitator. After the University of Minnesota refused Borlaug admittance, Frederick Hovde awarded the unpromising 19-year old a second chance. Just 25 years old himself, he was in his first year as administrator of the U of M Junior College (he'd finish as president of Purdue University). His decision kept Norm from slinking home a loser and set him on destiny's designated path to save the hungry.

A ctually, in those torrid times few sports counted for much. It's difficult to reconstruct how people felt in days so distant and dark, but in 1933 America's connective tissues were coming unstuck. When destiny died, so too did the communal confidence that shores up sports . . . as well as society. Now footloose *and* freed of civil constraint, the masses lurched toward what had been considered impossible in United States: class warfare.

Borlaug experienced this impossibility one afternoon when he set out for his first close up look at a city. Taking the Washington Avenue Bridge he crossed the Mississippi and wandered westward into a squalid section of the Warehouse District.

Hearing the echoes of a crowd in full throat, he strolled around a corner to confront a sea of cloth-capped workmen washing up against a tall fence fitted with high wire gates. Behind the gates stood a phalanx of company guards, shoulder-to-shoulder, each in a black peaked cap and black uniform and each embracing a black billy-club. And behind those blackguards stood a line of about a dozen white milk-delivery vans, engines ticking, drivers awaiting the order to bust through the blockade and proceed on their rounds.

The scene was fantastic; the tension tangible. Moving closer, the inquisitive innocent spotted a photographer erecting his tripod on the hood of an old touring car. For balance, the man rested his foot on the canvas roof. When that proved not quite high enough for his boxy Speed Graphic to capture the scene he levered himself up. Then, his foot tore through the fabric and along with that the action exploded.

As if the rip of canvas had been the director's cue, the gates were flung wide and the line of black goons charged the crowd, billy-clubs flailing. The first casualty Norm noticed was the camera; the second its owner. That hapless shutterbug tumbled from the top of the old touring car to emulate a heap of red wreckage impeding the pavement.

How the witless witness regretted his impulse to leave the campus cloister. He was directly across the street from the wire gates, and desperate to escape. In its panic, however, the human sea had ebbed backwards, surging around him like an undertow. Pinned against a warehouse wall, he couldn't move. Couldn't see. Could barely breathe.

Being trapped like that was frightening. The terrible truncheons were advancing ever closer, but just before his own head got cracked open the deputized toughs turned sideways into the thicker part of the throng, where more heads could be had with less hard work.

For a pupil from the placid plains this experience seared the soul:

I was freed from the crush only after the milk trucks had gone past. That's when the pickets took off down the street, screaming with frustration. Minneapolis got its milk delivered that day; the batons had beaten the strikers both ways.

The strikers, however, didn't realize they'd lost the skirmish. They kept on yelling as if their lives depended on it, which was certainly so because no job meant no life in those days. However, they were also yelling because the scene was so horrifying. Bodies and blood were scattered and spattered over the street.

By then, the company guards were back behind the gates. Again shoulder-to-shoulder, they stood stiff and seemingly unmoved by the sickening sights their own hands had created.

Ambulances arrived, but no police that I saw. However, I didn't stick around long. I took off running. Clearly, the caustic times had corroded the constitutional code supporting justice for all. That was the worst disillusion of all.

Given that the North Star State was traditionally as tranquil as its 12,000 lakes on a misty morn, mass disorder had seemed beyond possibility. However, out of this confrontation arose a period of anarchy since dubbed "one of the bloodiest and most far reaching labor conflicts of the decade."

The basic dispute had begun shortly before, when trucking firms serving Minneapolis's commercial establishments refused to negotiate contracts with their drivers. The crisis came to a head on May 12, 1934 when Teamster Local 574 voted a citywide strike. Without drivers, every business—department store, factory, grocery, laundry, bakery, construction project, warehouse, brewery and whatnot—ran out of supplies and could neither make nor distribute their wares.

Faced with civic paralysis, the authorities devised an ingenious plan: On the night of May 20 they dressed a deputy to look like a laborer and dispatched him to strike headquarters. Commandeering the public address system, the fake Teamster directed squads of strikers to a particular back alley near the Minneapolis Tribune Building. There, in the deep shadows, a reception committee quietly waited. When the unwary strikers showed up, the lawmen sprang. Surrounding their unarmed prey, they rendered them senseless with regulation nightsticks.

Back at strike central, the sight of the casualties sent the inner landscape reeling. Over a dozen comatose comrades—including several women—were drenched with blood; two or three had legs crooked enough to signify compound fractures; several lay unmoving for hours for the fellow travelers to salute and savor sweet revenge.

FOOD . . .

Minneapolis, 1934. During the 1930s, society ran amok. Borlaug inadvertently got caught up in a battle like this between the striking Teamsters (cloth caps) and the cops and their "Citizen's Army" deputies (uniforms) . . . .

. . . FIGHT

. . . The experience left an imprint indelible enough to become a blueprint for life. For the first, but not the last, time he'd seen hunger consort with hopelessness to breed violence. And eventually he'd dedicate himself to overcoming global hunger.

MAIN CAMPUS AND . . .

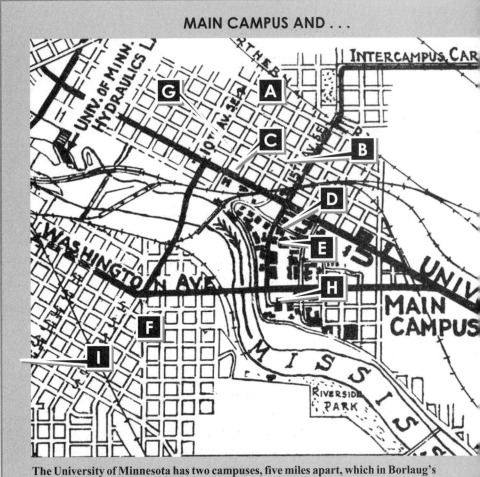

The University of Minnesota has two campuses, five miles apart, which in Borlaug's day were joined by a streetcar line that ran via 15th Avenue SE, Como Avenue and Hendon Avenue. Highlighted are: Dinkytown (A), Kearsarge Apartments (B) . . .

The next two days provided what history sardonically calls the "Battle of Deputies Run." The opening skirmish, on Monday May 21, brought mayhem to the marketing district when 1500 workers armed with batons, blackjacks, baseball bats and lead pipes attacked until the police turned and ran for their very lives.

Next day, the forces of law and order retaliated by fielding a "Citizen's Army" of 1700 cops and corporate deputies. The result was a City Square face-off. Being exactly matched, neither side wanted to precipitate pandemonium. Both waited.

Then, at the pinnacle of the pregnant pause, a picketer tossed a crate of

. . . FARM CAMPUS

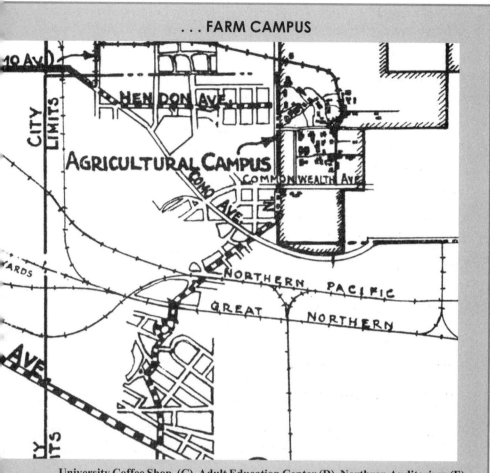

. . . University Coffee Shop. (C), Adult Education Center (D), Northrop Auditorium (E), Warehouse District (F), Alpha Omicron Pi Sorority (G), Student Hospital(H), and Independent Press (I).

tomatoes through a shop window, thereby shattering both glass and good sense. Following that almighty crash, more than 3000 combatants joined in battle. Within minutes a Teamsters attorney was killed. Then a company representative got knocked down and, while lying helpless on the road, battered to death.

Within the hour one side had triumphed. It was the strikers, and their satisfaction was complete. The cops and their conscripts had cut and run yet again . . . this time, permanently.

Good sense then abandoned Minneapolis. By default, the streets were commandeered by cloth-capped cronies who had neither employers nor executive powers. For 36 days the city remained out of civil control. Angry crowds like the one Norm had experienced denied all deliveries from the largest factory to the littlest corner grocery. "They had the town tied up tight," the sheriff later admitted.

For law-and-order types this civic surrender demanded an unconditional response. On July 20, they came up with just the thing: a Trojan Horse. In the interests of civil order, those morally superior personages first ran a large panel van toward a mass of picketers. Then, just as the union men moved forward to inspect the seemingly innocuous intruder, cops crouching inside opened fire at point blank range, wounding 67 and killing two.

With that, the governor had had enough. Floyd Olson called out the National Guard.

Minnesota morale was now the Mariana Trench. To a society so relaxed, so progressive, so certain of its decency, the dreadful act of ceding of public security to military might—let alone to the mob—was the ultimate disgrace.

Clearly the state needed new management, and in time that necessity invented a very youthful generation of politicians. The Teamsters strike propelled Hubert Humphrey, Orville Freeman and Walter Mondale to eventual prominence in the state's prevailing political force, the Farmer-Labor Party. Each would move into the governor's mansion and later migrate all the way to the ultimate den of iniquity, Washington, D.C. Both Humphrey and Mondale would end up vice president. Freeman would earn high distinction too, as we'll see much later in the Borlaug saga.

For Norm, the street strife proved just as influential:

> I ran back toward campus, trembling, frightened, rubbery-legged. My thoughts were racing: I'd seen how fast violence springs to life when hunger, misery, and desperation infect the public mind. I'd begun wondering too about the aftereffects of empty stomachs. Obviously, peace and prosperity couldn't survive without food; even the most serene society could turn violent. What have hungry people to lose?

The misadventure in the marketing district added yet another course of granite to the foundation of his maturity. For the rest of his life he'd be renowned for repeating: "Hungry people are angry people." Indeed, that simple mantra became the principle animating his ultimate career. You see, when he finally reaches his future he'll direct his immense energies toward keeping the peace by keeping people fed.

1934-1935
Margaret

A s payment for working the breakfast rush, the University Coffee Shop let its waiters take a cup of coffee, five prunes and two slices of toast. One morning, shortly after starting the job, Norm glanced up from this grand repast and noticed a pretty girl sitting nearby.

Margaret Gibson was bright and vivacious and looked—well, nice. Her cloud of thick black hair was strongly curled, with a sheen where the light struck. Her skin was smooth and healthy, giving an impression of well-scrubbed. Her lips were full and curved and sort of warm, not unlike the peonies blooming beneath the sunshine in his mother's garden.

Their eyes met. She smiled and asked what he was studying, and he noticed that her voice was low and cool. Embarrassed, he stammered he wasn't in the university at all—just Junior College. And he had no idea of what he was going to do. She smiled again.

By contrast to the introvert from the backwoods, Margaret was sophisticated, sure of herself, outgoing. Enrolled in the College of Education, she was a couple of years older and seemed to have descended from some quite unapproachable plane of existence. Her brother George had captained the most famous of all Golden Gophers— the 1929 National Champions whose star fullback had been bruising Bronko Nagurski. Nothing more was needed to confirm a higher order of origin.

Perhaps because of this connection with campus celebrity, the coffee shop's owner, Spencer Holle's mother, had taken a special shine to Margaret and had hired her as a waitress. The job was just for food of course, and from time to time while eating their pay the young acquaintances talked of their backgrounds and of this and of that.

Soon the boy whose only treats in life had been a few movies in Cresco found himself sitting beside Margaret quite often. He felt like a stranger in paradise.

CAREER SAVER #5

Fate's fifth facilitator, Margaret Gibson (later Borlaug). During her life, Margaret will often keep Norm's career from veering off track. Indeed, without her personal sacrifices he'd have accomplished little worth reading about.

Margaret had gone to the University of Minnesota to join her three brothers, George, Bill and Francis. George was then Campus King. An All-American during the era when college players outshone the pros, he captained the Golden Gophers to a National Championship and roomed with Bronko Nagurski, one of the greatest college stars of his time or maybe any time.

Margaret was committed to becoming a school teacher and probably dreamed of meeting a man like her brother. The greenhorn who waited tables in a seedy coffee shop must, by comparison, have seemed a poor prospect.

Given its social purpose as a supplier of scholastic welfare, Junior College was hardly challenging, and from the start Norm put in a more than satisfactory performance. Despite high scores on the first exams, however, he remained dissatisfied. He wanted to better himself, and these courses were too shallow for that. Thus it came about that in mid-October 1933 he mustered the courage to knock on Dr. Hovde's door. Standing on shaky legs (to say nothing of shaky ground) he requested permission to enroll in the university proper.

Far from persuaded, the Assistant Dean demanded details: "Why," he asked at one point, "do you want to leave so soon?"

It was a fair question—the boy had attended Junior College barely six weeks. "The work here," he replied, "is not taking me anywhere."

Unsurprisingly, that particular line of reasoning bombed. Hovde waggled his head, and quietly suggested the boy abandon his idea until the end of the semester. Only then would his progress be plain enough to make so momentous a verdict.

Norm thus dedicated the second quarter to serious study, and aced the exams. Then during his return visit he sat rigid with tension as the deity determining his future scanned the scores. For Norm, the slim figure fingering his fate was taking far too long; the pause seemed to portend rejection. But finally the momentous verdict emerged: "Well Borlaug, you can transfer to any college you want. Which will it be?"

That was easy. A few days earlier a friend had hauled him across town to see the university's second campus, the one on the outskirts of the state capital of St. Paul. The place was dedicated to agriculture, home economics and forestry, and he'd fallen in love with it. "The College of Agriculture," he blurted. "I'll major in forestry."

This declaration served only to re-furrow Dean Hovde's brow. Forestry was then something of a campus cult. Checked shirts and hobnailed boots seemed like student standard issue. Clean-cut young men from the best of families grew beards and swaggered like Paul Bunyan—tall tales not excluded. It was a peculiarly Northwoods rebellion against the establishment and the hard times the establishment had spawned. In addition, though, Frederick Weyerhaeuser had founded the world's largest forest empire here. Anyone seeing his mansion on Summit Ave knew that wealth could be made in the woods.

For a long moment Dean Hovde seemed to be steeling himself to deliver a rebuff. Then he relaxed, leaned halfway over his desk, locked eyes, and nodded. Yes, he said, suddenly grinning, Norm could enter the College of Agriculture.

The next few days were the happiest in memory. The mental pressure was relieved. He had a future at long last. Ahead lay a crystal-clear career path—one he reveled in contemplating.

He was going to spend a lifetime with lumberjacks!

Helium was still in the air as he hitchhiked southward for the Christmas break. Rising confidence and soaring spirits seemed to be floating him homeward in a state of weightlessness. The coming year would launch his entrance into the real university as well as into his designated field of study. Moreover, he'd now be eligible to try out for the freshman baseball team, which would set him on the road to the ultimate job site: second base at Wrigley Field.

Yes, of all his years, 1934 was going to be the greatest.

As you may have guessed, though, malignant fortune never quits the ring of life easily, and even then was preparing a one-two punch of epic proportion.

The left hook hit him at the farm: Granddad Nels had contracted cancer of the stomach. The tumor was inoperable, and the old man was already so weak he could barely get out of bed.

The body blow clobbered Norm when he returned to Minneapolis just after New Year: The University Coffee Shop had gone out of business. That put him almost down for the count. Without a source of food, how could he stay in college?

The search for something to eat now became the daily priority.

> Before anything else I had to find food—and not just for myself . . . Margaret Gibson also depended on that coffee shop.
> The university had no dining halls, so Dinkytown contained many restaurants. But finding work proved difficult. We did the rounds, almost begging for the chance to wait tables. At odd times one would let us in, but whenever business was slow the managers would shake their heads when they saw us standing in the doorway. For us, that was terribly disappointing. We were living meal-to-meal, so it meant we went off to class hungry.

This is when he hit the legendary bedrock. What on earth to do? There seemed nothing more to try; nowhere to turn. Deep in his heart he felt a frisson of fatalism and deep in his brain he sensed the psychosomatic tricks Hunger plays on people—the fear that burns out vitality, saps strength, slows reaction time and destroys the will, even the will to survive. He was mentally preparing himself to quit—famished, flummoxed and a failure in the foreign world, not to mention in Margaret's eyes.

CAREER SAVER #6

Fate's sixth facilitator, White Castle restaurant. In 1934 this company's coupon exchange allowed Borlaug to avoid starvation and stay in school. More than saving a career, its cut-priced hamburgers and milk provided life support.

For a few weeks coupons kept them alive. Some were clipped from the *Minnesota Daily*, the university newspaper. Others came from a boy he'd met in the coffee shop who'd acquired a roll of them (exactly from where Norm didn't want to know). Three coupons and ten cents were good for a bottle of milk and three hamburgers at the tiny, crenellated White Castle Restaurant near the campus.

He'd never eaten hamburgers before. Almost nobody had. Americans ate at home and quite properly stuck to the ethnic fare they'd been born to. In those days you were defined by how you dined. About a decade earlier, however, White Castle had broken the culinary bar. It was the first firm to serve what later generations called fast food. It took a very suspicious material, ground beef, and fashioned the modern hamburger.

This was a truly subversive product: a national rather than an ethnic food. Everyone could eat it without demeaning their ethnicity. More than ushering in a new cuisine, it ushered in a new culture. American.

Reflecting back on this distant and desperate episode Norm is amazed, yet immensely grateful, that the company from Cleveland sponsored that coupon exchange. With the Great Depression plumbing its greatest depths, corporations couldn't afford to have a heart. But this one did. What profit could there be in selling three hamburgers and a half-pint of milk for ten cents? The hamburgers were only bite-sized and were meant to be served severally, but they normally sold for five cents each, so providing three with a bottle of milk was a contribution to those terrible times that were both hungry *and* unhealthy.

Moreover it succeeded beyond what even White Castle has recognized:

> Thank God for those little burgers. They got me through the worst stretch of my young life! They allowed me to stay in school for the few weeks that made the difference. Without them, I'd have gone home.

This conviction Borlaug declares in a voice ringing with near reverence.

Without that hamburger helper he'd have been forced to retreat merely to eat. However, to stay in Minnesota he obviously required something more than charity. But what?

Just the day before he planned to pack his bags and slouch back to the claustrophobic confines, the answer materialized out of the ether. Charging up the stairs that evening, Scott Pauley burst into the apartment. "Food!" he whooped.

Scott was a fellow student. They'd met in chemistry class and struck up a friendship. He was bright, cheery and fun to be around. As Margaret also enjoyed his company, the three had formed a firm friendship. Several Sundays that spring they'd wandered into the countryside around the campus, identifying trees and admiring the glistening waters of the lakes bejeweling Minnesota.

Coming from a military family, Scott had enjoyed something quite beyond Norm's understanding: a roving life. He'd started college at Colgate in upstate New York only to renounce its scholarship—a blunder no one with a drop of sense dreamed of making in the 1930s—and flee westwards to face the hazards of working his way through Minnesota.

This was the friend who'd introduced Norm to the farm campus. The day they'd taken the university's intercampus streetcar the autumn sky was dulled a milky gray. Norm, though, found the somber scene at the end of the line glowing with promise—not from the intellectual ferment

CAREER SAVER #7

Fate's seventh facilitator, Alpha Omicron Pi. In 1934 this sorority's House Mother rescued from hunger the man who'd end up spending his life rescuing millions from hunger. For waiting on the young women eating here Borlaug was paid *all he could eat*. With hunger pains becoming unbearable, this proved his greatest compensation. Ever.

within the facilities but from the peace and quietude without.

This campus—so near the hooverville and the hooliganism—was clean and restful. Serenity was what catalyzed his interest in forestry, not rebelliousness or reveries of wealth. Despite the season's heavy mood, he felt happy out there in the quiet beyond the border of chaos.

Scott shared these feelings, and his outburst in the apartment had an impact difficult to overstate. When you've bottomed out in life food becomes everything, and suddenly Norm is offered an endless fountain of that stuff of life. To sustain his own need for sustenance Scott worked in a dining room of a well-to-do sorority, whose house mother had just asked him to find a second waiter. He marched his hungry friend straight over to Alpha Omicron Pi on Southeast 5th Street.

It was a critical turning point: Mrs. Nichols told Norm he could start the following day. For pay, he'd get *all he could eat*!

Incredible. The world had suddenly turned sunny-side up. Again.

Well, not quite. Yes, he now had food but the wallet was still running on empty. Of the $35 scraped together during winter break, tuition had absorbed $25. Not even he could make it through a college quarter on $10. By the end of February, more than $5 had gone for damnable necessities. He was back to the bedrock of bankruptcy.

This is where FDR's New Deal enters the saga. The program that saved Norm is nowadays largely forgotten. According to author Robert Caro, he should actually thank FDR's wife. "A civilization which does not provide young people with a way to earn a living," declared Eleanor Roosevelt, "is pretty poor." Then this most formidable of First Ladies pressed her husband for a program to help youngsters stay in school. "We have got to [make] these young people . . . feel that they are necessary," she explained.

The president resisted. There was no special problem of young people, he said, just a problem of society. Did she expect him to provide cash relief for everyone? Why, next he'd have all the 40-year-olds demanding government handouts!

But Mrs. Roosevelt knew her man's weak spot. Those young people, she quietly noted, were about to become voters.

All resistance then evaporated. Losing the next generation of voters was quite unthinkable. "There is a great deal to what you say," he replied, and surely his eye must have emitted a rascally twinkle.

Some weeks later when he signed the National Youth Administration into law "the friend in the White House" announced, "I have determined that we shall do something for the nation's unemployed youth. They must have their chance."

NYA devoted a portion of its funds to helping needy students stay in school. The University of Minnesota established an office to screen its candidates. Norm applied and was interviewed by a Mrs. Johnson, who checked his personal finances and was so appalled she sent him straight to the entomology department.

That was how the genie of salvation this time worked its magic. The department head, C.E. Mickel, explained that for a college student the work would be uninspiring. For one thing, Norm would pin insects onto boards for a graduate student studying the jack-pine sawfly. For another, he'd tidy up after professors and do other chores around the department. In return, he'd be paid 18 cents an hour in chits applicable to tuition. And he could put in 15 hours a week. Did he want the job?

Did he ever! $2.70 a week would cover tuition.

CAREER SAVER #8

Fate's eighth facilitator, Eleanor Roosevelt provoked her husband into creating the National Youth Administration, which among many things paid Borlaug's college tuition. Though less than $3 a week, it secured him, and in time millions more, a future.

Thus it happened that the ex-farm boy overcame the final impediment. At long last, he could put aside fears of financial failure and get on with his designated career . . . forestry.

Things now seemed as great as they could get. He had food, he had funding, and he had Margaret Gibson. Occasionally on weekdays they met on campus; Sundays, they spent an hour or two together. His schedule allowed no more than that. Indeed, burdened with the extra hours in the Entomology Department, his schedule threatened to break his health. Margaret was deeply concerned. "Norman, you really must slow down," she said, "you'll kill yourself!"

Margaret wasn't exaggerating. Each week the NYA job absorbed 15 hours and the sorority job 21. Somehow around those 36 hours he had to fit a full schedule of classes, homework and independent study. Some of the classes were in Minneapolis, others five miles away in St. Paul. The half-hourly streetcar, known formally as the Intercampus Special, took 30 precious minutes to make the trip. And of course he insisted on adding a daily session in the gym. Wrestling was sacrosanct.

It all seemed too much. Here's a typical weekday:

- 5:30 am—leap from bed and squeeze in an hour of study.
- 7:00 am—race to the sorority and serve breakfast.
- 8:30 am—take streetcar to St. Paul for morning classes.
- 11:30 am—return to Minneapolis to serve lunch.
- 1:30 pm—ride the streetcar to St. Paul for forestry lectures and lab.
- 5:00 pm—return to Minneapolis to meet Erv at the gym.
- 6:30 pm—take a quick shower.
- 6:45 pm—rush to Alpha Omicron Pi to serve dinner.
- 8:00 pm—walk back to the apartment and hit the books (except for two nights a week when Auditorium patrons need their cars parked).

Weekends brought little relief. There were no classes but he had to pin down insects and clean up professor's messes . . . for 15 hours.

By now, though, baseball was not a worry. At the start of the 1934 season he'd indeed gone out for the team, and been admitted to the freshman squad. During spring practice he was, in fact, among its more promising hitters. Then arose an exquisitely agonizing conflict: the team practiced *every* weekday afternoon. And on three of those he had a forestry lab class. What to do?

I was playing well enough that I probably could have gotten out of baseball practice for those three days, but two days of practice per week didn't seem enough to master professional level skills.

Suddenly I had to confront a career choice: baseball or forestry?

In one of the saddest days of my life I turned in my uniform. It was among the most difficult decisions I've ever made. The dream of playing for the Cubs was over; my one chance at the highest of all callings was gone.

That was a blow to my youthful pride. But even now in my maturity it still brings a pang of regret.

Though still fretting over his health, Margaret failed to realize that the manic pace was maintained because the horror of hunger and poverty had given way to the horror of flunking out. The fear of failure is a particularly compelling impulse, and at that moment failure seemed more probable than possible. Indeed, to avoid academic annihilation he had but a single hope: the upcoming winter-quarter finals. These, his first exams in the university proper, would determine his destiny. A pass was essential. Without that, he'd be packed off home to live out his days with the stigma of public humiliation.

Such self-inflicted pressures stemming from his own surreal sense of accountability would dog him and define him forever. But in March 1934 there arose a concern big enough to make him welcome the stigma of failure.

That personal tipping point occurred during the exam-preparation period. That's when a secretary called him from the classroom and told him to report to E.G. Cheney in the forestry school. There, Professor Cheney explained that Norm's father had telephoned. He was to call home, collect.

It was the worst call of his life. The voice from faraway Cresco was even softer than usual. Granddad Nels had passed on.

Norm was lost for words. He'd known it would come of course; leaving home after Christmas, he'd felt it might be the last goodbye. Still, the shock was tough to take. "Look, Dad," he said. "I'll come straight away. I can take the exams next quarter."

Suddenly the voice hardened. "You'll not do that, Norman. Your grandfather was very pleased at how well you're doing. He wouldn't want you to interrupt your work for *anything*."

Getting through finals was a struggle. However, as a memorial to Granddad Nels and his towering passion for self-improvement the boy called upon his deepest reserves. It wasn't so hard: During their last conversation the old man had grasped his wrist. "Education puts power into a man, Norm Boy," he'd said, glaring as though by look and touch he could transmit his own determination. "Governments come and governments go, but if you've got a good education no one can take that from you."

For those desperate days, if not for all days, it was good advice. And it's what tipped the scales in favor of the grandson proceeding past his freshman year and going on to great accomplishments.

You could certainly be forgiven for assuming that malign fortune had done its utmost to crush this upstart. But you'd be wrong. Within days it found an even sharper instrument.

In mid-March 1934—just as he was preparing for the last of those crucial exams—Norm's throat began burning. Then his temperature soared. Finally his throat tightened so much he couldn't swallow his own saliva. After struggling through the chemistry final he took his agony to the health service, and found himself whisked into the University Student Hospital.

Strep.

A very bad word, "streptococcus" was then akin to "cancer, a virtual synonym for death. For two days he cowered on a cot, boiling with fever, frustration and fear. The pain kept rising until it became almost unendurable. His wits began to wobble. But the hospital provided nothing more than warm salty water for gargling.

Only one of its staff wanted to do more, and his interest didn't seem exactly Hippocratic:

> The intern on my case was bent on cutting out my lymph nodes. The guy wanted to document some detail for his thesis. I'm sure he'd decided I was dying. Heck, I'd decided that too. And it didn't matter; living with such pain wasn't worthwhile.

In all his long life this was the sole experience with apathy. Only the intern's morbid quest jerked him out of the deadly decline. When Caifson Johnson dropped by the second day Norm croaked an urgent plea: "Get this intern out of here; he wants to carve me up!"

The wrestling team's light heavyweight scurried straight to the Athletic Department and collared the Assistant Football Coach, George Hauser, who was also an MD and member of the Student Hospital staff. "Please go over and look at Norm Borlaug," Johnson gasped out. "He's in real trouble."

Soon Dr. Hauser was bending over the cot, kneading the neck and peering down the red, raw, sandpaper throat. "You're a very sick young man, Borlaug," he said with obvious unease, "but we can't do more. It's up to you. You've got to make this on your own!"

Strep throat doesn't seem like much to us, but it was a terror of every prior generation. And that angst was anchored in historical precedent. Everyone knew, for instance, that George Washington had contracted the disease. One night in December 1799, after a day spent marking trees, he suffered a violent bout of "quinsy" (acute laryngitis, most likely from a streptococcal infection). Three hours later the doctor was called. During the fateful following day the medico bled the former president four times, forced him to gargle a concoction of molasses, vinegar and butter, and anointed his neck with a special curative prepared from dried insects.

None of this brought any relief. "Let me go off quietly," the First Father said. "I cannot last long."

At ten the following night he got his wish.

Norm knew exactly what Washington wanted and understood his morbid mutterings, but was unaware that a cure had already been discovered. Early in 1932 a German biochemist had injected a bright-red azo dye into mice and rabbits that had been massively infected with streptococcal bacteria. In his laboratory in Wuppertal, Gerhard Domagk, who worked for the German dye cartel, I.G. Farbenindustrie, was following a wild hunch based on the fact that a recently created red pigment was "fast" on wool. Both wool and a bacteria's cellular surface are composed of protein. Might the dye that binds to one also bind to the other? And if so, might a long red molecular tail affect the germ's ability to assail healthy cells?

Surprisingly, the wild guess proved out; the mice and rabbits recovered.

A human trial followed, when Domagk's own daughter pricked herself on an infected needle he'd left lying around the laboratory. Soon she was down with septicemia. This so-called blood poisoning was then an absolute death sentence. In desperation, the panicked scientist took the biggest chance a parent can.

The immediate effect was scary to see: the fragile dye-injected form assumed the aspect of a badly painted china doll. But in her bloodstream the color-fast compound was clasping the killer bacteria, breaking their grip, and keeping them from overwhelming the vital tissues.

In a few days the pinkness of proper health began returning.

And in a week little Hildegarde Domagk got her life back.

MEDICINE MAN

Gerhard Domagk. Most people died of infections until this German dye chemist discovered a compound that stopped bacteria cold. That was in 1934, when Borlaug was 20. Domagk's compound broke Mother Nature's reign of fear and repression. Suppressing myriad scourges, his "sulfa drug" moved mankind closer to mastery over fate.

Eventually Domagk would be honored with the Nobel Prize in Medicine. At the time, however, he kept his daughter's cure secret. His company also quashed the momentous discovery. Quite right, too: there was a patent to file!

Maybe that delay didn't matter. Even after the drug came available, the public showed little interest. The idea of injecting anything into the bloodstream was just too repellent to contemplate. Experts in ethics were adamant: playing God like that was too sinful to allow in the public purview. Deaths, after all, were part of the divine plan; no mere mortal had the right to interfere.

Widespread approval of hypodermic injections was achieved only after strep went so far as to fell the president's own beloved son.

Franklin Delano Roosevelt Jr. had been born the same year as Norm, and was a student at Harvard when his throat seized up early in December 1936. From the start it was a bad case . . . then the bacteria found an invasion route into his sinuses. Few victims survived once strep had seized their sinuses. Eleanor Roosevelt hurried up from Washington to become a fixture at her son's bedside. And for almost three weeks Ethel du Pont, a renowned beauty and prominent Delaware heiress, shared the death watch.

The press breathlessly ballyhooed all this drama in the presidential household. Soon the nation became transfixed by the doctor's dilemma: should he administer the new German compound? Public sentiment was opposed. For one thing, Domagk's dye was unproven. For another, it was not authorized for use. For a third, this was the adored president's son. Nonetheless, Dr. George Tobey decided to risk all.

With the manmade stain coursing his veins Franklin Junior turned the shade of fresh-cut beet. The moment was electrifying; science itself was on trial. But within a day the anxious watchers by the bedside sensed a hint of hope. Soon Massachusetts General Hospital was radiating cautious optimism. Finally, it announced that the patient was "expected to be sufficiently recovered to celebrate Christmas at the White House."

Those words leapt from newspaper stands in every state, every city, every town. Readers were more than amazed . . . they were thrilled. For the first time in American experience a body besieged by bacteria had been saved. The president's son had been returned from the edge of eternity. Of the modern miracles, this was perhaps the greatest.

And there was yet another twist to the story. During the two years in which the German company pursued its patent application, a team of French chemists learned the compound's secret structure and began their own experiments. Jacques Trefouel and his wife Therese were amazed to find that Domagk's dye had no effect on streptococcus outside the body. Then they discovered that living tissues broke the dye into two parts. One part did nothing; the other had been around since 1909 and was already patented for use in dye making. In the succeeding quarter century no one had thought to test this so-called sulfanilamide for medicinal value. Now, with the original patent ten years past its use-by-date no one could withhold it from therapeutic use. At a stroke, Domagk's camouflaged cure-all and his company's quest for cash were rendered moot.

Looking back, it seems criminal that lawyers dithered over patents while patients such as Norm were left to suffer—even die—for what amounted to nothing. Soon, though, British and American doctors tested sulfanilamide against meningitis, gonorrhea, undulant fever, childbed fever, pneumonia, appendicitis, peritonitis, strep throat—always with success. A major benefit was its lack of color; to anxious friends and relatives the loved ones no longer became cartoon caricatures.

Chemists next made hundreds of derivatives, some of which surpassed the original. Collectively, these "sulfa drugs" changed the human condition. Almost overnight the oldest of the mental manacles was unshackled. Infectious disease could at last be countered; the baby killers could be stopped. Clearly, mankind could control Nature in the medical field as well as in the farm field.

In Norm's case, however, all that lay in the future. In 1934, Domagk and his compound were hidden away in Germany awaiting a piece of paper from Hitler's patent office. Therefore, stoic endurance was his only recourse; just as Dr. Hauser had said, he had to get through his bout with the bacterium by himself.

Wrestling with the germ that sought his life proved a fearful torture. It turned into a sort of mind game, one he vowed to win. "It'll take more than this to knock me back," he told himself. And in a few days the fever abated a trifle. Then he felt a trickle of energy flowing into his ailing interior. Slowly stepping back from the graveside, he retrieved his throat from the devil. Soon he could swallow saliva and even indulge a smile.

He'd been extremely lucky. Some time afterward, the wrestling team visited Kansas State and after the Friday-night bouts the 165-pounder complained of a sore throat.

Saturday, the boy was delivered to the student hospital in agony and abject terror.

Sunday, he died.

After recuperating in the apartment for a couple of days Norm headed home. Both weak and worn out, he needed to pick up life's threads. And that summer of 1934 provided plenty of possibilities. During his absence farm country had turned into a social stew so unsavory certain Iowa counties had declared martial law.

Military power was required because penny sales had become too troublesome to tolerate. Public sentiment had tilted so far from the pillars of uprightness that the authorities would not execute the civil statutes. Even lawmakers favored lawbreakers. The state's beloved congressman Guy Gillette declared: "I sympathize fully with the farmers, and realize they are driven to desperation by conditions over which they have no control."

That was an era in which legal and illegal began diverging from right and wrong. Late in April 1933, for instance, a gang of farmers dragged a judge from his bench in the LeMars courthouse to a nearby tree where they threatened to hang him and, just for the hell of it, beat him up. The mangled magistrate, nonetheless, refused to press charges. Although he'd followed the law and foreclosed on indebted farms, he considered his attackers in the right on the issue.

All this grief had nothing to do with low production; hard-working prairie plowmen could produce more than ever. By switching to a tractor they could double their yield; by applying fertilizer they could double it again; and by planting the high-test hybrid seed they could double their output yet once more. Collectively, they could boost the food supply beyond any prior prediction, but the 1930s happened to be the one decade in which Americans had no way to indulge in extra food. The Great Depression had cut consumer's buying power past the point where they could afford to even eat their fill. The result was "food stagflation." Between 1929 and 1933—despite soaring hunger—net farm income actually fell by half.

This was perhaps the most vexing difficulty FDR confronted following his brave syllables spoken in the celestial sunbeams. It has been called "the biggest, toughest problem farmers had ever faced . . . the problem of surpluses."

The Secretary of Agriculture was the federal functionary caught in the headlights. And he was a newcomer—a stranger to politics, to Washington and to controversy.

Hopes in the heartland had sunk to such unbelievable depths in 1932 that Iowans had actually voted Democratic, and FDR had repaid the honor by designating one of their own to lead the nation's agriculture out of its agony. The politico now confronting the farm-country conflicts was

ROOKIE REFORMER

First week on the job. Taken on March 14, 1933, the photo shows the newly appointed Secretary of Agriculture, Henry Wallace. The daydream believer who'd made corn-picking a sport and high-test corns a success now must tackle the nation's most vexing social crisis: the food-price collapse spawning chaos throughout the rural regions. The task seemed so impossible that Washington observers wondered if this young (he was 45) political novice could meet the challenge.

none other than the reticent, unworldly, preoccupied romantic who'd once organized corn-husking contests and then almost casually created high-test corn seed.

From the start, Henry Wallace seemed to do everything wrong. No one could understand the path he selected; it made no sense whatever. On October 15 1933, just as the Great Depression hit its nadir, he announced that the government would pay the fantastic sum of 30 to 35 cents—more than twice market price (12 cents)—for each bushel of corn. But his offer came with a catch: recipients had to seal their harvest in bins on the farm and sow 20 percent fewer acres the following year. Stated bluntly, the agriculture secretary was bribing (the Fed's term was "financial inducement") farmers to be *less productive*.

This novel notion, denounced by every pundit as radical, reckless and even disastrous, had its intended outcome. Corn growers held onto their harvest and a month later the first reward check was delivered in Iowa's Pocahontas County; the second went to Woodbury County, near Sioux City. Thereafter payments poured daily into dozens of defiant districts.

The effect proved as soothing as oil on troubled waters; the sea of insurrection flattened out and rippled off into reeds. In a strange and roundabout way the Farmers' Holiday had worked. Food was being kept from the public . . . and—this was the truly amazing part—the Feds were paying up with their gold!

The Agricultural Adjustment Act epitomized lateral thinking. Though hundreds of thousands of citizens were slowly starving, it paid farmers *not to produce food*. America's 11th Secretary of Agriculture knew he was committing a flagrant violation of conventional wisdom, if not common logic. Though a budding tycoon, Wallace remained a rural idealist and it broke his heart to suppress farm output. He spoke for most when he said, "I hope we shall never have to resort to it again. To destroy a standing crop goes against the soundest instincts of human nature."

Yet, four months later when the price of pork sagged he authorized the slaughter of six million piglets, which seemed very much worse.

Such federal vandalism brewed up universal revulsion. The press declared it utterly unseemly. Even subversive. And such feelings were not found just in the cities; shame seared souls in God's country too.

Indeed, throughout Midwestern America the unholy blend of gratitude and guilt created a terrible tussle with both convention and conscience. Wasn't taking money from the government a sin? Prairie people never accepted charity; they were sturdy and self-reliant. Taking a handout was a terrible retreat from the path of righteousness.

THE FALLACY THAT FUELED . . .

Norman Borlaug's story is ultimately about the suppression of starvation, and here we leap ahead for a preliminary peek at that issue. You see, much of rural America's turmoil in the 1930s sprang from the belief that the Union of Soviet Socialist Republics had solved the "farm problem." Americans of all stripes were angry. Why wasn't Henry Wallace following the communist lead?

We now know that the basic belief behind the anger was false. Wistful, even willful, writers misled Americans through popular conduits such as the New York Times and Book-of-the-Month Club. While those pundits were praising communism, Soviet food production was actually in free fall and famine was soaring.

Fanatical about transforming Russia from a peasant society into a mighty industrial power, Stalin tried lifting the food supply by forcing all farmers into state-owned communes where they'd have to follow orders from the central command in Moscow. Stalin, in other words, took the exact opposite approach to Henry Wallace.

Communism was then new, and the Kulaks (food producers) continued to cling to their independence and free enterprise. To them the seizure of farmland was a crime and paying unfair prices amounted to confiscation. Many quit growing food for anyone but themselves; some assaulted the government goons who came to grab their grain.

In response, the Red Army dispatched troops and summarily executed farmers by the batch. That precipitated a life-and-death struggle between the Kremlin and the Kulaks, who produced the USSR's food.

Caught in the middle were the civilian masses. In towns and cities ragged lines waiting for bread and other necessities stretched down the streets. And the starving masses turned increasingly sullen, especially during the soul-sapping winters.

Stalin's mulish refusal to support the food producers induced the biggest famine the world had seen. During 1932 and 1933, the years when American writers were hailing his greatness, millions in the Soviet Union's *breadbasket*, were starving.

The loss of life became almost unimaginable. Figures are hard to come by, but one personal voice conveys the horror. In 1933, a young country girl sent a note to her uncle K. Riabokin, a professor at the university in the Ukrainian city of Kharkiv:

We have neither bread nor anything else to eat. Father is completely exhausted from hunger and is lying on the bench, unable to get on his feet. Mother is blind from the hunger and cannot see in the least. So I have to guide her when she has to go outside. Please Uncle, do take me to Kharkiv, because I, too, will die from hunger. Please do take me, please. I'm still young and I want so much to live a while. Here I will surely die, for every one else is dying . . .

Zina

Though the letter must have haunted the uncle the rest of his days, he was at the time powerless. Slipping a farm girl into the city would have sabotaged state policy, and likely occasioned his own end.

On receiving the next letter Professor Riabokin surely must have felt an awful mix of emotion.

The letter informed him of Zina's death.

. . . MASS FAMINE

Kharkiv, Ukraine, 1933. Inured to the sight of starvation, passersby ignore the corpses littering the street.

In total, the Soviet Famine produced about twice as many victims as the Bengal Famine a decade later. During 1932 and 1934 between 7 and 10 million Soviet farmers starved. Being the direct result of Politburo policies, this famine was premeditated!

Subsequently, Soviet farmers were subjected to the dictates of Trofim Denisovich Lysenko, a charlatan who'd gotten Stalin's ear during these years. Lysenko's gimcrack notion that plant breeding was a Western anti-Soviet plot would eventually bring the Communist caboodle crashing down. In 1991, weakened crops, failing farms, and falling food supplies combined to relegate the unlamented Soviet silliness to oblivion—worse, to obloquy.

All this demonstrates that a food supply is only as good as:

1) Its plant breeders;
2) Its seed; and
3) Its use of policies that foster the very best use of the very best seed.

Those three issues lie at the heart of the Borlaug saga, and as the action unfolds all will slowly move center stage and fearful famines like this one will fade from memory.

Thus did the citizens of the soil plumb the dark underside of the profit-making food production into which they'd so recently and so irretrievably cast their fate.

Yet despite all the revulsion, Wallace's topsy-turvy farm-relief efforts cured the canker threatening putrefaction in the country's core. Humble homestead folk reaped their recompense in both dollars and dignity. Millions in the heartland escaped just as they'd begun sinking into the slough of despond for the third time. Now country shoulders underwent a visible straightening. Frowns relaxed. Anarchy withdrew in confusion. And the national family began living with itself again.

All this mending and darning came just in time. The Great Depression had been testing the seams of the social fabric and finding lots of loose threads to work on. America had actually begun unraveling. Only the Civil War and the Revolution had ripped the society more.

The farmer's newfound income was what slowed the slide toward national dissolution. Yes, individualism had lost out to government meddling. But once again the rural dreamer's dizziness had done the job.

While the heartland was veering away from catastrophe Norm was struggling with college concerns. To him, outside events were minor distractions. Even the schoolwork was under control. Nowadays, wrestling was the only worry. You see, in 1935 the lawyer-coach decided to quit. That was bad enough, but not a single soul in the Twin Cities wanted the lowly, unpaid, twice-weekly duty of coaching a sport that lacked popular support.

This came as a huge blow to the athletes, who foresaw their own decline. Still and all, there seemed no escape. Then one afternoon when they were sitting around the mat glum and gloomy, Norm realized there was someone who might help. Erv backed him up; the others acquiesced; so he dispatched a brief note to Cresco High.

Within days the reply was in hand: David Bartelma would love to coach University of Minnesota wrestling, just as long as he could also study for a doctorate in psychology ("a subject," Norm notes wryly, "in which he needed no higher learning").

The boys then approached Frank McCormick, the athletics director. And in September 1935 Coach Bartelma breezed into town and got wrestling going with a rush. First off, candidates were selected for the different weight-classes. Then, a season schedule magically appeared. Finally, stomachs were prodded, biceps pinched, muscles worked on in the weight room.

In Norm's case, the results were not encouraging. "You've been eating too much up here in Minnesota, Borlaug," Bartelma brayed. "Got to get you down to a hundred and forty-five, *and keep you there!*"

From the start the coach's view stretched far. The boys had dreamed of winning a few bouts and having some fun, but Bartelma wanted a program to match the Big Ten's best. To that end, he mobilized his profound wrestling knowledge, contagious enthusiasm, and innate capacity to convince complete strangers of his sport's merits for building men, muscle and moral virtue.

Among other things, he initiated a statewide youth-wrestling program to develop a talent pool the college could plumb forever. In that regard, the big uncertainty was how to generate interest in high schools, where the sport was unknown, misunderstood or maligned.

Bartelma had an idea for that, too:

> He sent three of us—Erv, Caifson Johnson, and me—to Parent-Teacher Association meetings all around Minneapolis. We spent several evenings a week at it. He'd hand us bus fare and thirty-five cents for dinner and off we'd go.
>
> Most of the parents we met had no conception of amateur wrestling, and confused us with professional showmen bouncing around boxing rings. So we sought out the football coaches, explaining that by coaching wrestling during the winter months, they could ensure their players remained in top shape for the football season.

That connection was what made high-school wrestling catch on. And with surprising speed. The following year, for example, several high-school meets were held in different parts of Minnesota, and those led to district contests and a state tournament.

Under the new coach's fiery influence, college wrestling also caught on quickly. Indeed, it soon soared high enough to approach football's prominence. Among early fans was Lotus Delta Coffman, who, despite the pressures of being university president, even came to watch practices. Borlaug often saw this local legend observing from high in the bleachers.

Seeing his sport recover from collapse filled these days with interest and good fellowship. Among athletes he met were two future members of Minnesota's new and impossibly youthful political force.

One was a reserve quarterback and rising football star. Although they interacted only slightly, it was good Norm and Orville Freeman got to be locker-room buddies. At a vital point in the decades ahead their paths will cross again to benefit the world food supply.

Workout Place. David Bartelma is today called "The Father of Minnesota Wrestling." From this 1936 squad he built a powerhouse program. Borlaug stands behind the coach (with hands on hips). His Cresco friend Erv Upton is beside him, kneeling down. His other friend, Caifson Johnson, who helped start high school wrestling in Minnesota, stands on the other side, hands behind his back. Clinton Gustavson, standing far left, would become Big Ten and National AAU Champion. John Whitaker, standing far right, would in time also become National AAU Champion.

Work Place. The University of Minnesota Agricultural Campus provided Norm both comfort and a career. Only later would he discover that these buildings housed a sort of "horticultural hospital" wherein wheat underwent the therapy that brought it back from the dead following Marquis' collapse in 1916. And in time he himself would extend that therapy to wheat around the world.

Soon, too, he'd meet a second rising campus star—a student a few years ahead of him. It's been reported that in those days Hubert H. Humphrey couldn't afford textbooks, and was relying on library copies to master pharmacy. In future decades he also, without actually knowing it, would help the Borlaug saga unreel in the right direction.

S till and all, campus life was hardly a bed of roses:

For me, the fall semester of my junior year raced by and the new year of 1936 loomed ahead. By then Margaret Gibson and I were seeing each other regularly. She'd remained a student in the Department of Education, but that December she ended her formal studies . . . unable to tolerate the scrimping and scraping any longer. "I'm sick of going to bed hungry," she said.

Her brother made it possible for her to get a job. Bill Gibson edited the University of Minnesota Alumni Magazine and had learned that his printer needed an assistant proofreader. Thus it was that Margaret left school. Colwell Press paid her a pittance, but at last she could eat. And that was the main thing.

I was doing better too, although still facing financial difficulties. By then, the National Youth Administration had assigned me to a new job: cleaning cages and feeding mice, rats and rabbits at the Department of Veterinary Medicine. It took two hours, which I squeezed in before dawn. Three mornings a week I'd rise at three-thirty and ride the university streetcar to the St. Paul campus. That after-midnight service was called the "Owl," and I got to know it far too well.

One freezing January morning I stupidly left my overcoat on a seat outside the animal house. When I came out, it was gone. For the rest of the winter I had only a thin jacket and my varsity sweater [the gold sweater with the big blocky letter "M" he'd earned as a wrestler]. I joked about my carelessness, but Margaret worried I was going to get sick.

Truth be told, I did too. Surviving a Minnesota winter without an overcoat seemed suicidal. But, though very cold and very miserable, I fortunately stayed healthy.

Yes, things were looking up. Norm, however, still lacked the money to buy an overcoat for surviving temperatures that in January 1934 fell to *minus 34°F*. And Margaret had suffered such hunger pains she'd had to abandon her lifelong dream of becoming an educator.

For such a sorry pair what hope was there?

8

1936
Heavy Weather

T he 1930s may have served up the greatest social devastation since the 1860s, but that was just for starters. Weather happened to serve up the greatest physical devastation. No decade in history has devised worse weather, and few who survived the '30s doubted that Mother Nature was taking revenge on America's for its uppity challenges to her rule.

Natural forces struck from so many directions as to certainly seem purpose driven. For one thing, between 1930 and 1939 the Earth Mother delivered deluges to die for. Snows melted so abundantly and spring rains fell so ferociously that at one time or another the Allegheny, Columbia, Connecticut, Delaware, Merrimack, Mississippi, Missouri, Ohio, Potomac, Susquehanna and Tennessee roared through cities, ravished rural regions, drowned highways and sent houses and vehicles rocking and rolling down river valleys like rubber duckies.

March 1936 dispensed the biggest flood in East Coast history, inundating a dozen states from Georgia to Vermont and claiming 150 lives. At its height a newspaper reported that "The Potomac was up 26 feet at Washington. . . . Pittsburgh was under 10 to 20 feet of water and was without lights, transport, or power. The life of 700,000 people was paralyzed. The food supply was ruined, the steel industry at a standstill."

For another, during that already disheveled decade Nature seemed intent on blowing America away. In 1934 gusts atop New Hampshire's Mount Washington reached 231mph—a world record still unsurpassed. Then in April 1936 an F5 tornado crushed Tupelo, Mississippi (presciently sparing the Presley family's baby named Elvis) followed by Gainesville, Georgia. The only tornado to score a double on cities, it left over 200 dead and 2000 injured, and was then America's most destructive.

Moreover, during that decade hurricanes became altogether too enamored with handsome Uncle Sam. On the Atlantic coast, 1933 was the most violent year then on record, with a total of 21 tropical storms and hurricanes; 1936 strove to top that, but could only come up with 18. And on Labor Day 1935 the strongest hurricane of all—a Category 5 toting 200 mph winds—slammed into the Florida Keys, killing perhaps 800 people and unleashing a 20-foot wall of water that washed away 40 miles of the wondrous railway that had whisked spellbound tourists over the sparkling Caribbean to Key West.

Piling on the chastisement, Nature spent the decade desiccating the nation's eastern half. Her attack began with the drought of 1930, an epic event still ranked as the most costly natural disaster in the Mid-Atlantic region. Indeed, that year, Drought Relief Committees were established in 21 of the 48 states encompassing a vast empire of hurt whose boundary corners were Maryland, Wyoming, Texas and Alabama.

Even worse would follow: Florida's drought of '32 rewrote that state's record books. And the Great Plains turned to toast in '34, '35 and '36, when summers burned on month after endless month with wide skies, searing sunbeams, and dragon's-breath wind. "There's never been anything like this before," Granddad Nels informed Norm in July '34.

Nels Borlaug was absolutely right: 1934 is even now considered the hottest year before this century. That July the whole Midwest sizzled. Keokuk—an Iowa town due south of Saude—endured a month of 118 degrees, which was pretty much par for the prairies. Throughout the heartland chickens, cattle, hogs and horses gave up eating and slunk into the shade, preferring to starve than eat in the heat.

That same month, drought parched 80 percent of the nation, a record still unmatched. In places people walked across the Mississippi. And the soft rich Midwest soil cracked like crazy quilt, crops browned out, and national grain production plunged past the point of social safety.

And the following years were barely better. The 1936 fire that baptized Henry Wallace's novel corn was just one example. Indeed, drought would surpass the Farmers' Holiday or even Wallace's policies in jerking farm prices back to life. With weather like this, no farmer needed a bribe to produce less. Despite all the modern marvels, the wheat crop was the smallest recorded in more than two decades.

Moreover, those blistering summers were succeeded by winters that slammed the midsection like a deepfreeze door. The 30-below refrigeration Norm endured while working for the neighbors during January '33 and a year later when his jacket was stolen was far from unique. Indeed, January '36 delivered the longest freeze Iowa ever suffered . . . *for three weeks* the mercury stayed below *20-below*.

And Nature still wasn't satisfied. Plagues and pests added unique devastation to the already suffering people of the plains. In 1935, black stem rust returned to recreate the wheat-crop ruination of 1916. This is when Ceres, successor to the mighty Marquis, broke down bringing Middle America down with it. Moreover, between 1934 and 1938 swarms of grasshoppers and Mormon crickets consumed crops worth over $300 million, despite $2 million spent on arsenic sprays. And jackrabbits infested the Southern Great Plains in numbers that livened the landscape. With too many to shoot, town-folk spent Sunday afternoons marching over the land in long lines, herding terrified bunnies into netted fences, and clubbing them with axe handles.

But of all the elemental chastisements none caused more horror and hurt than the soil that took off to fly in the sky. This love of flight turned the decade into "The Dirty Thirties," a title applied more with shame than blame.

Airborne earth seemed to emigrate especially from the lands turned by the terrific new tractors for the food that won the World War. After the spring of 1931 rain refused to return to the Southern Plains. And three years later when Nature unleashed the searing summers and satanic winds millions of tons of topsoil rose as if in disgust and headed out in search of greener pastures. One observer voiced a common belief: "Here in the Texas Panhandle we were hit harder than most anywhere else. If the wind blew one way, here came the dark red dust from Oklahoma. Another way and it was the gray dust from Kansas. Still another way . . . the brown dust from Colorado and New Mexico. Little farms were buried. And the towns were blackened."

An area schoolboy told a similar tale: "These storms were like rolling black smoke. We had to keep the lights on all day. We went to school with headlights on, and with dust masks on. I saw a woman who thought the world was coming to an end. She dropped down on her knees in the middle of Main Street in Amarillo and prayed out loud: 'Dear Lord! Please give them another chance.'"

The dirt clouds sharing the heavens next moved on to see more of the countryside. Soon, they'd gotten as far north as the Dakotas, appearing on high like gray-brown ghosts and casting their all-too-real spoor over everything below. Finally they began barreling eastwards to batter Chicago, New York, Washington, D.C. Some even went so far as to muddy ships far out in the Atlantic.

BROWN . . .

Sure we complain about the weather, but we never face dirt storms.

. . . BLIZZARD

During Borlaug's 20s, however, dirt "drenched" Middle America like daily rain.

Those beneath the brown blizzards couldn't avoid the silt raining from on high. Despite oilcloth and gummed paper packed into windowsills, doorframes and even keyholes, indoor fans of fine sand rippled across the floor like little beaches. Grit also invaded every room, every cupboard, every closet. Between courses, children fingered pictures in the dinner-table dust. And millions woke up each morning inside a grimy silhouette on the sheet.

Almost half the nation's inhabitants suffered thus, and most considered it the end of existence. Nature had so forsaken Middle America that even the soil couldn't stand the place. Millions of farmland acres had been damaged; the remaining millions seemed ripe for ruination.

Of all the burdens Franklin Roosevelt and Henry Wallace faced, this was the most basic. Before they could restore the agricultural wealth, they had to at least keep the ground grounded.

Again FDR took charge. On March 9, 1933, just five days following the inauguration, he informed Congress: "I propose to create a Civilian Conservation Corps for simple work that will not interfere with normal employment. The young men will work on erosion control and forestry. They will build roads in state and national parks and fight forest fires . . . I estimate that 250,000 young men can be put to work by summer."

Two days later he called in the secretaries of War, Interior and Agriculture, the Director of the Budget, the Solicitor of the Interior Department and the Judge Advocate of the Army. "Your agencies will work together to run the CCC," he directed. "The Army will run the camps . . . the Agriculture and Interior departments will set up the work projects and provide the personnel to manage them. The Labor Department will recruit the men from families who are on relief."

By the end of July the new organization was employing more than 300,000 youths (200 of whom would die violently in the Florida Keys hurricane two years hence). They received handsome paychecks: $30 a month. However, $25 went straight home to the parents. Giving a kid a job may have been valid, but parents voted!

Although supervising the CCC, the Army was barred from directing the young recruits in their daily work. This, after all, was peacetime, and no one wanted to antagonize certain hysterical European bullies then showing signs of belligerent intent. Instead, hundreds of college students experienced in soil conservation or forestry were hired to manage the field operations. Among those was Norm. "I'm proud to have helped the CCC," he says, and he says it with passion because, beyond saving soil, the program saved his sanity.

This, his second New Deal involvement, started with nothing more than a fascination with the activity in Green Hall. The top two floors of that building on the St. Paul campus housed the Lake States Forest Experiment Station. This federal facility provided technical support to the "Shelterbelt Program"—a huge operation in which thousands of CCC kids planted trees in east-west strips, like rungs on a giant ladder whose feet rested on Texas and whose top touched North Dakota.

Behind this stunning idea was the Experiment Station's director, Raphael Zon. Placing lines of trees athwart the prevailing breezes of summer, he declared, would weaken the wind and rob it of the power to pick up dirt; he'd seen it happen in Russia. Roosevelt embraced the idea, and charged the CCC with suturing the vast belly wound, popularly known as the Dust Bowl, with healing bands of greenery.

The Russian refugee who urged this course is nowadays forgotten, a fact distressing to relate. While attending classes in Green Hall Borlaug often saw this intellectual dynamo. Indeed, Raphael Zon was so energetic, colorful and charismatic he seemed to be in all places at all times. Norm remembers him forever discoursing in a thick accent about trees and seemingly every other darn thing under the sun.

This wiry forester's firecracker spirit seemed forever primed to erupt from his average-sized body, and the slightest cerebral flint generated such fountains of opinions and speculations he seemed to explode. Accordingly, his wife made a point of attending scientific meetings, and whenever a detonation loomed she'd step up and say: "Ya, ya . . . that's enough Raphael." Anna Zon knew her husband had to be restrained before his searing syllables permanently branded resentment on his peers' psyches.

When Raphael Zon undertook the technical support for the shelterbelt project he was 60 years old and had already packed two full lifetimes into his unprepossessing frame. Born at Simbirsk on the mighty Volga, he grew up sucking the air of subversion. During the years of his youth that small fortress town (population about 40,000) standing on a bluff beside the rushing dark waters cradled the dissention that ultimately shattered the centuries-old rule of the Czars. Zon's high-school principal was the father of Alexander Kerensky, who'd govern Russia following the Czarist overthrow in the spring of 1917. Six months later, Zon's older schoolmate, Vladimir Ulyanov, would oust Kerensky and establish his own state, the Union of Soviet Socialist Republics. Ulyanov was by then using a nom de guerre: "Lenin."

THE GUIDE

When Raphael Zon stepped off the immigrant ship at Ellis Island federal functionaries first refused to him entry, contending that he had nothing to offer the U.S. Thirty years later he tamed the dust storms that were the nation's greatest disgrace.

Borlaug often saw this Russian firebrand at the St. Paul campus, from whence Zon directed the famed shelterbelt program. The 1930s was a terrible decade for tree planting on the Great Plains. But vegetation was the only way to keep the soil from lifting off; and by the time reliable rains returned Zon's shelterbelts provided a skeletal backbone upon which soil-saving vegetation could accrete.

Norm took lectures from Zon, and eventually he too combined hands-on fieldwork with a vision of putting plants to use on a grand scale to serve a great good.

But those horrors were still to come. Back in the 1890s, Zon was a schoolboy helping his buddies fight for representative government. Following several daring adventures the Czarist police arrested him and threatened dire punishment unless he ceased. The threats had no effect, and in 1896, following yet another arrest, he was sentenced to eleven years confinement in Archangel.

Somehow, the irrepressible pest avoided what amounted to a death sentence in the Arctic wastes. He could, however, no longer remain in Russia. Wandering westward, he bummed around Europe as a stateless nomad. Then in 1898 he headed out for America, taking passage on an immigrant ship and crossing the Atlantic squeezed into a bottom berth in steerage-class. You simply couldn't go any lower.

Or so he thought: Arriving at Ellis Island with nothing but 15 cents, he faced rejection. The immigration officer objected neither to his poverty nor his politics. The paucity of skills was what was unacceptable. This skinny youngster had no trade. He clearly was no laborer. What possible good could he be to the great United States?

Fortunately for us, Raphael Zon talked his way past immediate deportation. A New York druggist gave him temporary work and a local actress taught him English. Then he moved upstate to Cornell University and enrolled in the College of Forestry.

To professional observers that was a bad move. This particular college was then under intellectual siege for the sin of espousing practical tree growing. Worse, instead of lecturing down to students, its dean sent them to the woods to learn to do things for themselves. No wonder his associates were livid; this was a sellout to the lesser breeds below academe. The critics all agreed that a trade-school approach just wasn't good enough for the Ivy League.

Nevertheless, the hopelessly old fashioned professor prevailed, and in 1901 Cornell awarded Raphael Zon the degree of Forest Engineer.

By the time Borlaug knew him, 35 years later, Zon had applied his reviled training to rectify the American landscape. His ladder-like arrangement of tree lines was helping quell the dust storms that had been the government's greatest disgrace and the citizen's greatest distress.

Still and all, Zon remained a rebel at heart. To the end of his days, he resisted the ideals of academe, urging his students to maintain a realistic outlook on all things. More than once Norm heard him say that science was no place for speculation, sentimentalism or personal beliefs, and that many research claims would eventually prove wrong. "Temper every conclusion with common sense," Zon would say.

The shadow of this firecracker's cautions concerning runaway theories and theorists fell upon the boy Borlaug, whose schooling involved the same despised trade-school forestry. To graduate, Norm had to exhibit proficiency in using a surveyor's transit as well as in siting roads and fences and setting boundaries for tree-growing operations.

This was unlike anything required by today's top-tier universities. For days at a time Norm lived in the wilds bordering St. Paul, cooking on corncob-fueled fires, sleeping on the ground, washing in streams. His working hours were devoted to triangulations, altitudes, and azimuths as well as to identifying, measuring, pruning, doctoring, planting and thinning trees. Some exams were held way off in the deep dark woods. All in all, it didn't seem like tertiary education . . . and it wasn't. Ultimately, his grade depended more on surveying and silvics than on scholarship.

Little did he know that being a surveyor will eventually prove as vital as being a scientist. Indeed, that unique talent will keep the world fed.

This gritty apprenticeship with forest science's unloved underside led to his own CCC involvement. During the 1936 spring quarter, realizing he was broke and would have to bail out of school, he wondered aloud whether his newfound skills might secure a paying job for the coming summer. Margaret Gibson considered it a grand possibility. Using a borrowed typewriter she pounded out letters to Forest Service field offices. Night after night.

Norm thought her enthusiasm a bit over the top. "I'm just a junior," he said, "No one will hire me." Margaret replied that it should be tried. And as she slipped each letter into the mailbox she kissed it good luck . . . 55 kisses in all.

Then with naive optimism the young couple awaited a flood of responses from forestry research stations nationwide. In the outcome there was only one: The Northeastern Forest Experiment Station in New Haven, Connecticut offered summer employment. The pay would be $100 a month. He could come when ready.

Thus, following the exams in May, Norm hitchhiked along the two-lane roads that writhed eastwards toward the great Atlantic. Here's where he crossed the Third Great Divide and entered the truly wacky world beyond the Midwest. And he did it by thumbing lifts.

In that more innocent era hitchhiking was a standard part of public transportation. Getting a lift was easy, especially if drivers could see you were a college student. Norm's eye-catching sweater with the big blocky "M" got him to New Haven in three days, despite a 30 mph speed limit.

His nights were spent in private homes, which was customary before the masses got mobility and motels had to be invented. In the earlier era many families welcomed "roomers," who paid 50 cents or maybe a dollar for the joy of using Junior's bed. It was big business. Cities and towns were festooned with enticements urging passersby to come on in and spend the night. The plaintive missives were tacked on posts, trees and fences in front of ordinary houses on ordinary streets.

Arriving in New Haven, Norm found that the Forest Service had housed its Northeastern Forest Experiment Station at Yale University. Following an interview, the station director assigned him to a research forest 90 miles up the Connecticut River Valley. Then Ed Behre [BEAR-AH] handed over the bus fare, and, with a reassuring handshake, a friendly grin and a wave, dispatched the fledgling forester to the extreme northwest corner of Massachusetts.

Now alone with his first command, the 22-year-old novice was charged with the care and culture of a scenic hill tract enfolded within the beautiful Berkshire Hills near Williamstown.

At the heart of his four-square-mile realm stood a mansion with at least ten fireplaces and almost uncountable rooms. Amos Lawrence Hopkins (an associate of Jay Gould, the 19th Century railroader nowadays labeled a "robber baron") had built it in the previous century.

In 1924, however, Hopkins' widow moved away, sealing the place so tight that not even air could get in. Without ventilation, mold and ground moisture took up residence. Indeed, they thrived so mightily that twelve years onward the ancient pile, which the Forest Service had hoped to use as a regional headquarters, was collapsing under the impact of those crafty collaborationists, decay and gravity. Moreover, the pristine property surrounding the mansion was collapsing into a mirror-image wreck of rotting fences and riotous foliage.

To extract some order from his messy manor, Norm was required to survey the boundaries, create a topographical map, inventory the vegetation, plant hundreds of white pines to foil erosion, and set out sites for future tree-growing trials.

Despite his youth, he was provided four workers. That being a take-charge era when education included leadership, it was standard practice to honor the young with responsibility. Authorities in those daft dark ages trusted people more than paper; only later would the balance tip and red-tape reverence transcend all. (The switch being of course progressive: paper being so much better behaved!)

CAREER SAVER #9

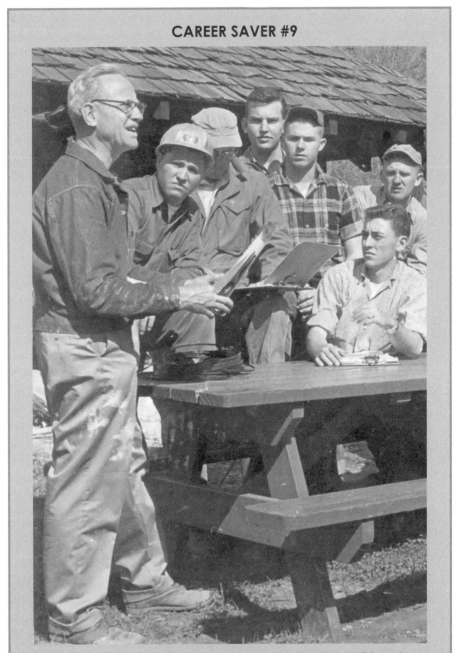

Fate's ninth facilitator, Edward Behre. A man of unbounded confidence in young foresters, Behre was the only research director who replied to Borlaug's plea for summer employment. The $600 he paid for six months work in the Berkshire Hills kept the Borlaug career from derailing before even reaching the main trunk line.

Norm's crew included two local Williamstown men paid by the Works Progress Administration, a New Deal program for unemployed adults. The others were Boston boys sponsored by the CCC.

Managing those youths was especially gratifying. They were about his own age and, like Coach Bartelma, he set challenging goals and acted more like a brother than boss. Such sensitivity was crucial because neither had been away from home before. They were savoring both the wonder of doing work and of being wanted.

Among CCC recruits the wonder at being wanted was widespread. During that dyspeptic decade melancholy ruled the young; and overcoming disillusion was a CCC mission. Beyond providing income and preserving the environment, the Corps kept despairing youths from drifting into anti-social sects, many of which were patently pro-Nazi.

Even more fundamental were the provision of food and nutrition. That American kids needed a good feed in 1936 is a fact troubling to narrate. Little had changed since the Great War. Visiting the large CCC camp in the hills above Williamstown, Norm noticed fresh arrivals slinking in bony and hollow cheeked.

This was a sight seen coast to coast. And the extent of this national disgrace is revealed by the War Department's biometrics for recruits. Inductees—almost all in their late teens or early twenties—had to weigh more than 105 pounds, be at least 5 feet tall, and possess no fewer than 12 of their original 32 teeth.

These biometrics—for the citizen soldiers soon to confront the "Master Race"—indicate that child nutrition was hardly a point of patriotic pride. Indeed, they are an indictment of the age. National Physical Fitness Director John B. Kelly would find in 1940 that 40 percent of the youths he examined were unfit for service. This Olympic rowing champion and father of future actress Grace Kelly reported their ailments as: bad teeth, poor eyesight, diseases of the heart and circulation, deformed arms and legs, and mental disorders.

For all that, though, Norm marvels at how fast CCC conscripts recovered health and strength. Those 17 and 18-year-olds went into the no-frills camp in the hills and literally disappeared. What emerged was an altogether different cross-section of humanity. Later it was found that the average CCC recruit gained 11 pounds in his *first three months*.

This pre-strengthening of America's youth is a forgotten facet of World War II. And it was decisive because during the 1930s American boys were woefully unprepared for war. Throughout the decade, a clueless Congress, blind to Hitler's mounting mastery of history, blocked

IDYLLIC INTERLUDE

The Hopkins Forest as it was in Borlaug's time. Here in this beautiful spot in the Berkshire Hills of Massachusetts he earned the cash that kept him in school. Seen in the distance is the Hoosic River Valley; to the left—framed by East Mountain—is Williamstown.

every military-buildup bill. By default, then, FDR's youth conservation efforts—the most humble and peaceable program imaginable—imbued 2 million lost souls with a sense of discipline and the requirements of communal living that would prove vital when confronting the regimented ranks of Hitler Youth. Moreover, it CCC imbued those 2 million lost American adolescents with hope just when the last dregs were about to disappear.

At the end of the summer, just as Norm was preparing to return home, his boss called from New Haven and asked him to stay on. Ed Behre also explained he was sending a second forester . . . one who'd just received a Masters from the University of California. This came as doubly disconcerting news because the newcomer was a forestry graduate while Norm, the nominal leader, remained an undergraduate, and a mere junior at that.

But Merlin ["Dick"] Dickerman proved no snob. He neither pulled rank nor tried to outshine Norm with his superior status.

> Dick and I had a great time. We shared the sleeping loft above the barn attached to the carriage house. Our accommodations were so poor that to this day I feel sorry for Mr. Hopkins' horses who'd once occupied the barn downstairs. Its walls were so drafty the snow blew through and piled up in the stalls. Some even swirled up through the ceiling and infiltrated our quarters on the upper story.
>
> The addition of Dick gave us a six-man squad, and together we finished a topographical map as well as a vegetation map highlighting the different plants in the Hopkins Forest. Our major achievement, though, was the boundary survey.
>
> The group got good at surveying: hacking through the under-growth, setting up the transit, and pegging out the lines. By happenstance, the last stretch was a long steep slope that ran right up to the intersection of Massachusetts, Vermont and New York. That point belonging to three states was so submerged in tangled undergrowth that I'm sure no one had seen it since the 1800s.
>
> On the morning of the survey's final day Dick bet me that we wouldn't come within three feet of the "Tristate Corner." However, in clearing the last bit of bush we uncovered a five-foot-tall granite cairn erected in British times. And the line my transit indicated was less than *two feet* off.
>
> That was a great day, made even greater by the bottle of bourbon Dick conceded. In 1936, that meant more than you'd think. The constitutional prohibition against liquor sales had been repealed and for the first time in our adult lives we could buy liquor legally.
>
> The Jack Daniels we shared that evening seemed like ambrosia. Yes, we'd found the secret spot where three states met; more important, though, we were free to toast our discovery!

By December 1936 Norm was back in Minneapolis. During the half-year absence he'd earned $600. Now a rich man, he seizes the chance for a trip home for Christmas. This time the sight proves surreal. The larval life everyone had deemed necessary for survival had gone forever and a new, almost gentrified, existence had emerged. Farming was now more than a life . . . it was a livelihood.

FREEDOM FROM CANT

Despite his bet with Dickerman, Borlaug is no big drinker. Nonetheless, to him, as to most citizens, prohibition's repeal in 1933 felt like freedom.

It's of course well known that the 18th Amendment did nothing to reduce crime and corruption, solve societal problems, reduce prison crowding, or improve health and hygiene. It's also well known that the earlier embrace of the Wartime Prohibition Act—the period during the Great War when Americans almost willingly gave up beer and cocktails to save on grain—paved the way for the "noble experiment" that from 1920 onwards prohibited the distribution of alcoholic beverages.

What's not well known is that the Wartime Prohibition Act was itself precipitated by the failure of the magnificent variety Marquis, which in turn was precipitated by black stem rust. This was another way the fungus changed the face of society, and sent cheerless effects cascading down the decades. Some of Prohibition's restrictions—the so-called "blue laws"—remain as history's hangover.

Behind the magical metamorphosis was yet another novel notion ginned up by FDR and Henry Wallace. Since 1933, a novel partnership the two schemers had arranged between the Feds, the power companies and the people had strung wires into hundreds of thousands of farms.

The Rural Electrification Administration was a self-help operation: It supplied wire, poles and electrical fittings such as transformers and insulators; power companies supplied electricity, but the users had to put in the poles and connect their houses for themselves.

As late as the mid-1930s, nine out of ten rural homes remained unserved by electricity. Husbands by the millions hand-milked cows by lantern light while their wives slaved over woodstoves and washboards like the Borlaugs. Absent electricity, rural life remained as straitjacketed as in days of the ancients.

Yet the local resistance to electrification was intense, widespread and amazing to contemplate. To receive an REA loan, every family in the neighborhood had to co-sign the request form that committed them to doing the work as well as contributing five dollars. The first requirement was okay, but the last created mass consternation. Farmers had no conception of this mysterious substance that inhabited copper wires, so there was always some cussed holdout who balked at putting up the deposit. Electricity, he insisted, could never be worth *a whole five dollars*!

In large measure the opposition reflected the fact that electricity had yet to expose its natural talents. But it also mirrored the power companies' propaganda, and for a while the corporate contention that rural power lines would prove a financial flop was born out. Indeed, the REA itself projected that farmers would use 75 kilowatt-hours *a month*, which made the whole effort a fiasco from the start.

Everyone—including the users—had, however, over-looked the countless farm chores electricity could shoulder with aplomb. That oversight persisted only until farmfolk found they could milk cows, elevate grain, grind feed, pump water, wash clothes, cook dinner and do myriad other tiresome tasks *all at the same time.*

With electricity suddenly exposed as a universal and ubiquitous assistant, farmers gleefully cooperated in wiring up their own enclaves. Even for professionals wiring one neighborhood was a challenge, yet farmers did it nationwide. During the latter half of the '30s, neighbors webbed most of Middle America with wire. Stringing the lines pole to pole, street to street, farm to farm, they wrought rural America's final transmutation. Whereas hybrid corn, fertilizer, tractors and sulfa drugs had already lifted heartland hearts, electrification brought the ultimate lift. Toil that had drained everyday existence now was performed by a Bakelite button on the wall. And in what seemed no time at all, farm families were using 1000 kilowatt-hours a month.

This is how the leaden life turned golden. At a church meeting in Tennessee a farmer summed up the significance: "Brothers and sisters, I want to tell you this. The greatest thing on earth is to have the love of God in your heart, and the next greatest is to have electricity in your home."

That's a sentiment Norm understands. He saw electricity help rural America finally emerge from the slough of despond. Energy is the most

POWER TO . . .

During the 1930s farmers webbed rural America with 300,000 miles of copper wire. With federally supplied materials, locals like these electrified themselves. By 1939, 25 percent of rural folks had powered their own barns and homes with the wondrous wires that did such hard work so well, so effortlessly and so quietly.

. . . THE PEOPLE

With electrons on hand America's rural half suddenly discovered the wonders of appliances. Radios without batteries, lights with real bulbs, stoves you just switched on, vacuum cleaners, irons, and washing machines all proved popular. Appliances opened a vast market for power as well as an industry to motivate the modern age.

basic ingredient of farming, and this miraculous modern form that was on tap seemingly everywhere gave America's forgotten half a future approaching what they considered "future perfect." While feeding themselves and everyone else, food suppliers could at last lead a grand life. Nothing like that had been known in agriculture's 10,000 year history.

Arriving home that Christmas of 1936, he discovered a house transformed. From every room light disputed the dark, making windows into beacons that pierced the country night that had been forever black. The family now inhabited a new age. When he and his father stepped into the pre-dawn darkness, the kerosene lantern stayed behind; in the barn a bulb was waiting to instantly banish the blackness.

And for his mother the wood-fueled stove and the washboard had gone the way of the work horse. When Clara Borlaug cooked, she no longer needed a boy to build a mountain of wood. On Mondays, clothes were washed with water that—quite incredibly—flowed hot from the tap. The old tin tub—previously allowed out of the basement only on Saturday nights—had been evicted and a real bath installed. An electric sewing machine mended and made clothes with mechanical fingers that neither tired nor contracted arthritis. Portable radiant heaters warmed rooms to meet the desires of the moment (luxury unimaginable). And evenings were given over to that cosmic companion that teleported enchantment right inside your mind. Radio had become part of reality.

From our comfort zone we cannot fathom how astonishing the effect of that final piece of the puzzle must have been. During his 22 years, Norm had seen lives mirroring those of Caesar's serfs made over not just with trucks, cars, concrete highways, and radio, but also with abundant food thanks to the combined powers of better seed, fertilizer and farm machinery. And now electricity has made rural living grand.

Indeed, he himself is feeling grand. At long last, he's ready to complete his training, commence his career, and clamber up the ladder of opportunity in the marvelous modern times.

As a forester.

Naturally.

9

1937

Wilderness

Refreshed in mind, and with the reassurance of $600 resting in his pocket Norm left the farm early in January 1937 and hitchhiked back to Minneapolis.

This time no hidden surprises lay in wait. Malignant fate had finally surrendered; he can now control his own destiny. Though no longer cleaning up after professors for tuition chits, he still serves meals to sorority sisters for "all he can eat." Heck, for one so wealthy not even that was necessary. The Forest Service's largess is sufficient to even treat Margaret to an occasional movie.

Her life is improving too. She's now Assistant Proofreader for Independent Press, a small publisher of books, magazines, pamphlets and folders. During their hours together the couple sometimes talked of the future, but the times remained distressed and not even Norm's gold could last forever. So before taking the relationship further he decided to secure his predestined profession.

As to wrestling, he was delighted to find that despite six months absence he's still listed on the varsity squad. This was a signal honor because in two years Coach Bartelma has worked such prodigies that the University of Minnesota is competing with the nation's best. Indeed, the upcoming season includes meets with mighty Big Ten and Big Six rivals. One particular contest promises a clash for the ages: The University of Iowa is coming to town!

Knowing that the reigning national champion will present an extraordinary challenge Bartelma assigns Norm to a lower-than-normal weight class, hoping to impart a strength advantage. "You'll have to starve yourself," he explains; "spend hours in the sweatbox and drink nothing for the last two days."

Cutting weight like that proved agonizing; made much worse by the sight and scent of the heavenly repasts he serves daily to young women, much of which went untouched.

Finally, his craving overcame his common sense:

> I waited tables at the sorority but scarcely ate or drank a thing—not even coffee. Handling food was sure hard, but my mind was fixed on the scales at the gym. And the damn things weren't cooperating. After the third day I stopped drinking water.
>
> That evening Margaret and I took a walk together, and she later told Scott [Pauley] I'd been extremely irritable.
>
> Early on the afternoon of the University of Iowa meet I spent an hour in the sweatbox. Bartelma came by and joked I was idling my time away while the others were hard at training. To me, there seemed nothing funny about it. For four days I hadn't eaten a decent meal, and the brass weight on the scales said 136. . . . I stared at it in disbelief: Oh hell, still a pound to go!
>
> Right then, one of the other wrestlers put his hand on my arm. "Let's see how you've done, Norm."
>
> Without even being aware, I swung round with a fist at the ready. "Take your hands off me or I'll break your arm!" I was about to smash his face when Bartelma stepped between us. "Take it easy; take it easy," he said, opening the sweatbox door and pushing me toward the showers.
>
> Standing under the cold water I was overcome by shame. "I'm sorry," I told the coach. "I behaved badly."
>
> He replied in soothing tones: "It's understandable," he said, "Don't worry. . . . it's over now."
>
> I went back, sweated away the last pound, and won my bout.
>
> The win brought no pleasure, however. At the following buffet I wolfed down a mountain of food but was too troubled to rejoice. It should have been a festive occasion; we'd scored an improbable victory over the reigning champs. But I left early. Had to get away.
>
> Margaret was living in a small apartment near mine, and as we walked home I told what had happened: "A friend just laid a hand on my arm, and I went berserk," I said.
>
> "You know, a hungry man can be as violent as a hungry beast!"

That night the man-child went home a man. He'd been stupefied by starvation, and the experience had seared another insight into his mind.

Early in 1937 the chance to sample his presumptive profession arose. The Forest Service offered him a summer position as a firewatcher in Idaho. He was then in the first half of his senior year and, although the job required no special preparation, he decided to take the National Junior Forestry Civil Service Examination. Indeed, in the few weeks before classes ended in May he studied hard enough to post one of Minnesota's highest scores.

Thus the day after finals, he and Scott Pauley headed west. Scott had been assigned a fire lookout in Montana's Flathead National Forest; Norm was to report to the Idaho National Forest.

On reaching this vast wilderness in Idaho's self-proclaimed "Heartland" he discovered a mountain hamlet with a gorgeous lake on one side and tree-clad slopes on all the others. It seemed like paradise, except that paradise would have had a sidewalk. McCall's main street was lined with the raised wooden-planking seen in wild-west movies.

In this quaint and woodsy spot, the Forest Service ran a boot camp for firefighters. Veteran rangers trained Norm and five other youths to extinguish blazes, maintain telephone lines and radio links, and survive alone in the wilderness.

After two weeks dishing out hard knocks, hard lessons and equally hard mental exercises, the crusty drill instructors ignited fires in the woods, assigned a student to each fire and then judged how well they handled their responsibility. Norm happened to handle his very well.

For the final test, compasses and maps were passed out and the trainees were dumped individually in separate sectors of the wilds. Norm was the only one to make it back unaided.

A day later he faced a row of three examiners, each squinting venom like a gila monster:

> I was put through quite a grilling. The questions mostly focused on moral issues and mental stability, which came as a surprise. But my answers must have been satisfactory. When the session was over the senior ranger stared at me: "Borlaug," he said, "we're assigning you to the most critical post in the system. Our whole fire-protection network will depend on you."

Perhaps understandably, Henry Shank, the Idaho National Forest supervisor, failed to explain that Norm would occupy the most isolated lookout in the lower 48. It was 45 miles from a trail—let alone a road. There, this 23-year-old novice will live beyond direct human contact. For months on end he'll have to survive by his own wits (not to mention his own cooking), while staying ever alert for any wisp of smoke over a seemingly endless forest domain.

Three days later he was given a horse and dispatched into the nation's biggest "Primitive Area," which meant it was wilder than a Wilderness because it was truly trackless. Accompanying him were an almost mute packer (on another horse) and three much-burdened mules.

FIREFIGHTER

At the end of the road, Big Creek Ranger Station. Norm inspects the first-aid kit upon which his life will depend during the months ahead. The fire lookout he'll occupy is so remote that help can't reach him for days. Those meager medical supplies are about to be packed on the back of a mule, along with his sleeping bag, a change of clothes, half a dozen sacks of flour, cartons of Spam, a block of dried yeast, and reels of wire. The wire is for repairing the telephone line that will link him to this ranger station at Big Creek. Winter weather having felled this, his sole connection to any other soul, he must first find the downed parts and get them working again. There in Central Idaho's vast, untrodden wilderness his companions will include bears, mountain lions and, scariest of all, forest fires.

On the afternoon of the second day they reached the destination, 8084 feet above sea level on the northeast slope of Cold Mountain. Here, in the primitive area's core, stood three structures. One was a tiny log cabin sheltering amid a scraggly grove of pines. This is where he'd eat and sleep during the months ahead. A few yards behind stood the second structure: an outhouse. About 100 yards further up the slope a tower soared skyward on metal poles. Topping the tower was a flimsy metal box that will be his place of work.

That evening, having watered the mules and stored the supplies, he climbed the ladder that zigzagged upwards between those 70-foot aluminum legs and pushed open the trapdoor in the floor of the box on top.

Though barely big enough to squeeze into, his workspace commanded amazing views through the walls of windows on every side. The 7-foot by 7-foot interior was dominated by a "fire-finder," a table fitted with a swiveling compass platform and something like a sniper-rifle sight. Attached to its pedestal was a crank-type telephone. And on the floor stood a tiny stool with feet wrapped in glass insulators. During electrical storms he was expected to stand on the stool because he'll be inside Idaho's finest lightning rod and he'll be no good to the Forest Service fried.

From this perch on the point of a metal spire soaring high into the sky over a mountain he was expected to protect a wilderness terrain covering perhaps 20 square miles:

> My duty was to watch for smoke and phone in any sighting to the Fire Dispatcher at Big Creek Ranger Station. Then, if Dan LeVan instructed, I'd go out and deal with whatever was causing the smoke *by myself*.
>
> Sending me out to fight a forest fire may seem foolish, but I was the only trained person within the Primitive Area. Helicopters and smoke jumpers were unknown in 1937. Thus, no other immediate help was available.
>
> Crazy as it may seem, I was required to keep the fire controlled *for several days*. The Forest Service needed that much time to round up a crew, get them to the Chamberlain Basin by horse, and keep them fed and supplied by mule.

To survive alone in a vast wilderness one must master living conditions sensible types consider unbearable. He has to care for himself, collect his own water, wash his clothes, and survive apart from everyone on earth. The only exception being the two days in July when the mute muleskinner

WORK SITE AND . . .

When he was 23, Borlaug spent his summer in this tiny box 72 feet above the ground. Being unneeded in the age of satellites most such fire lookouts have been destroyed, but by great good fortune in 1994 the top of this tower and the cabin Borlaug occupied (see opposite) 57 years earlier were saved. They can be visited in McCall, Idaho.

. . . LIVING QUARTERS, SUMMER '37

An Osborne Firefinder fills Norm's tower top. Lining its sights on a smoke plume, he read the location on the circular map. Then, cranking the phone beneath the table he reported the range and map-section to the fire dispatcher over the mountains. Here also are a Quick Lite lantern, a headlamp, Forest Service field glasses, a pulaski for fighting fires, and a stool with glass-encased legs on which he stood during lightning storms.

This is where Norm spent his nights, learning to live with himself and to survive by himself under crude conditions, two talents that will eventually help the course of history.

brought fresh supplies, a gruff greeting, and a pile of mail that swelled the spirit and filled the days with joy.

Best of all, he learned to cook camp style.

> Overall, my diet was simple: canned meats, beans and vegetables as well as bacon and a few basics such as flour and cornmeal. Mostly I lived on baking-powder biscuits, made each morning in the oven of the wood-stove in the cabin. After suffering through weeks of those, an urge for fresh bread became an obsession. I cut off a portion of my block of Fleishmann's Yeast and added it to the flour and water mix. Then, I kneaded the dough and left it overnight as Grandmother Emma had done. It was a total failure. The bread was like a slightly soggy brick; the altitude and the nighttime cold inhibited the yeast. I went back to making powder biscuits and eventually ate so many I got to hate the damn things, and cut back on eating.
>
> An old prospector named Charles Mahan saved my sanity. "Matty," as we called him, had built a cabin in the hills across the Chamberlain Basin and the Forest Service had installed a telephone so he could report any smoke he might see.
>
> The phone was strictly for emergency use, but Matty was lonely and called a different lookout each evening for a chat. "How ya doin' up thar?" he'd say in his cracked old-timer voice. When I complained about the bread, he told me to get a pencil and he'd explain what prospectors do in the high country.
>
> Soon I had a jar of batter warming beside the stove. By continually topping it up with yeast, flour and water I kept it in a high state of fermentation. To make bread I'd ladle out a few big spoonfuls, and knead them into the dough. The result was sourdough. Up there, above eight thousand feet, the bread still didn't rise fully, but it sure tasted great.

This was another step in tempering the cast-iron constitution that would serve him (and the world) well in the years ahead.

The panorama from the top of the tower encompassed a natural empire of untamed magnificence that staggered the senses. On three sides the terrain tumbled to the bottom of the Chamberlain Basin, a huge alpine meadow in the heart of the Continental Divide. Northward, in the far distance lay the Middle Fork of the Salmon, a ribbon of foam now called River of No Return or Whitewater because that very same summer a new pastime was invented there.

Norm learned about whitewater rafting only years later. For him the summer of '37 was all work and worry. With danger lurking on every side, he came to understand why the examiners had probed for psychological frailties. "Men go mad in the solitary confinement of the mountain peak," reports poet Edward Abbey, who has himself been there, done that.

Anguish fell on Norm too. However, after enduring days of self-doubt he came to terms with the solitude as well as the bears, mountain lions, rattlers, lightning strikes and other scary denizens sharing his territory.

A wise person has remarked on nature's ability to amaze, terrify, amuse and provide us profound and lasting insights *into ourselves*. And that's what the treed and trackless Rocky Mountain high did for this 23-year-old from the open prairie. In time, he grew more comforted than concerned; the place—so massive, majestic and mind-bending—became home, though its splendors and surprises also kept him forever humble.

During his first month on the job the days remained cool and damp, and might even have been boring except that he had to clamber down into the bottomlands a thousand feet below and repair the winter-ravaged telephone line connecting him to Dan LeVan.

Once that was working he had another voice for reassurance. Big Creek Ranger Station was on the far side of the mountains but LeVan's phone contact was a comfort, especially when July launched the first thunderheads. These black-hearted piles of cumulus powered into Cold Mountain, darkening his world and loosing liquid contents as if heaven itself had pulled the plug.

In August the skies cleared, the temperature rose, and the air thirsted for moisture. Thunderheads now came dry; their rain evaporating in the sky.

Now the fire season had begun. From his perch atop the 7-story metal poles Norm watched the charcoal-colored cloudscapes drift toward him, shooting hundred-million-volt sparks onto the ineffably beautiful, powder keg he was charged with protecting. It was far from comforting:

> Many an afternoon, I'd watch as a dry thunderstorm crept toward me. One memorable one started eighteen "smokes" . . . I counted each with mounting dread.

Smokes were low-intensity ground fires that tended to smolder for days before dying of natural causes. And he was infinitely thankful when all eighteen passed away to rest in peace.

The more energetic variety that refused to quit the land of the living constituted a threat to everything animal or vegetable within his purview. Typically they bided their time, patiently grazing leaf litter beneath the trees. The trick was to keep them that way. The main trees, such as pine and spruce, had bare trunks that were impervious to the gentle combustion creeping around their feet. Alpine firs, however, swept so

THE VIEW . . .

This is what Norm saw from the top of the tower looking northward into the Chamberlain Basin. The site, at 8000 feet above sea level, is on the highest point of a timbered ridge. The open area, Cold Meadows, is 2.8 miles distant.

low their branches could entice a ground-fire to a higher calling. One fir could spark an inferno in the forest crown.

Norm's job was to lop off fir limbs that sagged close enough to the ground to become fire ladders. It was a critical contribution because once flames hit the heights they could whoosh across the treetops with speed that seemed supersonic.

That's what had happened 27 years earlier. In August 1910 the area just north of his location was a tinder box. No rain had fallen since March, and Idaho and Montana had 1700 separate forest fires going at once. To fight this vast assortment of destruction the government dispatched 10,000 rangers, loggers, miners and ranchers, not to mention laborers enticed off city streets. That frontline force proving

. . . FROM THE TOP

For almost four months Norm defended this immense terrain, alone. Living here, far from help or human contact and surrounded by natural magnificence, made him mentally strong and boosted his growing self-belief.

inadequate, President Taft ordered in reinforcements: ten companies of U.S. Army troops.

Thanks to that quick action, by August 10 the fiery host was quashed. Despite a rash of lingering hot spots, the region remained quiet for ten days. Then on August 20 the humidity plunged toward zero and, just as at Hinckley 16 years before, the sky turned eerily yellow. Finally, a fury of devil winds hurrying straight from Hades combined the hundreds of hot spots and sent a flood of flame surging across the tree-top terrain. That fiery cascade moved with the irresistible ruthlessness of a hurricane. The noise shattered the eardrums. One survivor recalled it sounding like "a thousand trains rushing over a thousand steel trestles." A forest ranger simply reported that "the mountains roared."

In those days the Forest Service was young and vigorous and

commanded by tough types who thrived on adversity and adventure. Like astronauts of a later age, forest rangers were renowned for facing down danger as well as for daring escapes from desperate straits.

None better exemplifies their courage and can-do attitude than "Big Ed" Pulaski, who that infernal day would become a popular hero for the upcoming generation.

Having been a miner before joining the fledgling Forest Service, Edward C. Pulaski knew how to live by his wits in the wilderness. In 1910 he'd been on the payroll only a couple of years and still harbored a newcomer's gripes about the government's goofball regulations. Above all, he hated the forest-ranger's required tool kit: rake, axe, hoe, shovel. Humping all those through rugged terrain amounted to torture. So Pulaski erected a forge in his backyard and began tinkering. Among other things, he took a double-bladed axe and twisted one blade sideways to form a hoe. Thus was born the "pulaski," the firefighter's boon companion that has foiled fires and saved lives in the backcountry ever since.

During the ten days when the fire monster rested from its labors, Big Ed and his crew defended a superb stand of white pine in a dry gulch called Placer Creek. It was two miles from the hamlet of Wallace, about 100 miles north of where Norm's fire lookout was later erected.

Big Ed's 150 men included a handful of experienced woodsmen and a whole lot of rank amateurs who'd been induced to sign on by the promise of excitement as well as an exceptional wage: 25¢ an hour. In 1910 that meant a lot, yet the government had gone to the silly extreme of including "free board" and "all the room the applicants could ever want." Newspaper ads in Seattle and Chicago added: "Bring along a good pair of boots and your bedroll." Drifters and dreamers naturally signed up in droves for the adventure and the 25¢ an hour.

On the fateful August 20th, Big Ed was managing a 40-member squad of his motley mob when, late in the afternoon, a strange hush descended on the smoke-enshrouded gulch. Then from the valley's open end—their only escape route—came a wall of flaming fury.

In an instant, Placer Creek turned into a furnace fueled by the world's finest white pines. Being trapped inside a firepit was stupefying. The noise deafened the ears; the heat disoriented the mind; the smoke suffocated the lungs; and the sight of flames coming down the slopes turned the legs to tallow.

The men stood in shock and awe, immobilized by the sight of huge flaming tree-limbs being tossed to the four winds and young trees bent double in fiery circles. Old-growth trunks, filled with the sap of ages began exploding and ejecting burning brands that, like the legendary firebirds, ignited their own offspring in the air. In time, the heat vaporized so much pine resin that the sky itself caught alight.

Everyone wanted to run. But to where? No escape seemed possible. Fire stood on all points of the compass as well as the sky!

Then Big Ed took charge. Ordering each man to hang onto the one ahead, he led the file up the valley toward an old abandoned mine he'd once seen. It was a mile away, and due to the din, the darkness and the descending firebrands the men were a mere hairbreadth from hysteria as they slithered through the opening barely big enough for a body. Only 60 feet long, the shaft could barely hold all 40 occupants.

Pulaski was the last to squeeze in. Taking station at the entrance, he commanded each man to lie down, face to the ground. Then he hung blankets across the opening. When those began smoldering, he soaked them with water scooped up in his hat from a small seep in the mine floor. When the timbers at the entrance began burning, he soaked them too.

Despite his best efforts, the people-packed tunnel filled with smoke and fumes, and the hungry flames outside sucked away the air until the men knew they were caught in a death trap.

Then madness erupted. Surrendering to panic, man after man rushed the entrance. Brandishing his revolver, Pulaski drove each back until, one by one, all collapsed, unconscious, out of breath and out of even panic's reach. At length he himself crumpled, lungs seared, eyes in agony, muscles exhausted from fighting both fire and fear-crazed men.

Hours later one of the crew awoke and, to no one in particular, said: "Come on outside boys, the boss is dead."

The body slumped by the entrance did not move. But it did manage to croak: "Like hell he is."

It was five o'clock Sunday morning. Most of the survivors couldn't see. They counted noses by touch. Seared, sightless and smoke-choked, they might be . . . but they totaled 38.

Big Ed spent two months in hospital before his sight miraculously returned. By then, he knew how lucky they'd been. Practically everything in this firestorm's path, including trees, towns, wildlife and people, had been incinerated. Just counting the dead took 10 days (the number came to 85, including 78 firefighters).

Within 48 hours, the Big Blowup had consumed a forest empire 260 miles long and 200 miles wide—from the Salmon River north to Canada and from Spokane in Washington to Glacier Park in Montana. Three-million-acres lay wasted, and the world's finest forest was reduced to

MIRACLE SITE

The mineshaft following the Big Blowup of 1910, when bizarre winds merged hundreds of small fires into an inferno covering 3 million acres of Idaho and Montana. Flames engulfed this tiny tunnel, while 38 men huddled inside terrified by the heat, the ebbing air supply and the noise of these huge white pines exploding in the tremendous temperatures. Note the cloth, possibly a blanket Big Ed hung across the entrance and doused with water from a seep providentially discovered in the mine floor.

MIRACLE WORKER

Big Ed Pulaski, set the benchmark for what would later be dubbed "The Greatest Generation." His cool courage and incisive leadership saved his crew from the colossal conflagration. Yet this reserved, even reluctant, hero never sought fame and remained embarrassed by praise. Years later he penned a brief, bland article, his only account of the adventure. Although eventually enticed into posing for this photo, he appears discomforted and has come dressed as if for a trial . . . or perhaps a funeral.

a billion tons of ash and a billion tons of smoke particles, which roiled right across the continent. For decades, people in places as far away as New York and Montreal recalled the dreaded Five Dark Days of 1910, when the lamps had to be lit at midday.

This colossal effect, combined with lurid press accounts, seared the civic conscience. Soon thereafter Congress passed the first federal support for forest-fire protection. This helped erect the lookouts and explains why Norm lived on top of a tower in 1937. Behind the Weeks Act of 1911 lay the hope that clueless youngsters like him could stop another Big Blowup.

Now, 26 years later, he's required to do his part to save the priceless natural treasure spread out below him on Cold Mountain. Alone.

Though Ed Pulaski forever belittled his exploit, few others ever forgot it. Even a quarter century on, his story continued to inspire the Forest Service. McCall's gnarly staff bore the Pulaski stamp. Under their spell, Norm himself became a committed can-do forester. And in the long run being a Pulaski-clone would serve him well.

In the short run, too, that professional heritage would help him withstand a real-world trial of courage and character.

But that was some months ahead; during the first parched weeks, the fires probing the Chamberlain Basin's defenses quickly quit the contest. The only exception proved small, lethargic and unthreatening until it too perished from natural causes, for which he still offers up heartfelt thanks.

Not unexpectedly, as the menacing months marched onward without incident his thoughts turned homeward. By mid-August he'd decided to leave September 1st. That would allow him to indulge in some sight-seeing before heading to West Yellowstone, Wyoming, where he'd promised to meet Scott Pauley on September 20th.

By late August this desire to depart was dominating his days. So when Dan LeVan phoned and requested he stay on *three more weeks* it hit like a hammer to the heart.

The reason for the request was plain enough: For days Norm had watched a huge smoke plume billow up behind the hills separating him from the next watershed south. And each evening he'd followed the rising drama via his telephone hookup with the fire dispatcher.

On that Acorn Butte blaze the Forest Service experimented with using aircraft. Not for two more years would it test the seemingly suicidal notion of parachuting men into the path of a wildfire, and not until the 1940s would it deploy "smoke jumpers"—actually, brave World War II conscientious objectors. This time, the crews walked into Acorn Butte

Valley and were furnished food, water and supplies from the skies. It was not a success. Most of the packages burst on delivery; the underbrush swallowed the rest. LeVan soon had 200 men battling a blaze in a vast wilderness without sustenance, support, or water.

For that reason Norm suppressed his personal desires and stayed at his post three more weeks. He was doing his duty, which felt good. But the days nevertheless passed on leaden feet.

At sunrise on September 20 he stepped from the cabin to fill his canteen at a nearby seep. This was a truly glorious morning— the one in which he'd begin the long march home to the life he'd left behind almost six months before. Already his schedule was in tatters; this was the Monday was supposed to be in Wyoming. But his bags were packed and he hoped Scott would wait, and would understand.

Then, suddenly, far off in the northern dawn shadows, he spied a curling wreath of ruin. Racing up the steps to the observatory, he swiveled the compass platform, took a quick azimuth, cranked the phone, and reported the white plume's bearing. Next, following instructions, he headed out with his shovel, daypack, canteen, and pulaski tool to confront nature's demons . . . and his own.

The smoke was miles off, and reaching it became a nightmare trek through treacle. For almost six hours he scrambled over the Chamberlain Basin's treed bottom, hoping he was heading in the right direction. At last, he climbed a spruce. Even at 40 feet the fire remained hiding in deep cover behind the tall timber, but at least he could sense the direction from which arose the smoky odor.

The rangers had not taught tree climbing, and for good reason . . . it was stupid. Norm left his perch and had about six feet to go when the branch under his left hand broke, tumbling him to the ground, legs painfully doubled-up beneath his body. This was serious, deadly serious. Anyone incapacitated here might not be found for days, other than by fire, thirst or perhaps a grizzly.

Luckily, though, the spruce had created a pad of needles thick enough to safely cushion a young and supple body. Shaken but still sharp-witted, he rose, dusted himself off, and with rather more wariness proceeded toward the smell souring the sky up ahead.

At last the quarry was located. The fire had taken residence in a stand of Engleman spruce that, thankfully, happened to be on terrain that was relatively open, flat, and almost devoid of alpine firs. Although the gentle combustion had singed several acres and still grazed greedily, it

The Idaho mountains that toughened up Borlaug. Foolishly, he traversed them alone and by moonlight to reach Big Creek Ranger Station, located on the small, easy-to-miss meadow seen in the middle distance. Although he and the wilderness were on friendly terms, this journey constituted one of his worst decisions. As no one knew where he was, a fall would have been fatal.

was moving in one direction . . . northeastward. Hustling back and forth along that leading edge he used his pulaski to remove any fir frond that might flirt with a spark.

Through the afternoon he struggled—alone with the flames, the firs and the fears that fluttered the stomach. Then at about 4 o'clock, a ranger from the north side of the Chamberlain Basin arrived on horseback.

The pair then took the offensive together, scratching little firebreaks in the needles ahead of the greedy glow. When the final flickering threats seemed properly corralled they patrolled the scorched perimeter in search of places where an eager ember might effect an escape.

At about 7 o'clock the ranger finally remembered Norm's situation: "Hey," he said, "you'd better get going."

That curt dismissal came as a huge relief because the arrangement with Scott was by now dominating the mind. Racing against the sunset, he scampered back to Cold Mountain, grabbed his belongings, filled his canteen and, as the sky fell, turned his back on his summer abode. Then, by the lingering light he headed down one of the spidery drainage lines traced on his map. The goal: Big Creek Ranger Station on the far side of the mountain range.

For a while the completeness of the night made it impossible to step out safely. Near to bursting with frustration, he rested up, sitting on a boulder.

Then a full moon rose to light the land, and he moved onward, hopping from rock to shadowy rock down the almost dry creek beds. The dread of letting his friend down was now so all-consuming he pressed on through the night, stumbling into Big Creek Ranger Station about nine the next morning.

Imagine the apparition that appeared out of nowhere: eyes bloodshot, feet blistered, clothes grimy—to say nothing of the stink of smoke and sweat. Ranger LeVan took one glance and barked: "Hell, you go to the crick and take a bath. We'll get you some breakfast; then you're going to bed. I don't care where you have to go, you're not going today!"

Though Norm was exhausted in body and brain, the words sent his resentment into overdrive. He spent the day in a cot and a craze, furious at being held a prisoner at Big Creek Station by a purblind jailer.

Next morning, in high dudgeon he grabbed a ride with a young cadet, and fled toward the liberating horizons of sense and civilization.

When he arrived in McCall, however, events took an unexpected turn. Hank Shank, the Idaho National Forest supervisor, made a special offer:

A Junior Forester position was coming available in the new year. If Borlaug wanted it, it was his.

That changed everything. Norm quickly calmed down and made the easiest of decision of his life. Without wasting a second thought on alternatives, he accepted the offer. A delighted Shank informed his new recruit he could start right after graduation.

This brought another miracle moment. No longer was there uncertainty about what to do for a living; he had only to endure one last quarter of college and then come right back here to McCall. His first day on the Forest Service payroll would be January 15, 1938.

Professional life thereby touched the take-off point. He's now 23 and the career path extending ahead is positively, absolutely, unchangeably settled. In less than four months he'll be earning a steady income and absorbed in the vocation he loves and for which he's trained so very hard. For the rest of his days his beat will be woodlands and his companions will be wild.

Yes, this is where doubt was finally defeated. One other thing was sure: he's definitely left the world of farming behind.

Of course, he nursed a secret hope that a certain someone would be by his side sharing the endless joy in Idaho's magnificent Inland Empire.

C rossing Montana, North Dakota and much of Minnesota took an age. Scott's decrepit Dodge couldn't top 25 mph. Finally when that moveable museum piece creaked into Minneapolis late in the afternoon, Norm took the streetcar straight to Independent Press.

Standing outside the gates at 89 10th Street S, he surprised Margaret as she emerged. He grasped her hand and in a voice turbocharged with tension explained he'd landed the perfect job. His career was settled. There was no reason to wait any longer.

"Will you marry me?" he said.

That was a different era from ours. Both were struggling too much over the trials of life to worry much about the trappings of love. They had no money for a fancy wedding, nor any need. There was no cause for delay either. They scheduled the event for the coming Friday.

Given this press of circumstance, there could be no standing on ceremony. For the service Margaret's brother, Bill Gibson, offered the sitting room in his house in the suburb of Robbinsdale. Norm phoned his father and mother, but as the harvest was in full swing they (the only workers left on the farm) couldn't spare the time to travel 160 miles. His sisters Palma and Charlotte, however, said they'd come by train.

TOGETHER FOREVER

Wedding Day. Margaret and Norman Borlaug, September 24, 1937.

When that fateful Friday arrived, Margaret quit work at noon and treated herself to the naughty luxury of a professional hairdresser. Her brother's wife Lois took her shopping to complete her trousseau. And at seven that evening the Lutheran minister was standing at the front door. Behind him stood Norm clad in a spanking new charcoal-gray suit right off the rack at the local haberdasher. Scott Pauley was best man.

In the simple room with its couch and chairs and flowery wallpaper, the two exchanged vows. It was brief, quiet, tender. Then they went home to Margaret's apartment at 1325 7th Street SE. And over the weekend Norm moved his meager possessions from the Kearsarge Apartments, eight blocks away.

Honeymoon? That was never considered. Why should it? In less than four months they'd be glorying in Idaho's stunning scenery; within the mighty embrace of the Rockies they'd honeymoon a lifetime. Until then, Margaret's apartment would do just fine.

Well, that's what they told themselves. But even as a temporary shelter, this single room—containing a table, two chairs, a daybed, a stove and a sink in the corner—was hardly enticing. The bathroom was down the corridor, and shared with another family. Margaret had brightened the room with snappy curtains, her few pieces of good crockery and vases of fall flowers. For Norm, this was palatial. Less than a week back, he'd been alone in a little box seven-stories high in the sky and his companions had included million-volt lightning bolts. With a guilty grin he settled into domestic bliss.

The days that followed passed in a wondrous haze. Everything had changed for the better. He'd become both domesticated and a dedicated, can-do forester, and soon he and his wife would begin a great life in the western woods.

It was all so simple. His Bachelors courses would take just three more months—October, November and December. Then they'd head to their private piece of the Promised Land.

There, he'd help Hank Shank train firefighters.

And who knows where that would lead!

10

1938
Course Correction

By the final quarter of his senior year Norm had dropped in and out of school often enough to scramble his coursework beyond rational recognition. "Borlaug," the dean of forestry said jokingly, though in a decidedly anguished tone, "your schedule is so loused up I can't understand the first thing about it. Why don't you either go to work or come to university?"

Forest pathology was among the dean's top concerns. Norm was merely months from graduation and yet was just getting around to this tree-disease course for sophomores. Nevertheless, he enjoyed the experience, and was unfazed by being the lone senior amid a sea of underclassmen.

Then one afternoon when the semester had less than six weeks to run something strange occurred. That particular lab section started out quite uneventfully. Professor Christensen distributed thin sections of wood cut from a diseased pine and told the students to sketch the blotchy blue stains a fungal intruder had pushed out between the tree cells. Then as the class members absorbed themselves in their artistry, a dignified-looking gent ambled into the room.

Neither tall nor imposing, he radiated a personal nimbus that enlarged his presence until it dominated the room. That authoritarian aura gained nothing from his clothes . . . he wore a commonplace tweed suit and carried a pipe loosely in one hand. Nor had it anything to do with his face, which, though tinged with grayness around the temples, was handsomely good-humored. Instead, it came from a piercing gaze and a steely voice that penetrated like a dagger.

Actually, with every student glued to a microscope the intruder attracted little notice until he stopped at the sophomore next to Norm. Peering over the boy's shoulder, he started firing questions . . . not about the fungus, but about the wood. What species of pine was it?

Why did one part stain and not another? What is this cell? What is that?

Fortunately Norm was left alone, but his companion collapsed into catatonia, and for good cause: One of the U of M's most honored scientists Elvin Charles Stakman [STAKE-man or STAKE for short] was a campus colossus. Dean of the Department of Plant Pathology, he was renowned for challenging students as well as for discovering great things about wheat disease. Only much later did Norm learn how great those things were, and only very much later would he learn that Stakman had once lectured freshman foresters on wood anatomy.

A month after that episode, on a day when he was just two weeks from heading for the western wilderness, Norm noticed an announcement tacked to a campus bulletin board. The Sigma Xi Society was sponsoring a special lecture entitled "The Little Enemies that Destroy our Crops." This same professor Stakman would talk about rust diseases affecting cereals.

That topic seemed irrelevant; Norm had no earthly interest in cereals. Still, he decided to go. Certain rusts affect pine trees, so perhaps he'd pick up some tidbit that might prove useful for his future.

Only years later would he realize that this casual decision was the pivot about which everything turned. For his career, for the fight against hunger, for the future of a billion souls, this seminar was the tipping point. And it was all thanks to Stakman's personal nimbus.

Norm recalls the scene in the cavernous Northrop Auditorium:

Stakman lit up the skies that night!

The subject was black stem rust. The miniature menace that drains wheat's will to live had frequently felled the food supply right back to the great plagues of the Bible. Yet its lifecycle had remained a mystery into modern times. Sure, it was known to be a prolific breeder, but where did it come from, where did it go during winter, why did it only periodically achieve epidemic proportions, and how might it be stopped?

Indeed as recently as the year 1900 people knew hardly more about this bundle of menace than when it had swept the empires of Egypt, Greece and Rome into famine. Ancient Romans may have prayed to the Goddess Ceres to provide a good harvest of her "Cereals," but they prayed even more fervently to Robigus, the God of Wheat Disease, whose anger brought hunger. And in 2000 years not much had changed; praying was still about the best anyone had could do.

Given this plague's powers of destruction, calls to the Almighty are not to be wondered at. August brought the prairies not only withering weather but also overwhelming worry. August was when wheat farmers began scanning their fields for any hint of the wrong color or odor. A rusty look and a sour smell provoked the paralyzing fear that accompanies failure, foreclosure and ruin. A broken crop, you see, brings broken lives.

In the distant past the ebb and flow of rust had been almost bearable. But during the first third of the 20th Century the fungus had begun ebbing less and flowing evermore frequently. The century was just four years old when rust launched its first attack. A second was loosed in 1911. And five years later came the catastrophe of 1916, when flour stocks ran low and the government had to ban booze, not to mention buying bread on Wednesdays and Mondays. And the assaults kept on coming: the Septembers of 1923, 1930 and 1935 all saw millions of acres of North America's wheat blacken, bend and kick the bucket.

Basic research had of course been done. It was known, for instance, that different fungi cause different rust diseases and that the main threats came from stem rust (*Puccinia graminis tritici*), leaf rust (*Puccinia recondita tritici*) and stripe rust (*Puccinia striiformis*). During the growing season their spores penetrate wheat stems or leaves, robbing the tissues of moisture and nutrients and erupting in dusty yellow-to-red stripes or spots. Worse, the fungal cells clog the capillaries and weaken the fibers so the plants weep and wilt and give up the ghost. Even the survivors typically yield grain that is too sparse or too shriveled to be worth sharpening the sickle.

In his lecture, Stakman reached beyond such detail to portray our dependence on the suppression of plant disease. His stiletto voice carved graphic memories on the mind. Hunger, he warned, had always been humankind's companion. Every society had lived under its shadow, and historically hunger had ranked among Mother Nature's most lethal weapons for capping the number of people.

Even in modern 1937 no person was safe. Black stem rust remained the protean enemy, forever changing its chromosomal clothes to circumvent whatever wheat variety farmers planted. Even varieties with the exquisitely rare, mysterious and almost mystical ability to deny the microbe access to its innermost tissues couldn't be trusted for more than a few years. Though then quiescent, rust was merely resting and awaiting the right moment to reappear. Somewhere in the years ahead the fickle fungus would slash the food supply as deep as it had in the past. And finding ways to prevent that should be society's greatest priority.

"Rust is a shifty, changing, constantly evolving enemy," he thundered during his peroration. "We can never lower our guard. Rusts are relentless, voracious destroyers of man's food, and we must fight them by all means open to science!"

As Norm listened, the sincerity of the delivery and the style and sharpness of the rhetoric sent his imagination soaring. While Margaret cooked supper that night he got out his notes and quoted passages. "Rust is a shifty, changing, constantly evolving enemy," he told her. "We can never lower our guard." "Rusts are relentless, voracious destroyers of man's food, and we must fight them by all means open to science." "Biological science, crop disease, soil infertility, human population and world hunger, all are interwoven."

Here was a cosmic vision, and this was the very first moment Norm entertained the possibility that he himself might tackle crop disease as a means for reducing world hunger. He mentioned the idea to Margaret, but they both knew it was a flight of fancy. Within the month they'd be heading to Idaho to make trees succeed and forest fires fail.

He buried the notion in the well-turned mental soil of what might have been.

As to the bargain struck in Idaho, he held to his part. Dan LeVan's plea that he wait in the wilderness three weeks past his due date set back his studies, but by dint of dedication he made up the classes and completed his BS on time: December 18, 1937.

Now his brilliant career was at hand. It was exciting; in just three weeks the newlyweds would wend their way westward. They'd already begun packing for the move and for a calling in government service.

However, two weeks later—in the opening week of 1938—he stood in the apartment staring bug-eyed at the letter in his hand. Postmarked "McCall," it stated that unexpected budgetary problems had arisen; funds had been cut; the Junior Forester position could no longer be offered. Could Norm hold off until the first of June?

His heart fell at his feet. College was over. The Depression still reigned, so this was his only possible job. Worse, he was basically broke and rent alone required $30 a month.

In an instant everything in the young couple's compact seemed to have shattered. For a week they endlessly discussed their plight without finding any satisfactory solution. Nonetheless, their thoughts always circled back to a single unassailable conclusion: one of them had a job in Minneapolis. Regardless of their dreams, they had to stay put.

CAREER SAVER #10

Fate's tenth facilitator, Henry M. Shank. A career savior only in a backhanded way, this husky forester with a leathered face and hard voice hired Borlaug as a junior forester for the Idaho National Forest. At the last minute, however, budgetary limits forced him to rescind the offer. This bureaucratic blunder awarded Destiny its due. Thanks to Shank's rejection letter, Borlaug would never become a forester.

Norm took the decision hard:

As a breadwinner, I'd failed before even getting a chance to begin.

Margaret tried to soothe his injured pride. There must be other jobs around, she said; he just needed a temporary position until June. Then in a flash of inspiration she recalled his enthusiasm for the lecture. "That professor you told me about . . . couldn't you take courses with him?"

She laughed away his doubts. "Oh come now, Norman," she said. "I'll go on working. We can make do on my wages."

Thus it came about that the dispirited forestry student approached the heartless interlocutor who just weeks before had reduced his classmate to the point of catatonia.

It was another of the seminal moments that would influence the future for much of humankind.

Although a campus bigwig, Elvin Charles Stakman was, as we've said, of medium stature and modest demeanor. Then 53, he had an athletic build, close-cropped gray-brown hair and a penetrating, unsmiling, brown-eyed gaze that never seemed to stop sizing you up. Always difficult to know, he was especially harsh toward the subspecies designated "Student." His power evidenced itself almost *sotto voce*. Despite their seeming softness, however, his words carried the force of command. Some sliced egos like swords; others slid rapier like through brain tissue. All too often they incited a rebellious response, which was his intent because it helped him probe past the grade-point average and see how well the youngster disbursed his wealth of accumulated knowledge.

Perhaps such a propensity sprang from his background. Stakman came from a family that was Germanic both in origin and outlook. He'd grown up in Janesville, Wisconsin and Brownton, Minnesota (about 60 miles west of Minneapolis), and from earliest days had been attracted to botany and microbiology.

In that interest he was far from alone. The 1890s saw the microbial world unveiled. The germ theory was born then and a new universe of invisible organisms was found to be living in, on, and around each person—a reality barely believable, quite inescapable and, above all, scary as hell. One day, you thought you ruled the world; next day, you found microbes did. The society suffered shellshock—we'd nowadays diagnose America as suffering from "post-traumatic stress disorder."

Exposing the prevalence of fungi, bacteria, viruses and the rest was the cutting-edge of science, if not of civilization, and Stakman's boyhood interest later blossomed into a lifelong mission to master black stem rust. Approaching this chameleon-like crop-killer from half a dozen different angles, he devoted himself to exposing its innermost secrets.

One such investigation arose out of the nation's most memorable brush with hunger. In 1916 Stakman determined to find out where the disease, which requires living wheat or barley plants, sprang from with such annual regularity. This he did by exposing Vaseline-smeared microscope slides to the skies over the wheat belt.

Each spring for decades, this prestigious professor sent hundreds of boxes—each containing 24 bits of greasy glass—to every state from Texas to North Dakota. Most ended up in rural grain elevators, and during the prime rust period the operators hung out a slide a day— usually attaching it to the front of a weather vane so it would face the wind. Other boxes went to Army- and Postal Service pilots, who held the slimy slides up in their open cockpits, noting down the date, altitude and location as they traversed certain stretches of Texas, Oklahoma, Kansas and Nebraska.

The grease was the key. Particles blowing by stuck to it, and under the microscope rust spores could be seen and counted. Year after year, boxes streamed back to the St. Paul campus, and throughout the spring, summer and fall graduate students in the plant pathology laboratory peered down microscope barrels and recorded all the spiky, dark-centered specks they could spot on the thousands of slides.

That work was far from uplifting, and its seeming absurdity baffled the students, not to mention other professors. Researchers, after all, are paid to develop theories and probe hypotheses, not merely count things. Why would this accomplished academic persist with an unimaginative, tedious, empirical survey that seemed less like science than stamp collecting?

But the pursuit in the end turned out to be far from trivial. Those glass slivers led Stakman into the core of an unknown world. They showed, for instance, that stem rust undergoes an annual migration. In the fall the fungus retreats south, riding the wintry winds blowing out of Canada. Then, like some abominable snowbird, it winters in southern Texas and northern Mexico, where warmth keeps wheat plants ripe for rust. Then in spring a new (and perhaps "improved") spore generation roars back northwards, riding air currents up whole length of the Great Plains.

Stakman thus proved that the insidious infection migrates astonishing

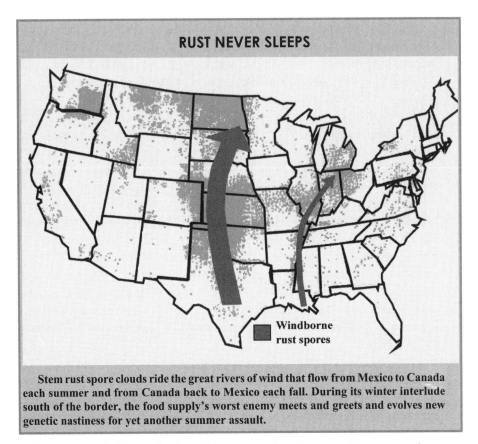

RUST NEVER SLEEPS

Windborne
rust spores

Stem rust spore clouds ride the great rivers of wind that flow from Mexico to Canada each summer and from Canada back to Mexico each fall. During its winter interlude south of the border, the food supply's worst enemy meets and greets and evolves new genetic nastiness for yet another summer assault.

distances and, like a duck, relies on regular flyways. He reported one example: "During the first week of June 1925, there was rust on wheat as far north as central Kansas. For almost a week the wind swept northward at 17 to 26 miles an hour, carrying rust spores 600 miles northward on a front more than 400 miles wide, thus inoculating grain in an area of a quarter of a million square miles almost simultaneously."

Even more astonishing was the aerial infection's density. The gummy glass showed North Dakota receiving up to 50,000 rust spores *per square foot per day*. And the peak load came six weeks before harvest, the exact moment to establish residence and grow fat by gorging the juices meant to nourish the grain and eventually assuage human hunger.

As if learning the migration patterns weren't enough, in the fall of 1916 Stakman found something of even greater significance. Acting on a brainwave, he took the Great Northern Railroad and headed west to collect rust samples beyond the Rockies.

His trip coincided with Marquis's collapse. "For a thousand miles

CAREER SAVER #11

Fate's eleventh facilitator, Elvin Charles Stakman. This Minnesota professor bribed Borlaug to quit forestry and commence agriculture. Previously, he'd built the basic understanding of the fungus behind the hunger in 1916 and had brought North America's wheat back from the dead. Borlaug's contact with this visionary would later inspire him to fight the same fungus and rescue wheat—this time for the world.

from eastern Wisconsin out to the high plains, almost to the mountains in Montana," he wrote. "I didn't see any wheat fields that would yield more than six or seven bushels an acre of chicken feed [shriveled grain]. We went through some of the best wheat-growing areas. [The crop] was ruined. Everything was ruined all the way along the line."

That of course reflected the scene across Middle America that season when the magnificent Canadian variety sickened and died and the wheatland turned wasteland from Missouri to Montana and even into the upper reaches of Manitoba.

At the first whistle stop past the Continental Divide in Montana, Stakman jumped from the train and grabbed a handful of rusted wild barley. Analyzed back in his St. Paul laboratory, those diseased stems proved to carry a previously unknown stem-rust variant with genomic powers capable of devastating the nation's wheat crop.

In the history of agricultural science, even of civilization, those scraps of tawny straw were seminal: they established that pathogens could exist in distinct variants. Researchers now knew that rust came in genetic forms that looked and acted alike but attacked wheat plants using discrete gene combinations. To use a modern metaphor, this fungus was fitted with multiple warheads to overwhelm the host's defenses.

The professor now could appreciate what had gone wrong in 1916. A new rust race—one for which Marquis's carefully crafted genes offered no protection—had invaded the Great Plains. This revelation meant that foiling this phoenix-like fungus would require wheats capable of countering not only the races on hand but also those that might show up in future. Scientists needed, in other words, to prepare for the full fungal diversity, including rare genetic variants hiding beyond the mountains. Indeed, beyond the seas.

This discovery sparked the third phase in Stakman's lifelong campaign: the creation of a cluster of wheat varieties whose pattern of reactions could "fingerprint" the different fungal strains. Eventually, this tedious process distinguished more than 300 stem-rust races. Now he could see that our most vital crop was being subjected to something akin to 300 flu strains every year. Luckily, though, only four were capable of taking out *every* wheat variety. Nevertheless, those four posed extreme danger; they were embedded in the landscape like a sixth-column, and each could *by itself* bring down the sustenance upon which society relied.

In turn, this new revelation led to Stakman's ultimate achievement, the creation of a wheat variety capable of resisting all four killer strains. At its outset this mission seemed foolhardy. No one had attempted breeding wheat to resist even a single pathogen race. And Stakman was no wheat breeder.

Indeed, only one wheat variety had ever been bred for reasons of health. During the Great War, L.R. Waldron had crossed Marquis with a hardy Russian variety named Kota. Sorting through the progeny in 1918, this North Dakota wheat specialist spotted a single plant that survived the red rain. The times were so desperate that after just eight years of development the seeds were rushed into farmers' fields, and from 1926, that plant bravely shouldered North America's wheat supply. Waldron called his creation "Ceres."

Ceres was the predominant spring wheat when Stakman launched his wheat-breeding mission with two colleagues and a cluster of students. One of the colleagues, Herbert Kendall ["HK"] Hayes, was well known to Norm. A man of strapping frame, mastiff features and powerful bark, he was a legitimate plant breeder . . . just not of wheat. Throughout his career he'd developed corn hybrids.

From the early 1930s the all-amateur team of Stakman, Hayes, colleagues, and students crossbred different wheats, doused the resulting progeny with spores of the four extreme rust races, and subsequently scoured the fast fading combat zone for any sign of life. From the few, exquisitely rare, survivors the group perfected the wheat variety they named Thatcher.

Luck seemed on their side when in 1934 they passed out small gifts of Thatcher seed. But that year's drought—the one surpassing even Granddad Nels' comprehension—wrecked the farmers' field test, not to mention the farmers' faith. Nothing useful resulted; Nature had repulsed the half-baked assault. Then Stakman threw in all his chips and committed the precious reserve. In the spring of 1935 the final few pounds of Thatcher seed were provided to farmers.

Again providence seemed unsympathetic. That's when rust rose to epidemic proportions and took down Ceres en masse. By season's end the wheatlands were as wasted as in 1916 and farmers faced a unique form of financial torture. Some set fire to their fields and lost everything; the rest cut, stooked, and threshed whatever grain remained, and went broke.

In the tiny, last-ditch test plots, however, Thatcher plants remained perky and productive. Stakman's genetic quadruple-bypass had given the crop a future just when its survival was in doubt. His newly tooled wheat withstood stem rust's four-pronged gene probes.

When that became known, wheat growers across the prairies embraced Thatcher, not to mention Newthatch (new Thatch), the

A PLAGUE OF . . .

Rust fostered famine for thousands of years. By rotting the stems or leaves of wheat it affected ancient Greece and probably triggered the fall of Rome. Genesis, however, records an even earlier epidemic.

The story starts about four thousand years ago with Jacob, his sons, their families and flocks living contentedly in the green hills of Palestine. Jacob's favorite son, Joseph, was indifferent to farm work, and this together with the father's favoritism angered the other brothers so much they sold him to a passing trader, dipping his cloak in goat's blood to prove their "beloved" brother had met a violent end.

. . . BIBLICAL PROPORTIONS

After carrying the boy into Egypt the trader sold him to a captain of Pharaoh's guard. There, despite his slave status, Joseph prospered and became the estate's overseer. Later, however, the captain's wife accused him of attempted rape. And, although the charge was fallacious, the handsome Israelite was bundled into jail.

As chance would have it, two of his cellmates had been servants of Pharaoh. Joseph happened to interpret their puzzling dreams, predicting that one would be released and return to favor while the other would be hanged. And so it proved.

Two years later Pharaoh himself had a puzzling dream:

. . . and, behold, seven ears [of grain] came up upon one stalk, rank and good. And, behold, seven thin ears blasted with the east wind sprung up after them. And the seven thin ears devoured the seven rank and full ears.

Pharaoh challenged Egypt's wise men to interpret his dream. None could.

Then the reinstated servant mentioned the brilliant young prisoner. Called before Pharaoh, Joseph explained that the seven good ears of grain meant Egypt would have seven plentiful harvests, and "the seven ears blasted by the east wind" meant Egypt would suffer seven subsequent and sequential crop failures.

Much impressed, Pharaoh awarded the young man control over the food supply. Joseph thus moved from prison to palace, and during the seven good years caused granaries to be built and filled with surplus grain.

Then came the seven years of crop failure, during which Egyptians were grateful for the sustenance in the storehouses. In Palestine, however, the east wind "blasting" the fields produced famine. Hearing that Egypt had great stores of grain, Jacob sent his sons to buy some and save the family.

When his brothers arrived, Joseph (without revealing his identity) commanded their sacks be filled. Then, exercising executive authority, he ordered that his father, his brothers and their manservants and maidservants be brought into the land of plenty.

Thus it was that the Jews entered Egypt.

Several centuries later Moses would lead them back to the Promised Land, along the way receiving the Commandments that ultimately codified Western moral underpinnings.

The relevance of all this to the Borlaug saga is the biology behind the east wind blasting the grain crop. That crop was almost certainly wheat and "blasting" refers to a fungal disease. But which one?

The original Hebrew Bible calls it "yeraqon," a disease that *yellows plants*. Scholars who provided the King James Version of the Bible translated "yeraqon" as "blast" or "mildew." Although both are fungal diseases, neither yellows the plant. The translators therefore selected the wrong English name, which is not surprising because in King James' time, the early 1600s, bread was a luxury and wheat a minor crop in England.

German bibles, on the other hand, render "yeraqon" as "rust." Being better acquainted with wheat, German translators appreciated the connection between yellowed plants and this particular disease. Additional support for rust as the culprit comes from the seven bad years in a row, which is consistent with rust's lifecycle, the farming of wheat, and Middle East wind patterns.

Thus it's only slightly farfetched to say that by inducing the Jews into Egypt black stem rust stimulated the events that set the boundaries of Western morality and thought.

upgrade that soon followed. Australia, Argentina, the Soviet Union, China and other nations adopted it with equal fervor. Newthatch became the gold standard for stability and survivability. And the consequences were so sublime that next decade and a half came to be considered wheat's golden age.

This was the great discovery Stakman was famous for. Based on better intelligence, he and his colleagues stole the initiative from Nature and brought wheat back from the dead. By interrupting the endless rumba with rust, they endowed the world's top food crop a future and, arguably, did more to save humans from hunger than anyone to that time.

In addition, they contributed to winning World War II. In total war, you see, food becomes Raw-Material Number 1, and this time around no scenes of ruination, wheatless days or johnnycake diets scarred stateside existence. Meat, butter and cheese were rationed in 1943, but cereals, the fundamental fuel of humanity, flowed forth in such plenty that no one in Washington dreamed of demanding a nationwide diet.

Again, we see the power of a super seed. In December, 1940, the U.S. actually had 400 million bushels of surplus wheat in storage and Canada had 500 million. This overstock was used to keep Britain from being starved into surrender as she held the line against Hitler. And in the long run Britain's survival led to the victory over tyranny.

Newthatch made that outcome possible.

Sadly, though, Elvin Charles Stakman is unsung in military history.

Political history.

Social history.

Any history.

Years would pass before Norm could properly appreciate Stakman's contributions. In January 1938 he was a boy forester beset by an outsider's resentment of the cereal research dominating the Plant Pathology Department. But at that moment, thanks to Margaret's urging, he approached its most daunting authority figure.

Despite an open door policy, Stakman seldom allowed a sympathetic hearing to the lower life forms. Leaning forward on his office chair, as if on the point of rising, he heard-out the nervous youth. For long minutes he remained rigid, fingering his pipe but otherwise not moving. Then he cocked his head to one side and, peering from beneath bushy brows, shook his head: "Fill in a few months between jobs, Borlaug?" he charged, fixing the frightened supplicant with his birdlike gaze. "That's a pretty poor reason for staying in graduate school. You should know better. You'll have to get more serious than that."

Next, the stiletto sounds rose, hardened and sharpened the well-tempered thoughts: What exactly did Borlaug want to study? Did he have any idea? What was his career goal?

Norm explained that he wanted to stay with forest pathology.

"Look here, young man, you do that and you'll lock yourself into a single profession. You'll lock yourself out of everything else." Stakman was shaking his head with resignation, almost disgust. "Forest pathology offers so few positions. You're young . . . keep your options open . . . USE A LITTLE COMMON SENSE!"

The by now thoroughly shaken supplicant was urged to widen his vision. "Get a broad education, and leave the specialization until later," Stakman barked. "Forego forestry and study general crop science. Take plant pathology and round that out with agronomy, genetics and soil science. Then you'll be equipped for dealing with much more than trees. You'll have a breadth of perspective that'll serve you well in your future. And you can always return to forestry should you want to."

Finally, he tossed in the ultimate inducement: an assistantship for the coming year. That was a bequest impossible to refuse during those dismal days when money had gone AWOL.

In return, though, Stakman required a momentous concession: *Norm must commit to being a proper graduate student.* "Put away this idea of taking higher education in dribs and drabs!" he said, jerking his pipe stem toward the bewildered plaintive. "Aim for your Masters degree and I'll go to bat for you. Play about, and you must go somewhere else to find help!"

So it transpired that, with the utmost reluctance, the young forester enrolled for postgraduate study in plant pathology. Here's where his career left the branch line and finally took the main trunk track fate had decreed. Neither he nor Margaret would ever live in the West with the wildlife and the woods. That is still sometimes regretted; even decades on, the dream has yet to die. In truth, were the Idaho job still on offer he'd seize the chance to return to his first love: trees.

But at the time who could foresee all that this office visit signified? The decision was merely a convenient stopgap allowing them to remain in Minnesota where Margaret had a paying job.

Not for years to come would the sterling-silver lining lurking in all those dark clouds expose itself. Now, though, we can see that Stakman did more than deliver a dose of reality to a student he'd never previously met. During this office visit he induced Norm to cross another Great

Divide and enter the world of agricultural research wherein he'll ultimately find personal satisfaction and global success.

Also, by insisting the young man abandon a specialty and broaden his career course to encompass the health of crops the perceptive professor helped save much of yet unborn humanity from hunger.

Stakman's grant paid the year's tuition and provided a modest stipend. In turn, though, Norm had to spend 10 hours a week peering down a microscope barrel at bits of greasy glass and counting stem-rust spores, each a red blob about the diameter of a human hair and cloaked in a mass of fine spines that made it look like some microbial seamstress' pincushion.

That duty was so visually demanding it permanently damaged his right eye. Still, he never complains, because it got him on with life at a point when life seemed to have died.

Also that year of 1938 saw him undertake a line of investigation leading to a Masters thesis. Unable to stomach a total break with trees, he chose to study the then-unknown cause of a red stain commonly seen in the wood of box elder.

Thanks to Stakman's iron-clad stipulation, he also studied genetics, plant pathology, plant physiology, and cytology. Beyond that, he took a memorable course in plant breeding taught by the bipedal bulldog, H.K. Hayes. The co-developer of the famous Thatcher wheat drummed into the class the vital need to "fit the genotype to the location." Varieties, he barked, must be bred for specific sites. And plant breeders must work *in the place where their crop will be grown.*

Norm was *soooo* Old America he never dreamed of questioning that guiding maxim of crop development—the most basic rule in the plant-breeding manual. Come to think on it, why should he? Professors know best, right?

The maverick streak had yet to evolve, and the young grad student had no clue that Destiny was setting him up for a duel with Hayes' dogma. Somewhere down the road they'd duke it out. And in the outcome the world food supply would soar.

11

1938-1941

National Service

The rest of 1938 and the first half of 1939 brought a big change. Having transcended hunger and destitution Margaret and Norm enjoyed a happy household routine.

The struggle to stay within their meager means certainly seemed endless. But with the Depression stubbornly refusing to depart or die millions had nothing whatever; so the young couple's life was in reality the good life. Both at least had jobs. She remained a proof reader at Independent Press; he was "being a proper graduate student" and earning his tuition by peering down microscopes for Stakman's stem-rust studies.

Then in June 1939 a puzzling letter arrived. It came from the nation's capital and asked Norm to again man the firelines. There was urgency in the phraseology. Experienced forest-firefighters were needed. Fast.

This missive caused much mischief. He talked the situation over with Stakman as well as with Clyde Christensen, the professor overseeing his box-elder research. Finally, following much high-level deliberation, the school agreed to let him put his studies on hold *yet once more*. The approval, however, came very grudgingly; this rackety Iowan was going back on a solemn promise to stay a proper graduate student. He was again proving unreliable, if not unworthy.

For Norm and Margaret the choice proved awkward too. They'd been married less than two years and the U.S. Forest Service wanted his services *six whole months*. After they'd agonized a week, Margaret told him to go. It was, after all, his country that was calling.

His country had called because nine months earlier Mother Nature had dreamed up an indignity to top all the deluges, droughts and dust storms that had already made the 1930s the Decade of Devastation. This time, her climatic chaos came from an altogether unforeseen quarter. More than a stealth-attack, this one was a sneak attack.

On the morning of Wednesday, September 21, 1938, the skies along the eastern seaboard seemed of sinister aspect. This, however, did nothing to faze the local weathermen. Although during the previous afternoon ships had reported powerful winds off Florida and North Carolina, the New York and Boston meteorologists predicted the day ahead would be mild. On its front page, a New York newspaper parsed the forecast down to: "Rain and cooler."

The experts of course realized a hurricane was out there somewhere. But it hadn't touched land, and everyone knew that kind always curved out to sea. This time, however, a high-pressure system dominated the North Atlantic and a separate front happened to be piling in from the Midwest. Squeezed between twin highs the storm barreled straight on northward gathering speed as it got squeezed.

No weakling of the weather world, this tempest torment had sapped energy from a sizable portion of the planet. Thanks to its strength, barometers plunged almost off the scale; tide gauges disappeared under rising seas; and anemometers spun so fast they flew apart, one clocking the wind at 186 mph when it shattered.

Early that afternoon the circling storm tested its strength against New York, doing its damndest to sink Long Island. And nearly succeeding.

Then, around 4 o'clock, sun-seekers crowding the Rhode Island shore observed what one called "a thick and high bank of fog rolling in fast from the ocean. When it came closer we saw that it wasn't fog. It was water."

This giant wave, Weather's real weapon of choice, rolled right into Rhode Island's soft underbelly. A hissing, white-capped, misguided missile of the restless Atlantic, it seemed intent on striking the state capital 30 miles up Narragansett Bay.

That vast estuary's wide open jaws captured the ocean that had strayed, and its funnel-like shape focused the power of destruction right on Providence. The capital's inhabitants, wholly unsuspecting of what they were about to receive, happened to be enjoying a lovely midweek break. The previous four days had brought heavy rain. Now they were out strolling in the streets, window shopping, resting in the parks, imbibing what just might be the last sunshine of summer.

At the very moment of maximum high water the tidal bore, all of 50 feet tall, hurtled into the host of harmless humanity crammed into the compact capital. A local journalist described it as "a cone of water rushing at express-train speed."

Those waves gone wild then treated Providence like a private plaything. Among many indignities, they hefted a 70-foot-high lighthouse and hurled it into the sea (along with the keeper and his family). They tossed breakwater boulders around like marbles, despite the 20-ton weight. And they turned the business district into a bathtub filled with 14 feet of feral ocean.

The sea surging through the city center made an astounding sight, with hundreds of vehicles, including large streetcars, swinging and swaying like toys amid the foamy surf cascading through the straits between the skyscrapers. Within the hour, everything up to the second story had succumbed to salt water. And the region's second largest metropolis had become its largest junkyard.

Finally, having taken their pleasure with Providence, the winds tore onward to violate another attractive victim: the grand old-growth forests of that serene and sylvan region known as New England.

No hurricane having passed this way in 120 years, the myriad woodlands of Connecticut, Rhode Island, Massachusetts, Vermont and New Hampshire stood verdant, vulnerable and equally unaware of what they were about to receive.

That night they learned.

At dawn on September 22 the sky opened clean, clear and a shade of blue verging on heavenly. However, the sun peeping over the curve of the earth that Friday morning saw only hell on earth.

Not only were the towns trashed, but seemingly every item fashioned by man was vandalized. The debris included the most treasured of possessions. "Automobiles were lying on their sides, half buried in mud," the Providence Journal reported. "Houses were flattened out as though crushed by steamrollers. At one spot nearly fifteen houses were whirled together as though they had been in the grip of a giant egg-beater."

The physical devastation included 9000 homes, cottages and buildings demolished and 15,000 damaged. The human devastation amounted to almost 700 dead and 63,000 homeless.

The survivors, moreover, were cut off. Downed wires webbed most of New England like giant ground spiders. Some 20,000 miles of telephone, telegraph and power lines were down. Both electricity and ground communications were thus comatose too. Even the airwaves were empty: scores of radio towers slept on their sides, silent.

Transportation too had been totaled. Trains were stuck in place—the New Haven Railroad, alone, having 1200 trees, 700 telephone poles and an oceangoing ship piled on its tracks. More than 2600 boats had been destroyed and 3300 more were too unsafe to use. Trucks couldn't operate

"OCEAN...

On September 21, 1938 the Atlantic surged into the heart of Providence, Rhode Island. Photographer Walter Adler captured the scene with pedestrians marooned on the steps of City Hall and ocean waves pounding the Biltmore Hotel.

. . . CITY"

The surge occurred at 4:45 p.m. and in the gathering dusk Adler's small Zeiss camera exposed stoplights, street lights, and vehicles consumed by the tide. Unlike a normal flood, the salt water surfing these streets had hurried here straight from the sea itself.

because bridges were broken and streets blocked. Connecticut, for one, had no operating highway. Moreover, without electricity gas pumps couldn't disgorge fuel, which actually didn't matter much because vehicles of all kinds were either wrecked or unable to reach a road.

New England could be accessed solely by air, a possibility of little importance because commercial air travel was in its fledgling decade. Flying remained a gamble with gravity, and the public recoiled at the prospect of leaving the ground. Now, however, there was no alternative, and September 1938, so it is said, saw the birth of the airline business. Indeed, 1939 was the first year the industry made money.

In terms of property damage this was America's greatest natural disaster to that date. Insurance companies put the overall loss at $400 million, or more than the San Francisco earthquake, the Galveston tidal wave, and the Florida Keys hurricane.

Yet the human landscape was not as bad off as the natural one. With the soil presoaked and softened by the prior four days' rain, the wayward winds had lifted old-growth oaks, elms, pines, beeches, birches, maples, and walnuts and waltzed them around like Johann Strauss. The once immaculate, shady, sylvan paradise now resembled the aftermath of some climactic scene from reel life rather than real life. Across seven states 275 million titans of the tree world lay like exhausted marathon dancers. Among individual horrors, a third of Vermont's celebrated sugar maples and half New Hampshire's noble white pines had been castled.

With a thousand square miles submerged beneath fallen forest giants, New England's situation seemed hopeless. Workers couldn't access, let alone unravel, the muddles of branches, trunks and roots that were knitted, purled and cross-stitched into arrangements not even film studios could conjure up.

And what could be done with all that timber? Just the logs big enough to mill contained 2.5 billion board feet, which would take New England's sawmills eight years to process. Who could wait eight years? Besides, dumping all that timber onto the market would drive saw-millers out of business, slowing down the removal rate.

Beginning that September, individuals, corporations, state agencies and federal authorities undertook to bring the prostrate region to at least its knees. The Feds created a special agency, the Northeastern Timber Salvage Administration, and structured it along military lines. That confident can-do decision made it one of the most efficient federal programs ever. By 1939, NETSA had 275 sawmills in operation and was storing wood in 800 locations, many of them under water. New Hampshire alone had loaded logs into more than 125 lakes and ponds.

Despite that huge effort, most of the forest fatalities still lay where they'd fallen. And every passing month raised the possibility of a blaze breaking out amid the jumble of trunks, branches and sun-dried roots.

New England needed trained forest firefighters, a breed unique to the west. That is why the Feds needed a Minnesota grad-student's assistance. He wasn't required to go of course, but deep down he relished the chance to give something back to the society that had saved him.

This, then, is the point of pivot where Norman Borlaug turned from a petitioner to the provider he'd be the remainder of his days.

In June 1939, Norm reported to the Forest Service office at Gardner, Massachusetts and was dispatched to Winchendon, a likable little community hard upon the New Hampshire border. His title was "Foreman of Laborers" for the hundred-man camp known as DA-14.

As before, he oversaw jobless youths and older workers. Primarily, he had to meld them into a cleanup team capable of clearing tree debris, cutting firelines through the scrambled wreckage, and countering fiery flare ups. Chainsaws being unknown and machinery unavailable, the only aids were axes and two-man hand saws, each four feet long.

Again the 25-year-old student bonded with his workers, many of them teenagers. They shared an army barrack, slept on cots and washed their clothes with bar soap on wooden washboards leaning like ladders into tin tubs. Camp cooks fed them in a military-style mess. Despite poor pay— less than $5 a week—harsh conditions and hard labor, the teens took to their tasks. In those hopeless times it was pure joy to have something to do, let alone to sample life out of sight of the folks.

As before, Norm reported to what he calls "shellbacks"—hard skinned Forest Service professionals who were demanding but also practical, positive and properly prepared for the unforeseen. Those Pulaski-like professionals he admired immensely. FDR, however, had entrusted New England's clean up to the Works Projects Administration, whose director was the president's long-time friend and political advisor Harry Hopkins. Accordingly, many New England camp managers had been selected for party ties rather than professionalism.

As Norm heard it, the one directing the neighboring Camp DA-13 at Ashburnham had obtained his appointment through the indulgence of Boston's labor bosses. The man was prickly, quirky, emotional, loud and querulous. The fulltime foresters hated his petulance almost as much as

On Wednesday the 21st September, 1938 New England was a sylvan wonderland. The Harvard Forest Pisgah tract in southwestern New Hampshire shows what much of it looked like.

On Thursday the 22nd the Harvard Forest Pisgah tract was wrecked. Indeed, most of New England looked this way. In mere hours the region's age-old idyllic character had gone with the wind.

his ineptness. Three had quit in as many months.

Despite having heard of the problem, Norm was baffled when headquarters telephoned and requested he come to Gardner right away. There the story emerged. "Look, Borlaug," supervisor Dean Rowland said, "our patience has run out. We can't afford to lose any more foresters, but we can't fire the guy because he's a political appointee. How about going over and working for him? We need someone with a calm temperament who knows what he's doing. Will you try it?"

So Norm packed his kit and was driven the eight miles to Ashburnham.

In the upshot, he and the prickly boss got along fine. Norm and a crew of about 20 men and boys steadily cleared away downed debris. The site had been a highway that had traversed a beautiful forest. Now the trees were scattered like the leavings of clumsy giants after a rowdy round of pick-up-sticks. Norm divided the men into two-man crews and for an hour or so each evening he put on a special training session in which they practiced Western firefighting methods.

Though mere precaution, two months later it proved prescient:

> It was about lunchtime, and I was in charge. My boss had gone off somewhere. Suddenly we saw smoke and then some sparks. The situation demanded instant action. It was early October; the downed timber had been drying for over a year and all around us flames were roaring skyward like a bonfire.
>
> Within mere minutes, the blaze exploded to encompass several acres. With a breeze from the south was urging it on, there was a good chance it would consume thousands more acres. It might even get out of control and prove unstoppable.
>
> I was out on the fireline directing every man in sight. There were about a dozen, and we were trying to pinch off the northern front where the flame was spreading. The heat singed our faces and stung our eyes. Because my novice workers had never considered confronting anything so terrifying they were very skittish. I had visions of them running away and our worksite starting New England's Big Blowup. And I'd surely be blamed.
>
> There was only one thing to do. We needed outside help, and rapidly. So I radioed Gardner and Winchendon.
>
> Within minutes my boss stormed into the already chaotic scene. He'd heard my call on his own radio and was offended because I'd asked for reinforcements without his permission. He strode past me and addressed the crew, loudly countermanding my orders. It was already hotter'n Hades and a catastrophe could result if we let those leading edges get out of hand. I yelled at the crew to ignore him. And without another word I pitched in and worked like the devil.

LUMBER JILLS

June, 1943. Florence Drouin, Elizabeth Esty and a colleague bring logs into the sawmill slip at Turkey Pond, near Concord, New Hampshire. Lakes made perfect repositories for hurricane leftovers. They held a lot of logs and quenched any possibility of fire. Hundreds were pressed into service.

When the Turkey Pond sawmill ran out of man power in 1942, these women took over—an action both handy and highly heretical in the macho world of lumbering.

During Norm's time in Massachusetts, war broke out in Europe. His fire-prevention efforts might seem irrelevant to hostilities so far away, but the logs the Feds scavenged in New England ended up doing military service of the highest order. Wartime Washington's myriad "temporary" structures were erected using timber sawn from New England's fallen elms, pines, oaks, maples and the rest. The wooden crates used to transport war materiel as well as thousands of barracks and facilities serving 2 million GIs dispatched to Britain for the D-Day assault were also built of timber salvaged from the tragedy. All told, by war's end the government had salvaged and put to wartime use 631 million board feet of building supplies.

Moreover, the fire-hazard control operation—the part Borlaug participated in—proved a stellar success. By 1941, it had cleared more than 10,000 miles of roads and trails and eliminated 214,000 acres of "blowdown." In all, almost 5 million man-days and woman-days had been spent tidying up seven states—all of it by hand.

The men looked first at him and then at me . . . and went back to deflecting the fireline. Working side-by-side, we collectively contained the flames in a rough but steady and organized way.

That rejection of his rank and respect left my boss livid. He was so beside himself he refused to join our fight. In fact, he stalked off and I never saw him again.

After perhaps half an hour truckloads of new crews began arriving from Gardner and Winchendon. Soon we had maybe 50 firefighters. And by late that afternoon the flames were finally under control.

A few of us patrolled the area through the night, but thankfully the wind died at dusk and there were no flare-ups.

First thing next morning, even before snatching some sleep, I went straight to Gardner. "I've had enough," I told Dean Rowland. "I'm going back to school!"

Norm never recounts this story with relish. He'd broken civil society's age-old covenant. Regardless of provocation, overriding one's supervisor was unacceptable. It was very troubling.

This was the very first time that practical needs demanded he defy authority. It would not be the last because this incident in the great state of Massachusetts taught him that public functionaries don't necessarily act in the public interest.

After returning to Minnesota in the fall of '39 Norm completed his class work as well as his investigation of the fungus that reddened box-elder wood.

His MS degree was awarded in May 1940. Attending the ceremony in St Paul were his parents—still reserved but nonetheless radiant over their son's stunning success within the wondrous world beyond their purview.

The lone lament was Granddad Nels' absence. To see the family's first postgraduate would have made the old man glow like the Viking conquerors of old. What joy he'd have taken in seeing Norm Boy free at last. And the fact that it was all thanks to the education he'd urged almost to his final breath would add to the satisfaction.

That summer was the best the young couple had had. Even the financial woes had gone to ground. Norm now enjoyed a steady cash income: General College (as the Junior College now was named) had made him an instructor. He taught a survey course on basic biology and natural resources. It was especially pleasing to contribute to the second-chance school that had kept his own career from crashing on take-off. This was the ultimate affirmation that, despite all that cruel fate could devise, the country bumpkin had flourished.

A HOME AT LAST

Thatcher Hall, Paul Campus, 1940. Their two rooms in this newly built dorm for graduate students constituted Norm and Margaret's first reasonable accommodations. To these Great Depression waifs, this was putting on The Ritz!

Home life was flourishing too. After three years crammed into Margaret's single-room they'd moved into Thatcher Hall, a brand new apartment block built to house married graduate students. Now their living quarters came with two rooms as well as a reasonable rent. Wow!

Life was so good there was even time for wrestling. Shortly after Norm returned in the fall of '39 the St. Paul campus' Athletic Director buttonholed him: "I've got all these kids with nothing to do in the evenings," Marshall Ryman said. "Let's start a wrestling program."

For the next two winters Norm coached at the University Farm School, a unique institution that helped rural high-school graduates sample college. Following the October harvest, students trickled into the St. Paul campus, took a handful of courses, and trotted home happy in April when the soil's relentless demands required attention.

This academic innovation awarded farm kids the chance to sharpen their wits within the wider world. For most it was a mind-altering experience with lifelong benefits. Given his own tortuous history of getting into university, Norm was a huge fan:

University Farm School was a great thing. It benefited a critical portion of Minnesota's youth and did a huge amount of good. I'm still mad as hell the university abandoned it after World War II.

The fact that the University Farm School wrestling coach was unpaid did nothing to diminish his zeal. He relished the new chance to push young people and raise their performance. His wrestlers competed against high school teams, which by then had become common. Just five years following Bartelma's arrival, 260 high schools had embraced wrestling and the sport was part of growing up Minnesotan. Norm recalls the encounters:

> We had some good times with the Farm School squad, and even won some meets.

This was yet another step in what would become an iconic feature: piloting young people to extraordinary attainment.

At Stakman's urging he now undertook a line of study leading to a PhD, the supreme scientific degree. His new research dealt with flax. Why? Mainly because Stakman had scholarship funds earmarked for that obscure crop; more importantly, though, Norm wanted to avoid rust research. At Minnesota, rust inevitably involved wheat, and that was something he wanted no part of. No sirree! With the rest of Stakman's students researching wheat, a recently re-treaded forester could never compete for the rare job openings after graduation.

Thus in the spring of 1940 Norm undertook to defeat *Fusarium lini*, a soil fungus that infects flax plants. There was no known control; farmers whose soil turned "flax-sick" had to abandon flax and grow something less profitable.

For starters, Norm established that *Fusarium lini* occurred in genetic strains differing in the ability to infect various flax varieties. In that sense it was like wheat rust. Then, following Stakman's precedent, he began breeding plants capable of defying the worst variants of their worst enemy.

In this, his first experience in fighting crop disease, he staged a "survival of the fittest" test, sowing a wealth of different flax seeds into the sickest patch of soil he could find. Although the resident infections turned his flax patch into a disaster zone, a handful of plants made it to maturity. Despite a wan and weak appearance, those few survivors were also wonderful because some hidden inheritance had helped them ward off the fungal foe. He saved their seeds and plowed back all the other decayed and dying plants to concoct a super-killer culture.

In the spring of 1941 he sowed his few seeds into that malevolent concoction. By that summer, it was clear that more plants were surviving. Then when they flowered he cross-pollinated them in all their possible permutations. By season's end, a few were even healthy enough to produce a passable harvest. Those second-generation seeds opened a new era for the crop that American farmers grew for linseed oil, but that also produces linen and (nowadays) the food supplement known as flax seed.

Although this work was not under Stakman's supervision, Norm routinely participated in Stak's plant-pathology seminars. He began as a suspicious outsider, shrinking from anything to do with wheat research. Soon, however, he caught the spirit of the man and the significance of the mission. And in time he became a lifelong devotee:

> Looking back, I can see that Stakman's program was unique. During that era students came from across the country as well as from around the globe to study with him.
>
> Stakman did more than teach to the textbook: he produced cereal caregivers. These self-contained "general practitioners" were capable of diagnosing disease and counteracting it wherever they might be in the world. Much of their skill was learned during his outdoor seminars in which he required all of us to interpret the symptoms of scores of wheat diseases and to recommend remedies.
>
> In the fields next to the departmental building Stakman maintained 40 acres of diseased wheat plants, and made us pit our wits against smut, scab, rust, blast, blight, bunt, wilt, mildew and the rest. Every Saturday afternoon the students and faculty trailed through those acres of sick and dying plants. Stopping at each one, Stakman would stimulate arguments over what we were seeing. The sessions sometimes went for hours; and sometimes got very heated.
>
> This was his style. His laboratories and classrooms were open intellectual forums full of fire and light. He threw out sharp-edged thoughts like grindstones throw sparks. He thus illuminated young minds, but often enraged his peers; more than once the rhetoric turned so rancorous that fists got clenched in preparation for use.
>
> Despite being surrounded by academic antagonism, Stakman was universally admired because plant pathologists face huge challenges and carry enormous responsibility. A misdiagnosis might unleash a disease that destroys a food supply and dooms millions to hunger.
>
> Stakman's Thursday evening seminars were also amazing. In fact, they were the most stimulating and wide-ranging academic discussions I've ever attended. Since those distant days I've often said that you only had to audit his seminars to get a rounded education. Into the immediate scientific issue he integrated history, geography, current affairs, philosophy and whatever else engaged his probing, catch-all mind at that moment.

Yet for all his defiance and confrontation the man was soft inside. Once you'd earned his respect he became a kindly mentor.

And his dozens of associates returned the warmth. Stak could travel the planet and find a welcome from former students and admiring colleagues wherever he went.

With those associates, he unreservedly shared his seed and his research findings. And they shared their own with him. The loyalty was strong enough to transcend personal, parochial, commercial, national or international interests. They were interested only in keeping humanity's main food crop healthy and productive.

With today's wide-angle view we can spot Stakman's spirit behind all that would transpire in the Borlaug saga. With his intellectual penumbra extending outwards to the farthest corners of the agricultural world, the plant-pathology professor inspired something like a can-do clan of food-crop medicos, whose members shared a common vision as well as methods, motives and materials. All worked easily together, enjoying mutual support and a clan loyalty that outsiders couldn't fathom.

Theirs was more than research collaboration. The professor and his pupils sprinkled across the Americas as well as Europe, Canada, Australia, Africa, and China remained always alert for the appearance of any new wheat disease. When one appeared, they share seeds they thought might resist the new threat. They were, in actual fact, lifeguards patrolling the beaches of the food supply, nay of civilization.

Two of those graduate-student classmates became fast friends. One was a very quiet, even reticent, young Minnesotan who was not easy to know. Although a year behind Norm, Joseph A. Rupert had begun as a forester before succumbing to Stakman's blandishments and switching to agriculture for his master's degree. Strangely, Joe and Norm looked so much alike they resembled twins.

The other was Albert H. Moseman, a doctoral student also studying flax. Unlike Rupert, Moseman was confident and outgoing, and he and Norm shared information, compared data and collaborated on certain experiments. This was a partnership of mutual benefit—Norm's specialty being plant pathology; Moseman's being plant breeding and agronomy.

Just as well Norm got to know Joe Rupert and Al Moseman. Much of the ultimate suppression of famine across a great swath of the world would be founded on these youthful friendships forged within the warmth of E.C. Stakman's stern, caring and far-sighted humanitarian embrace.

B y October 1941—just when he'd gathered the second-generation flax seeds and was preparing to document his discoveries in a dissertation—Norm received a summons to Stakman's office. There, he found one of his former undergraduate forestry instructors, which seemed more than weird because he barely knew the man. Several years before, Frank Kaufert had moved up in the world to direct a biochemical laboratory at E. I. du Pont de Nemours & Company, which was somewhere on the East Coast.

Then things got truly weird: Kaufert explained he was returning to become Dean of Forestry. The company he was leaving had a peculiar policy of letting successful scientists nominate their own successors. The new dean wanted to put Norm's name forward for the position he was vacating in Wilmington. Was he interested in going to work for a corporation in Delaware?

Norm recalls the stunning impact this had:

> I couldn't believe my former teacher would consider me a suitable replacement for himself. That didn't seem right. But then he explained I'd control my own research and have an annual salary of $2800! On hearing that, I struggled to keep from grinning. The sum was so enormous.

Stakman was encouraging: The flax research would be completed in a month; the dissertation could be written in the evenings after work in Wilmington; the doctorate could be awarded next year, 1942.

Despite the attraction of landing a job, an especially interesting one, Norm was far from swept off his feet. He said he'd like to talk it over with Margaret, explaining that all their dreams lay in the west.

Within a week another DuPont scientist showed up. Wendell Tisdale headed the newly acquired DuPont division known as the Grasselli Agricultural Chemicals Laboratory. That was where Kaufert's chosen successor would spend his time. Tisdale explained that it was a most desirable berth, being new and well equipped and engaged in finding ways to grow more food and protect forest products. Norm would be its resident microbiologist.

To the 27-year-old that particular angle raised red flags. DuPont was famed for developing Cellophane, Rayon and especially Nylon, which had been on the market barely a year and was sensationally changing the look of women's legs (then an imperative fashion accessory). What chances for advancement would a microbiologist have in a company transfixed by chemistry?

He kept raising his unease with Margaret, who was much more positive. She noted that he had no other prospect. "At the very least," she said, "it's a good place to see if you like working in industry."

In the end he faced up to the dilemma, and the answer came in a rush: Yes, he concluded, she's right. I'll give corporate research a try. We'll go "out East." It might be our only chance to see that section of the country.

Margaret then withdrew $300 from her savings (built up dollar upon dollar from her meager assistant-proofreader paycheck) and bought her boss's father's old car.

On the first day of December, a Monday, the young couple headed eastwards out of Minnesota with rising spirits and a purring 1935 Pontiac. That broad-shouldered, tan-colored boxy conveyance was their only significant possession and it held all their worldly belongings.

By today's standards, travel in 1941 took forever. With the interstate system still undreamed of, highways were cramped, crooked and clotted by country towns that typically padded their payroll by arresting lunatics reckless enough to zoom down Main Street at 26 mph.

Pulling into Philadelphia late the following Sunday afternoon, both Norm and Margaret were relieved that the weeklong almost 2000-mile journey wiggling across half the nation was nearly over. All but the last stretch—the recently opened, astoundingly modern, Pennsylvania Turnpike—had been by two-lane roads bejeweled with red stoplights.

Now Wilmington lay just down the Delaware River; in 30 miles they'd discover the delicious delights of East Coast living.

Then, in the heart of Philadelphia they saw people gathered on a sidewalk. For a Sunday afternoon this seemed unusual. Moreover, the group radiated a strange impression of jittery fear. A nearby newsboy shouted out the evening headline: "Pearl Harbor Bombed!"

Having never heard of Pearl Harbor, Norm assumed it must be in China. The name certainly suggested that; China had a Pearl River, didn't it? But Japanese forces had been bombing China for four years. Why would anyone be gawping about it now?

Today, he chuckles over his naiveté:

That shows how much I had to learn. It was December seventh. Next day I'd start my new job, and it'd be unlike anything anyone had imagined.
Least of all me.

1941-1944
Wartime

Following that fateful Sunday America lost its mind. The Army designated the three Pacific-coast states as the "Western Combat Area." College-football authorities moved the Rose Bowl game to North Carolina to place players and spectators beyond the Japanese flyers' bombsights. San Franciscans lined their streets with sandbag walls thick enough to withstand the blitz to come. Government agents distributed 50,000 gas masks for West Coast women to protect themselves from poison gas. Troops of the National Guard cut slit trenches into famous California beaches so mighty invasion forces could be defeated. And the Feds hustled citizens of Japanese descent into inland camps so they couldn't tell the invaders where to go.

Following that fateful Sunday Hitler lost his mind too. Within four days he declared war on the United States and thereby set the world (and ultimately himself) ablaze. After that, no one, least of all a trained microbiologist, could indulge in peacetime pursuits. Indeed, the career of Norman Borlaug here again veered wildly off course.

Although every scientist suffered weird stresses during this new World War, Norm's were bizarre.

At the start he was informed that the enemy had designated DuPont as a priority target. The company produced lactic acid by fermentation, and his first job was to save samples of the bacterial cultures so the fermenters could be restarted once rebuilt from the rubble. He found, however, that the cultures weren't worth saving. Not having been exposed to Stakman's training, DuPont chemists didn't appreciate the importance of genetic selection. They'd been wasting money culturing mixed races of bacteria, some of which produced little lactic acid.

On the organization chart, Norm's lab was but a blip, barely noticeable within the company's elite research facility, the Experiment

Station. Located on a park-like campus on Brandywine Creek near the city's edge it was directly across the street from the stately DuPont Country Club. Although the Grasselli Agricultural Chemicals Laboratory was the sole life sciences group, it counted for nothing amid this huge industrial research operation. No wonder its staff felt like flotsam bobbing among an ocean of corporate chemists.

During those early wartime months he met some of the chemists holding the keys to the company. One was a fellow Iowan who was trying to make urea practical for farm use. A simple compound found of course in urine, but easily made from ammonia and carbon dioxide, urea seemingly held huge promise as a fertilizer. This white solid was safe, stable, nitrogen-rich and cheap to make. The synthesis, however, formed trace impurities that damaged plant tissues and made the product worthless. Frank Parker hoped to find how to eliminate the contaminants and release mass-produced urea as a new power for food production. Sadly, though, he was having no success.

I n those early wartime days everyday events could easily generate the jitters or even produce public panic. Norm can attest to that:

Early in 1942, DuPont sent me to Pensacola, Florida to check on some tests of antifungal agents. Months before, samples of wood, fabric and paint had been treated with various organo-mercury compounds and placed in contact with soil. My job was to record how well each of the different treatments had done.

Wartime travel was always tedious, but this was my worst trip. The train was so overloaded even the aisles were crammed with passengers, ninety percent of them soldiers.

Then as we pulled into some place in rural Georgia the sound of smashing glass reverberated from up front. Suddenly, a maddened crush of humanity came screaming and struggling toward me. Next came a wave of sensation . . . invisible but unmistakable: the breathtaking stench of ammonia. I instantly knew it was not to be feared and shouted for everyone to relax. But panic had taken charge. Soldiers near me broke windows, and crawled out. Thank goodness we'd by then reached the station.

For some reason, a passenger at the front of our car had been carrying a bottle of concentrated ammonia. I guess in preparing to detrain he'd dropped it. In the outcome that poor guy had to run down the platform for his life. He could quite easily have been strung up by locals convinced he was a saboteur delivering poison gas. In that part of the country there was no guarantee anyone would wait for the cops; with the furies stirred up by war, lynch-mob mentality was back in force.

As you might expect war soon sucked DuPont's main microbiologist into its ravenous maw. Indeed, the federal government's War Manpower Commission quickly classified him "Essential to the War Effort."

What may sound like an honor was more like a hostage situation. The Feds now ran his life, freezing his salary and demanding he stay affixed to his desk. In that, he was far from unique; during the war years Washington determined what millions did with their days. It was an un-American age, and no one cared . . . national survival was at stake.

Even private life became regimented, although less by public fiat than by personal feelings. Several million young men had by then been called to active duty, and volunteers were needed to maintain the hundreds of home-front happenings that had lost their manpower. Many 12-year-olds, for instance, went out and picked crops on local farms.

> With millions being called up for military duty, those of us still in civilian life had to fill in. I, for example, spent three nights a week substituting for Boy Scout leaders who were away in uniform. Someone needed to keep the activities going. Although I signed on as a Troop Leader, I eventually was elevated to Neighborhood Commissioner, with authority over several Wilmington troops.

In light of all the horror and happenings in the world, his help for the Boy Scouts may seem inconsequential, but it was yet another step in his lifelong mission to help the young as he himself had been helped.

At about this time Norm brushed up against one of the war's great secrets: a chemical safe enough to spray on skin but effective enough to kill critters carrying mankind's greatest diseases. Those critters included the mosquitoes carrying malaria, a disease that annually killed millions throughout the world, including the U.S. They also included the lice that carry typhus, an unstoppable scourge that had ravaged Eastern Europe following World War I.

His brush with this medical marvel resulted from an incident a year earlier, when Soviet troops blunted the German army's northern thrust on the outskirts of Leningrad. During the city's subsequent 900-day siege typhus broke out among the inhabitants, 5000 of whom were already dying of starvation *every month*. This age-old plague—a fellow traveler of famine, fighting, filth, and poverty—gets around by hitchhiking on the lice that populate armpits and groins. As there was neither cure nor treatment, the only answer was to kill the lice.

At some point in 1941 Soviet forces had pushed out from the city and captured a few German soldiers, whom some sharp interrogator noticed were typhus free. This miracle appeared to be thanks to the white powder in a little pillbox attached to each soldier's belt.

Subsequently, a deeper Soviet push captured a facility that filled the pillboxes. A sample of the mysterious powder was seized and sent to Moscow. Subsequently, the Soviet government shared it with the British government, who sent it to Imperial Chemical Industries, Britain's chemical giant. In turn, ICI shared its portion with its American counterpart, DuPont. As ICI and DuPont were bitter commercial rivals, this was probably part of Churchill's technology package given to the U.S. in exchange for armaments critical to Britain's survival. (Other British goodies included the jet engine, certain atomic secrets and the Klystron tube that made radar a reality.)

Norm became part of the story purely by accident:

One day my boss, Wendy [Wendell] Tisdale, asked me to sit in on a meeting of DuPont's senior scientists because a microbiological problem was going to be discussed.

Dr. Bousquet, a very creative senior organic chemist, started the session by showing us a sample of an unknown powder. "I've got something new here that's just come from ICI," Bousquet said. "In a week I'll know what it is."

Leaving that meeting he went to test the sample's solubility and to sniff it for a clue to its chemical class (which was about the level of rapid chemical analysis then). Next he went to the library and perused the recent patent literature, where he found a Swiss patent for a compound of the class he'd sniffed. It was dichloro-diphenyl-trichloroethane. The patent claimed it killed clothes moths.

Within about two months DuPont was producing the compound, which after the war would be called DDT. The speed with which this was accomplished was truly remarkable. Wartime constraints made getting new equipment impossible, so engineers at the Grasselli Heavy Chemicals Division co-opted the small test-facility used to scale up laboratory-level processes. By operating that "semiworks" in Cleveland, Ohio round the clock, they produced two hundred pounds of the insect-killing powder each week.

Every Friday, the week's production was driven to Detroit and loaded onto one of the new bombers rolling out of the factories. Those then flew it straight to a war zone. That way, DDT controlled mosquitoes in areas as far away as North Africa and the South Pacific. It proved especially valuable in New Guinea, the Solomon Islands, the Philippines, and other paces beset by malaria. All in all, it saved the lives of many marines, sailors and GIs.

Because I worked for the company's Grasselli division, I was among the first to experiment with the powder that relieved man's greatest menaces. However, my tests were on garden pests, and it proved amazingly effective against flies, Colorado potato beetles, cabbage moths and other crop-eating insects.

For a couple of years I had the powder all over my hands and clothes and was as thoroughly exposed as anyone on earth. Yet I had no adverse health consequences then or since.

Nor did I ever see evidence for environmental damage. In fact, in the years after World War II hundreds of thousands of American families kept chickens near the house and used DDT to rid their coop of flies, mites, lice and mealworms. As far as I'm aware, none ever reported seeing a thin eggshell as a consequence.

This is why I've always been skeptical of the claims of calamity that today surround DDT.

As Norm notes, DDT later got blamed for so much evil that the very sound of its name induces a shudder of horror. But in 1942 it came as a savior. This simple, cheap compound dramatically reduced the incidence of a dozen or more previously unmanageable diseases. And it could be applied directly to people as well as their clothes and abodes.

To keep this an Allied secret, the Army code-named the powder AL63. It regularly sprayed it onto soldiers' clothing, especially underclothing, to kill lice. Special dispensers were devised, and proved their worth in the European Theater when malaria broke out in Morocco and later when typhus erupted in southern Italy.

Italy's typhus problem only became apparent after the Allies liberated Naples on October 1, 1943 and found the devastating disease gaining a grip. Though AL63 had never been applied on a massive scale, a large louse eradication campaign was quickly launched. Between December 15, 1943 and May 31, 1944, three and a quarter million Neapolitans were forced to loosen their shirts, skirts, and trousers and get their armpits and groins dusted.

To us powdering millions of private parts may seem indelicate, but in war-torn Europe death was too prevalent to worry about personal dignity. The vital thing is that it worked. The louse that inhabits body hair disappeared from Naples with incredible speed: After peaking in January, the epidemic was over by March.

Reports of the miracle flashed around the world and were received with jubilation. The unstoppable disease had been stopped. The camp follower of famine, fighting, filth and poverty had finally been conquered. History had hit a new high.

Later the Allies discovered Hitler's extermination camps—Buchenwald, Bergen-Belsen, Dachau, Flassenberg, Mounthausen, Auschwitz, and others. All were rotten with typhus. At Dachau, some 40,000 inmates were housed in unspeakable conditions, the living and dead jammed side by side with lice crawling over both, and no soap or water for washing. In June 1, 1945, there were more than 2000 typhus cases and 300 deaths. Then DDT was applied, and the plague vanished along with the lice.

At Bergen-Belsen, typhus had broken out in January 1945. Here, too, camp conditions quickly turned terrible. Jammed into confined spaces without sanitary facilities, thousands of the sick spent their days covered in common excrement and lice. When British forces liberated the place on April 15, 1945, they counted at least 3500 typhus cases. Anne Frank and her sister Margot had died there just weeks before . . . both from typhus. For the living, though, the Allies' powder again proved its worth. With liberation from tyranny came liberation from typhus!

Looking back, we can see that World War II's aftermath could have surpassed in horror the great epidemic following World War I. Raging amidst the famine and mayhem of the Russian revolution typhus infected 25 million Eastern Europeans, killing 3 million.

World War II, however, ended with no typhus epidemic. The louse had met its match. It was the insect powder the Soviets had discovered on enemy soldiers . . . the one Borlaug's tests had helped prove out.

W ithin a short time so many men had been whisked off to war that the Grasselli laboratory ran out of technicians. Stand-ins were needed, and obviously they couldn't be male. Thus it happened that DuPont recruited girls right out of high school. Norm was required to teach them the science and practice of microbiology, and do it virtually overnight.

By now he was 28, and had twice been told to cross the Delaware and report to Fort Dix for induction into the Army. All that kept him from combat was his Federal designation "Essential to the War Effort."

By then, the label was no sham. Despite an almost total lack of administrative experience, he was managing contracts of consequence. Indeed, as the conflict consumed the world his modest laboratory provided support to all the services, which were then suffering more from microbes than from military matters. In the Pacific Campaign, for example, bugs were felling more marines than bullets.

Such problems were DuPont's to solve . . . and on the double. Every few days Norm would glance up from his desk to find an agitated officer from the Quartermaster Corps, the Navy Department, the Army Department or some other critical agency glaring down and demanding he fix

DUSTING THE DRAWERS

DDT powder applied against the lice that live in body hair. Displaced persons' camp, Linz, Austria, 1945. The collapse of Europe saw millions stranded on the wrong side of a continent in which there was little transportation and a large threat from typhus.

Borlaug's friend the late George Knaphus described how this vast swap was accomplished using railroad boxcars made for animals. Their capacity: "Cinq Cheveaux, Quarante Hommes" (five horses, forty humans) was stenciled on the side. As the cars were loaded and unloaded the passengers had their armpits and privates dusted with DDT. George himself helped dust tens of thousands.

Perhaps this seems gross, but in the aftermath there was neither typhus nor toxicity. Indeed, DDT averted many millions of deaths—a feature the future would sadly forget.

some frightful difficulty from a distant fighting zone. The typical unilogue ended with an order: "Find the answer before the end of the week!"

For him, this opened a new window: speed science. Solving pressing problems became his basic business; working out the answer within a week was top priority. Freedom's future hung on what he'd recommend in seven days. Settling for less than perfection was necessary. One practical actionable answer surpassed any perfect possibility.

Norm vividly recalls an incident late in 1942 when a Marine colonel and a Quartermaster Corps captain marched in bearing cartons of canned rations—tomatoes, he thinks. They explained that the marines on Guadalcanal were desperate for food and supplies, yet the Navy couldn't deliver the goods because enemy warships controlled the nearby seas. To keep its fighting force from starvation the Navy sent fast destroyers close to shore, where sailors on the decks pitched cartons of rations overboard, trusting the waves to wash them into the shallows. The cartons, however, quickly came unglued, dumping their contents straight to the bottom. "Fix that," the Marine officer barked. "Before the end of the week!"

Cardboard boxes were then bonded with sodium silicate, a weak and soluble adhesive. Luckily, Norm found a DuPont chemist who suggested polyvinyl acetate, an insoluble adhesive all but immune to water, damp and mold. The military services adopted it, and as far as Norm knows, polyvinyl acetate still seals cartons and food-can labels. At any rate, the once common aggravation of cartons in civilian life falling apart on humid summer days (to say nothing of labels floating off beer bottles in the ice bucket) is gone.

That was just one out of a dozen incidents in which a stranger marched in, dumped objects on this greenhorn's desk, and bellowed outrageous demands. Given the South Pacific's hothouse climate, molds were messing up seemingly everything. Electrical equipment was sprouting fungus, thereby killing radios, ships, bulldozers, jeeps, trucks and aircraft. Camouflage fabrics grew molds that dazzled the eye. Binoculars bloomed fuzzy interior growths, beclouding lenses no cleaning cloth could reach. Rotting tents and sandbags exposed troops to weather and weaponry. Decaying medical supplies endangered the wounded. Cracked conveyor belts, transmission belts and hosepipes, brought engines to a screeching death rattle. And gaskets broke down before even seeing the inside of a cylinder.

In truth, tropical microbes were attacking anything based on wood, silk, wool, leather, glass, rubber or paint. And that meant most things in those days before plastics grew up and learned to perform miracles. Microbiology was, at least for a time, more crucial than munitions.

In dealing with such challenges Norm needed help, so the company hired a recent PhD from Rutgers University. There, just up the railway line, Elizabeth Horning had been isolating soil molds and assessing them for medicinal effects. Her professor, Selman Waksman, was the genius who (to help out a harried editor) casually coined the word "antibiotic" and later would be awarded a Nobel Prize for discovering streptomycin, a soil-mold compound that suppressed TB and introduced the second generation of bacteria slayers, ones that surpassed Domagk's sulfa drugs.

To handle the never-ending battlefront demands, Norm and "Betty" Horning created what they called the "Jungle Room." This walk-in enclosure contained heaters that kept the interior space at 90 degrees and troughs of water that kept the air sodden. Both floor and walls were seeded with fungi and bacteria capable of degrading any part of man or machine: skin, hair, toenails, leather, wool, cellulose, rubber and whatever else might hinder or help the war effort.

Among many products getting a steamy stint in Borlaug's hellish little hothouse were electrical and telephone equipment, sandbags, trousers, paints, and fabrics. DuPont's own chemists adopted the room to evaluate the worst that rot, mildew, decay and corrosion could do to their wondrous new fibers called Rayon, Nylon and Dacron, which then were strategic commodities too vital to victory to share with civilians.

One day a colonel from the Quartermaster Corps trounced in, tore open a cardboard box, and tipped out a pile of paper packets. "Would you use any of these?" he growled. Norm admits they looked revolting. The paper was sprouting green and black molds—Penicillium and Aspergillus, respectively. "We've got a tremendous number of our troops down with gonorrhea, but they won't use these damn things," the colonel added by way of explanation. "Do something about it!"

Inside the packages were condoms.

On that problem he appealed to the Cellophane Division, which specialized in packaging research. The connection was especially convenient because Betty Horning's husband worked there. Norm hoped he'd overlook the impropriety of his wife working with devices that were furtively dispensed from hidden places beneath drug-store counters as if selling them was a criminal act, which in the previous decade it had been.

Late one afternoon, after the young laboratory assistants had left for the day, the Cellophane Division delivered dozens of differently packaged samples. "I'm going to put these under test right away," Norm explained to Betty. "But in the morning you're going to have to explain to the girls what this is all about, because it hardly seems related to the war effort."

In proper scientific style the separate coverings underwent replicated tests. Norm inoculated each packaging type with cocktails of decay microbes and by nightfall the Jungle Room looked like some macabre Christmas Grotto, hung all about with weird ornaments.

Two weeks later he penned his report describing the ability of the various coverings to resist fungi. He drafted it at night, finished about two in the morning and left the handwritten copy for his very efficient (and very frank) secretary. About 10 o'clock the next morning Gertrude McCarthy bustled into his office, the normal cigarette dangling from the corner of her mouth: "Mr. Borlaug," she announced, "you've got a misspelled word here; you've got the wrong word completely."

"Is that right? Let me see it."

"It's this word condom."

"No, that's right."

"Godalmighty," Mrs. McCarthy exploded, "I thought we had a fighting army!"

To this day, Norm can't imagine how Betty Horning introduced the teenage girls to the details behind this decorative scenery while keeping intact both their purity and patriotism.

In these tests the perfect packaging proved to be cellulose acetate, a material made simply by treating highly purified wood pulp with the active ingredient in vinegar. Heating these natural materials together generates a surprising product: a clear film. In his report for the Quartermaster Corps Norm noted that cellulose acetate resisted most of the Jungle Room's fungi and would answer the government's immediate need. He added that it could have other uses as well: It was tough and stayed strong even when wet. It also kept its shape, showed little tendency to shrink, and was neither especially flammable nor likely to melt in everyday use.

Problem was, cellulose acetate was hard to get. Since 1929, when the Cleveland Clinic's store of X-ray film caught fire and killed 124 people, it had been used to make "safety film," but not much else. Soon, however, the federal government invested in factories to mass-produce this rare material. It would have done so anyway, but it's nice to think Norm's recommendation expedited everything.

In the outcome, cellulose acetate proved a modern marvel. Following World War II demand soared. For one thing, fabrics treated with it remained soft and pliable but repelled mischievous wrinkles and mortifying creases. That aptitude ushered in permanent press—a thrilling advance because clothes had always demanded endless ironing.

The astounding new duds both retained their lines and dried in an instant. Manufacturers of swimsuits, sleepwear, rainwear, umbrellas and the rest adopted "acetate" with abandon. And to this day packaging relies on it. From candy bars to cotton briefs, products by the thousands come in the film that Norm suggested the government wrap its rubbers in.

Projects like these brought him to the cutting-edge of chemistry, not to mention of the Allied cause, but his greatest personal take from the war years was a streetwise approach to science. This is when he perfected his rugged research style. From here on, he improvised as opportunity unfolded openings for advances. From here on, too, he used whatever lay at hand, rather than waste time searching for something better. And from here on he conducted experiments more like an action sport than an academic search.

He's often described his just-in-time jousting with fate in terms of quarterbacking a football team. The idea, he says, is to work the ball forward with speed and purpose; always seeking the big play but falling back to avoid a sack when nothing comes open.

This also is where he learned to focus with half an eye on the horizon. By concentrating on the present, while constantly casing the future, he'd press ahead in an orderly way and produce advances of proven value. And like Herbert Hoover of old, he dispensed with plans, and never tried to predict what his subsequent steps might be.

In the end, these traits are what would set him apart from his peers. Scientists commonly scamper back and forth chasing the latest fads, ever seeking the big play that brings prestige, prizes and perhaps profits. Mostly, they receive only the pain of a sack. By contrast, Norm worked with wartime efficiency, without preconception, and with each result leading to the next step in a methodical forward movement.

This is where we first glimpse his ability to conjure magic when every avenue for progress seems closed. For decades to come his days will involve a seemingly endless struggle to bust through the opposition's defense, scoot through holes that open, and dash for daylight and the end zone, thereby overcoming some impediment to a fully fed world.

Home these days was as calming as the laboratory was creative. Norm and Margaret lived in the quiet comfort of their third-floor apartment at 1407 Delaware Avenue. Despite their contentment, though, life was not pure pleasure:

I still had to write up my PhD research results. Stakman and Christensen [his box-elder research advisor] kept sending notes: "Get that thesis written before you go into the armed forces—or you'll never finish it!"

Thus, in addition to working at the lab and taking care of home life, I had to also put in long nights of writing. Trying to squeeze in even a little relaxation was impossible. But the wartime atmosphere was all the incentive we needed to stay focused. In those days we all felt invigorated and willing to work without complaint.

Being in private industry certainly proved a change from anything I'd ever experienced. DuPont was a remarkable place. It's personnel guidelines, for instance, amounted to a credo for balancing home life and career. They included three special instructions:

Involve yourself in activities outside work;
Never talk shop at home; and
Avoid idle talk about colleagues.

Obviously, the corporate officials knew that researchers fall into obsessions, that mixing job and family affairs can affect both, and that gossip undermines even the best-run group activities.

These were good dictums. I've followed them ever since.

Given DuPont's demands on his days it was particularly gratifying to finish his thesis at night and receive his PhD in 1942 . . . right on schedule. Although unable to attend the graduation ceremony half-a-continent away, he was more than happy.

Perhaps it's strange that happiness could show its face during history's most violent decade. But this time the home front was eerily upbeat. By displacing the Depression war accorded each American personal worth. During the 1940s ordinary people became partners in a great enterprise; they had things to do . . . important things. There was a rare sense of shared sacrifice and common purpose. And millions finally found what had been missing for a decade: a cause and a career in which to confer body and mind.

The Borlaugs felt that way of course, but this young couple loved each other enough to overlook externalities beyond their control. For them, this was an interlude of domestic sunshine. Indian summer.

WARTIME DIGS

From December 1941 onward Margaret and Norm spent the war years in Wilmington, Delaware. Their apartment, 3B, was on the top floor and on the left hand side (as seen in this view) of this building. In the evenings here at 1407 Delaware Avenue, Norm finished writing his PhD thesis. During his days, he took the bus across town to the DuPont Company's Experiment Station, the famous research facility that had just produced Nylon, Neoprene, Dacron, Teflon and other marvels of modernity.

And the pleasure of those days wasn't just from relief as the horrors of the past faded into forgetfulness. In their second year in Wilmington Margaret announced she was pregnant.

With excitement, they awaited the great moment, imagining what their expanded future would be like and trying out names. As the due date approached, they settled on Norman or Norma Jean.

The baby, born on September 27, 1943, was a sparkly, blue-eyed daughter. They quickly shortened her to Jeanie.

Although his experiences at DuPont gave him a handhold on history, there was one experience whose significance he came to appreciate only much later. In this case he'd brushed the greatest war secret of all.

When I'd arrived, the Graselli Research Division was directed by Crawford Greenewalt, a young and dynamic chemist married to a Du Pont. I got to know him a little, but then he left us to head a special project that involved extraordinary secrecy.

By 1943, many of the DuPont staff had joined Greenewalt's secret venture. None, however, was allowed to even remotely refer to their work. Whenever we'd ask about it, they'd fall silent. Among ourselves, we outsiders called them "hush-hush boys."

One hush-hush boy was a metallurgical engineer named Jim Maloney. Jim was my age and lived on North Broom Street, just around the corner from me. We'd gotten to know each other pretty well; we went to the same church, and his wife Dorothy had become friends with Margaret. I sometimes kidded him that he was just one of those "hush-hush boys." Even at a little teasing like that, he'd clam up and kill the conversation.

Only once did I ever get more out of him. It happened because each day we rode the bus together. No one drove in those days; even if you could get a gallon or two of gas there was no tire rubber.

I recall one particular afternoon—it must have been toward the end of September 1943. Jeanie had just been born, and Margaret hadn't yet come home from the hospital. Despite the fall season, the day was particularly hot, and as we left the bus I said to Jim: "Come on up to the apartment, we'll have a Coke."

Ordinary folks had no air conditioning then, and with the heat in our apartment Jim removed his jacket. After a while we finished our cokes and left. I was heading for the grocery store to get myself the makings for dinner. As we parted at the corner of Delaware Avenue and North Broom Street, he suddenly looked concerned, and blurted out in a worried tone: "Damn it Norm, I forgot my coat."

"Well, that's no problem," I said. "I'll bring it to you tomorrow."

"No," he said, with panic shaking his voice. "You don't understand.

I've got something in the pocket, and if anyone challenges me and I don't have it I'm in trouble . . . and if they find it's in your apartment so are you!"

"Oh come on now," I said. "This hush-hush stuff can't be all that important."

"No, this is a flow sheet; and it's *really important*."

After he'd picked up his jacket and we were back at the corner where he turned toward his apartment he said: "As of three days ago, we're feeling pretty good about things."

That is all Norm ever got out of a hush-hush boy, and it was very little and very enigmatic. However, an incident in Norway around that time did indeed relieve a burden from the Allied scientists' minds. This occurred in Telemark, the county from which Norm's mother's ancestors hailed. The nearby mountain range is so precipitous and the snow so prolific that the locals call the melt water "white coal." Indeed, the tumbling tide generates so much electricity that the government power company, Norsk Hydro, had begun distilling vast amounts of seawater to separate its infinitesimal amount of deuterium oxide (aka heavy water).

Since 1940 the German army had run Norway, and the Allies feared that this vital ingredient of atomic weapons would fall into Hitler's hands. Several overt and covert operations had failed to destroy it, and Norsk Hydro finally filled drums with the precious liquid and dispatched them to Germany.

Doomsday was then in clear view. Basically there was only one chance to avoid the possibility of a Hitler wielding a weapon of total destruction and holding humanity to ransom. Between the remote distillation facility and the world lay a deepwater lake. Daring Norwegian saboteur Knut Haukelid managed to trick a guard and plant explosives on the ferryboat carrying the "heavy liquid." At exactly the point where the waters were deepest, his detonation sent it to the bottom, destroying Hitler's hope of fomenting a second Holocaust, a nuclear one.

Given those events and Jim Maloney's comment, Norm believes the hush-hush boys were part of the Manhattan Project, and the flow sheet left in the apartment contributed to creating the atomic bomb.

Other than the Boy Scouts, Borlaug had avoided outside activities, but in the fall of 1942 he learned that the Phytopathological [plant disease] Society was holding its annual meeting in nearby Philadelphia. Trains from Wilmington were quick and convenient, so one afternoon he snuck out to sample a couple of hours of lectures.

More than indulging in a little hooky, he was indulging in nostalgia. He'd heard that Stakman would attend. And it turned out that another of Stakman's students was there as well.

Norm had never met George Harrar [ha-RAR], who'd earned his doctorate in 1935, before Norm got to graduate school. Nonetheless, everyone in the department had heard breathless tales of "Dutch" Harrar. A man of commanding presence, with a rare combination of iron will and engaging charm, he was one of those rare personalities who impress the air others breathe and who's always referred to in tones of awe.

After the afternoon's final session, Norm happened to be passing through the hotel's main lobby when Stakman and his charismatic colleague sauntered in from the other side. The old professor introduced the two. "This is fortuitous," Harrar said, "I've been wanting to talk with you." He waved toward the bar: "Let's go have a drink."

Over a beer Harrar, as was his habit, came straight to the point. "You know," he said, "I'm working with the Rockefeller Foundation. In a couple of months we're starting an agricultural research program in Mexico. Stak says you'd be a good person to have on our staff. We need a pathologist to help with the diseases of corn and beans and wheat. Why don't you join us?"

"Well," Norm said, "I'd like to consider it, but I'm under government control. The War Manpower Commission says I have to stay where I am, and there's nothing I can do about that."

They had another beer, after which Norm traipsed off home and pretty much forgot the offer. But eighteen months later, in May 1944, the War Department freed anyone 30 years or older from federal employment restrictions. As he'd passed that cutoff point on the 25th of March, he could now accept a raise . . . even change jobs.

Still, he did nothing about the job on offer below the border.

Then one day Harrar telephoned. He happened to be visiting the Rockefeller Foundation headquarters on West 49th Street in Manhattan; would Norm come up? There was something to discuss.

Borlaug explains the upshot:

> I took an afternoon off and rode the train to New York. George laid out a grand scheme of lifting the poor people of Mexico out of hunger and poverty. It was exciting and inspiring. Again he asked me to join. This time I explained that while I was no longer under federal restrictions my work was still war related, and he'd need to contact my chiefs at the company.

CAREER SAVER #12

Fate's twelfth facilitator, George Harrar. By cajoling Borlaug into trying international agriculture this powerful personality steered the career into its proper path. To succeed, though, he first had to face down DuPont's finest, a task for which he was eminently suited. Without Harrar's strong persona and timely intervention, Norm would have spent a career in chemical industry.

So Harrar did exactly that, to the intense annoyance of DuPont's executives. Wendell Tisdale immediately called Norm in. "We understand why you're unhappy here," he said. In this he was assuming that low pay was the problem. That conclusion was certainly understandable: almost everyone working for Norm was earning more; some, including Betty Horning, took home more than twice his pay.

Actually, though, he felt lucky. He explained to Tisdale that money was not the concern; he did, however, worry about being adrift in a company whose key interest was chemistry.

A few weeks later this notion of swimming in a scientific sea wherein chemistry sharks controlled the food chain got to him. He approached the chief of the Grasselli Research Division, explaining that he didn't seem to fit well in DuPont now that the war work was winding down.

"No, no," John Woodhouse replied, "we want you here. If you feel out of place in research you can go into sales." Then he added a special inducement. "Seeing how well you've worked and considering the injustice of your salary, we'll give you two afternoons a week to go up to the University of Pennsylvania and take graduate courses in chemistry."

This seemed perfect . . . it settled all doubts. Norm called New York, only to find that Harrar had already returned to Mexico. So he left a message: he was grateful for the offer but would remain Stateside.

That was it, then. He'd finally, absolutely, for the last time, stumbled upon his true vocation. After attending the famous university and getting a grounding in chemistry, opportunities in the corporate world would open. Perhaps, as Woodhouse suggested, he'd become a salesman.

It would have happened, too, but on his next visit to New York, George Harrar called again. This time, he wanted to come to Wilmington and bring a Rockefeller Foundation vice president with him.

"Sure," Norm said, "that's okay."

"But we want to talk to your boss."

"Well, I don't know about that. Security is very tight and getting into the Experiment Station could be difficult."

Heedless of the warning, Harrar and the foundation's VP showed up, wangled their way through the security screen, and collared Wendell Tisdale. A microbiologist by training, Tisdale appreciated the grandeur inherent in helping a hungry nation lift its food production. "If Borlaug is important to you," he said, "we should not stand in the way."

With John Woodhouse, however, the fireworks flew. In temperament, both Harrar and Woodhouse were emotional pyrotechnicians. Norm made the introductions and scuttled from the room. Later he heard that a professional exchange of rockets ensued. Among other niceties, the infuriated executive charged Harrar with unethical behavior: "I resent you coming down here and hiring away our employee!" Woodhouse had yelled across the table.

Nonetheless, the decision ultimately came down to Norm. And it wasn't easy. Among issues to face were:

One. He'd have to leave United States and live in a foreign culture.

Two. He'd be expected to conquer the elusive enemy called Hunger.

Three. The job would have to be taken sight unseen.

Four. Mexico was a scientific wasteland, having no research establishment, technical library, or facilities for experimentation.

Five. Americans by and large despised the place as well as what they considered its backward and brutal people—an attitude that was heartily reciprocated.

Six. He'd have to sacrifice all material advantages because his annual salary would be $3500, and after four years of wartime inflation that no longer seemed excessive.

To colleagues, the decision was a no-brainer. All advised him not to throw his career away. Immured in a technically primitive society he'd lose his professional edge . . . he'd fall behind the curve of advancing knowledge. He'd be unhappy. And, unable to land another job back home, he'd become an exile.

But after mulling it over he decided to go.

Margaret agreed. And for good cause: She'd noted a special sparkle in his eye whenever the prospect of lifting Mexico's food supply came up.

There was only one catch: She was again pregnant, and wartime Mexico seemed hardly the best place to bear a child.

She'd have to stay in Delaware a while longer.

AFTERWORD

BY NORMAN BORLAUG

The previous chapters reflect the hardscrabble life and tough times experienced during my first 30 years. This was my awakening, and without the selfless support of others I couldn't have gotten through. Thus, I'm especially glad these pages honor those who helped me escape the subsistence life and enter the world of wider prospects.

Among family, Granddad Nels, my parents, my cousin Sina Borlaug and, later, Margaret made possible the first part of my passage.

At the New Oregon Rural District School Number 8, Lena Halvorson, Sina Borlaug and my classmates provided a sense of place that helped ever after, no matter where or among how many thousands I happened to be standing.

My Cresco High friends Erv Upton and George Champlin contributed selflessly to my progress at critical moments when I seemed stuck firmly in place. And the wrestling coach Dave Bartelma enhanced my ability to cope with all the perils that would ultimately befall me.

At the University of Minnesota, Scott Pauley found a source of food just when I'd gotten too hungry to stay in school. Then E.C. Stakman opened a broad future at a moment when there seemed to be not even a narrow one. Professor Stakman also provided the tuition funds that allowed me to enter graduate school, an option otherwise beyond all reach.

Finally, wartime work at the DuPont Company taught me to apply science and solve practical problems with speed and dispatch, an aptitude that proved helpful during my later efforts.

Because so many people lent a hand I've since made a special effort to assist young people. Down the decades I've addressed many college classes and campus groups. Typically, I tell them to:

1). Reach for the stars, and keep in the front of your mind an image of everything you plan to achieve.

2). Remember what Granddad Nels drummed into me, "Think for yourself! Fill your head now to fill your belly later!"

3). Remember also the words Stakman yelled at me: "You're young... keep your options open . . . USE A LITTLE COMMON SENSE!"
His message is still good, and I say with the same ardor he employed: "GET A BROAD EDUCATION, AND SPECIALIZE ONLY AFTER YOU'RE PREPARED TO APPLY SCIENCE AND NOT JUST ADVANCE IT."

4). Remember Raphael Zon's charge to scientists to mistrust abstract theorizing and temper research findings with reason. Beware of sensationalists and their correlations, projections, and pronouncements masquerading as proofs. Even professors fall for fads or for the latest research fancies. I've often said that the textbooks should be burned every 10 years to rid the collective mind of intellectual corruption.

5). Be courageous in your career. Remember the Bartelma maxim: "Give your best . . . Believe you can succeed . . . Face adversity squarely . . . Proceed with confidence that you'll find the answers when problems arise. *Then go out and win some bouts!*" Those are still great words to live by.

7). Always keep in mind the DuPont Company dictums for preserving comity during a career: involve yourself in activities outside work, don't talk shop at home, and never gossip about coworkers.

Beyond acknowledging the people who helped make my long journey possible, the previous chapters also highlight an important phase of American history that is today unknown. For one thing, the old days were not like today . . . they were very much worse. For another, during the 1920s and 1930s, the years of my youth, rural America experienced a Green Revolution. The benefits of better seeds and better farming technology uplifted my life and drove all my subsequent endeavors. In later decades, whenever I saw struggling subsistence farmers in Africa,

Asia or Latin America I wanted to provide them the same updraft that had let me reach for my stars.

Helping struggling subsistence farmers produce a food surplus is the way to rid the world of much poverty and misery. It's what happened in rural America during my teens and twenties, and the cash earned from our own labors lifted my parents, sisters and me into a better world than any previous Borlaug generation.

Moreover, it was a permanent improvement. And not just for the rural regions or that era. Indeed, the benefits from that homegrown Green Revolution continue today for every American. In that sense, I hope my story helps modern readers appreciate the wonders we all nowadays enjoy. Those wonders may not be perfect but they give us lives that no previous generation ever had a chance to even sample.

Finally, I want to thank Dr. Vietmeyer for so ably integrating that larger and mostly unappreciated history with mine.

NORMAN E. BORLAUG
September, 2008

AUTHOR'S NOTE

This volume has covered just the first of Norman Borlaug's four distinct and separate lives. The next transports us to Mexico, where he transforms himself into a Hunger Fighter. The character you find in Volume 2 is poles apart from the one you've just met, as is the environment, the work, the challenges, and the social scene. So far he's been fighting to find food for himself; from here on, his competence will be continually tested as he fights to provide food for others so they needn't suffer as he had.

Volume 2 starts in 1944, with his arrival in desperately hungry Mexico. Local food production is so poor that massive imports of wheat are required to keep the 22 million citizens in flour tortillas. He discovers that the main cause is the fungal infections that each winter roar through Mexico like box cars on a freight train. This is the same black stem rust that opened this current volume when in the fall of 1916 millions of acres of the magnificent variety called Marquis sickened and died, and from Missouri to Montana and even into the upper reaches of Manitoba the wheatland turned to wasteland.

Now it is the 30-year-old Norman Borlaug who faces the nearly impossible task of finding a wheat variety that survives the fungal assault, thrives in cultivation and meets all the quirky concerns of commerce and consumers. Just like the magnificent Canadian called Marquis, which he'd eaten as a boy.

To get a new stellar performer he must first beat the highly mutable microbe that has broken Mexican wheat's protective genetic code and is poised once more to transform thousands of square miles of lush fields into miasmas of putrefaction.

Despite having never worked with wheat he embraces the challenge. Without hesitating, he harnesses all he's learned from pressured wartime research, from living alone in the wilderness, and from David Bartelma's dictum to give his best, believe he can succeed, face adversity squarely, and proceed with confidence that he'll find the answers when problems arise. *And then he goes out to try and win a bout!*

Philosophically speaking, he never forgets where he came from. Thus his approach to feeding a whole country is that of a problem-solver who, like Herbert Hoover of old, favors results over all else. Also, he plunges ahead without worrying about anything so trivial as plans.

Scientifically, he builds on what he learned listening to Stakman arguing with his peers as they wandered through the 40 acres of diseased plants (sometimes with fists clenched in preparation for use).

The campaign to suppress the fungus will continue for 13 years, and in each of those years he'll breed two huge generations of wheat—a winter one in the Sonoran Desert of northern Mexico and a summer one 700 miles to the south and high up a mountainside near Mexico City. All told, that's 26 battle royals in a row, each involving planting, managing, inspecting, judging and selectively harvesting millions of plants. It is history's greatest campaign to keep a crop healthy . . . and it's waged by a lone researcher racing back and forth between remote regions of a hungry backward nation without a break for rest, let alone a holiday.

The story has never been told. Not even Norm has recorded the sequence of amazing events and twists of fate that unfold in Mexico between 1944 and 1959. None of it was easy. Initially, his director provided neither money nor equipment because he'd not budgeted for two plantings per year, let alone any work in the distant and remote northern desert.

Several times some local functionary's ignorance or stupidity carries the program perilously close to unraveling all Norm's achieved. Then at year 9, the wily microbe nearly achieves the same outcome by changing its spots and sending him hurtling right back to the beginning—18 immensely laborious seasonal cycles earlier—to start almost from scratch. About that time he also comes perilously close to losing his life: first when a canyon wall collapses the road around him and a few days later when he gets swept into the depths of a river raging in full flood.

All this he endures in the service of feeding hungry humanity, yet while busy fighting wheat's worst enemy he's inadvertently becoming a center of controversy. To achieve the vision occupying the frontal lobes of his mind, he breaks canonical rules that all his peers agree *must* be followed. His bosses in faraway New York send committees to investigate, and more than one reports back that this rookie wheat breeder doesn't know what he's doing and is wasting the sponsor's dollars and everyone's time.

Mexico's senior scientists are no fans either. The saga is peopled by purblind public servants who designed dirty tricks to get this Yankee interloper deported. Angered, or perhaps embarrassed, by his obvious success, they move in print and in politics to get him expelled.

Worst of all, local farmers show no interest in his results. His first demonstration day draws only one farmer who is genuinely interested in using his seeds; the other 20 have come just for the free beer, whose availability Borlaug has advertised all over town.

The apathy is understandable: no scientist has ever before helped Mexico's farmers; how could this crazy gringo be any different? Surely, families that have tilled the land for generations cannot trust anyone silly enough to live and work all by himself in a derelict research station in the desert. Moreover, this preoccupied foreigner has no help, no tractor, no equipment, no accommodations other than a tumble-down building without windows, sanitation, running water or stove. The only thing it has in abundance is rats, among which he spends his nights with a sleeping bag pulled tight over his head!

Is it any wonder this lone ranger of research feels beleaguered? For half of each year his wife and daughter (and later a son) seldom see him. However, while never quite understanding his obsession with the fungus called rust, they remain sanguine and supportive down the endless years.

Despite what you might imagine, he's not one of those above-the-fray superior scientists. Instead, his research is what you might call "of the people, for the people, by the people." He works not in a laboratory but out in the dirt, dust, heat, and flies of Mexican farm fields.

His farmer neighbors eventually come to recognize the prospective progress behind his madness. They befriend him, thereby saving his sanity. They teach him Spanish so he can function in society. Then, slowly, they become his ally. And in the end they go to extraordinary lengths to pull off miraculous rescues just when his expulsion from Mexico is imminent and his continuance as a hunger fighter seems impossible.

During this seat-of-the-pants thrill ride, which just happens to involve the crop that produces the most food for mankind, young students and a ranch manager at loose ends are moved by this scientist's charismatic qualities and ask to work with him. Without pay. He treats them as colleagues and they quickly turn into acolytes and true believers in problem-solving research that favors results over everything, including senseless rules and silly reporting requirements.

In time, more and more students volunteer to join his effort, and these develop into a fresh new generation of Mexican crop scientists as dedicated and committed to hunger fighting as he. Finally, the ranch manager shoulders the task of distributing the seeds that defy black stem rust and this American cowhand thereby saves the food supply at the very moment the fungus is preparing to take down every variety Mexico grows.

Along the way, a few uneducated boys too young to be called teenagers also throw in their lot. Norm treats them like colleagues too. And when one asks to crossbreed plants, the scientist with the PhD somewhat reluctantly shows the almost illiterate 12-year-old the complex routine. In the upshot, the nimble-fingered kids develop into master craftsmen and make wheat crosses leading to varieties that eventually lift food production in scores of countries worldwide.

By the end of Volume 2 Mexico—following 15 years of Borlaug's presence—is producing more wheat than it can eat. Farmers by the thousands are flocking to his annual demonstration days because his seeds and methods are lifting their own lives to levels they'd never imagined possible. By this time they admire, even love, the gringo with the sky-blue eyes who's transformed their own prospects, and their nation's.

Still, not everyone appreciates the awful challenges he's facing. The New York bosses who sign his paychecks continually demand he redirect his efforts to comply with standard methods, and when he goes merrily onward heedless of the directive they wrap up his research.

With that rejection, the scientist who is poised to feed a hungry nation becomes a ward of a foreign government, which removes him from the leadership and turns his research over to the students he's trained. The Doctor of Plant Pathology now works for his Mexican understudies who lack graduate degrees . . . and he likes the arrangement. Teacher and trainees remain close and collegial and, if anything, make an even more powerful hunger-fighting team because he infuses them with the Bartelma and Stakman mental imprints.

It's no wonder the Mexican government wants to keep him. The wheats he's bred have doubled the farmers' productivity to a level of 1000lb an acre. But by then he's looking ahead to wheats like none ever seen before—ones that can best 5000lb an acre. The new plants are tiny and dedicate their main energy to producing grain rather than stem or leaves. But they're still far from perfect and are unready for use. Indeed, at that moment the challenge to re-engineer the second-oldest food crop seems an impossible dream.

This is the point where Volume 2 ends. Mexico is feeding itself. But the great new 5000lb-an-acre wheat varieties remain works in progress. Worse, they seem likely to remain unperfected because his bosses completely abandon their pesky employee who's always been a center of controversy and nearly impossible to manage.

The subsequent phase—while he's orphaned from his nation and profession, a ward of the Mexican government and working for his former students—is the stuff of Volume 3, which tells his third phase of life and the ultimate triumph over Famine. The character you find there is yet again distinctly different, as is the environment, the work, the challenges, the social scene and the consequences of failure. By then, he's dealing not only with dirt farmers but also with presidents, prime ministers and leading politicians on the other side of the globe. And he treats them all alike, sometimes even honoring the presidents, prime ministers and leading politicians as highly as the dirt farmers.

And I'm not giving away much of the plot to mention that the remotest of remote research conducted half a lifetime ago still feeds the world. The exquisitely rare genes he and his pre-teen Mexican boys teased out of the wheat genome are in the bread, cookies, crackers, cakes, pastries, pancakes, doughnuts, breakfast cereals, rolls, bagels and very much more that we all eat today. Those genes have kept wheat plants healthy and productive worldwide for over half a century. They have also kept food cheap, and kept the fields that grow humanity's biggest food crop free of fungicides.

That's why his peers honor Norman E. Borlaug as the man who saved a billion lives. It's also why, despite a quadrupling of the number of mouths, humanity is better fed than it had been when he'd been born in 1914. More than anyone, he is the father of the food supply.

But it's the untold back-story that is so fascinating. Who knew agricultural science could be more enthralling than a beach-blanket bestseller? Maybe that's because it's all real and also because the hope for humanity's future hangs on the myriad decisions, coincidences, strokes of fortune, friends and supporters, none of whom had any clue they were helping feed the world. Heck, on that score he himself had no clue. He was just following his mental image of the next good thing he'd like to achieve. Maybe also it's because the Borlaug saga foreshadows how to feed the expected billions of new arrivals that makes the prosaic so heroic.

Borlaug is a member of what Tom Brokaw calls "The Greatest Generation." No question, he's its greatest exemplar. Behind that generation's big-tent successes are the same character lessons Norm boy learned during the years described here in Volume I: courage, can-do confidence, common sense and a commitment to results not rhetoric.

A feature of moral transcendence is that everything that happened in the first stage of Borlaug's life arose from the democratic experience. Harry Emerson Fosdick neatly summed that up in 1937. Here are that philosopher/preacher's words written when Borlaug was just starting graduate school:

> PRIMARILY, democracy is the conviction that there are extraordinary possibilities in ordinary people and that if we throw wide the doors of opportunity so that all boys and girls can bring out the best that is in them, we will get amazing results from unlikely sources. Shakespeare was the son of a bankrupt butcher and a woman who could not write her name. Beethoven was the son of a consumptive mother, herself daughter of a cook, and a drunken father. Schubert was the son of a peasant father and a mother who had been in domestic service. Faraday, one of the greatest scientific experimenters of all time, was born over a stable, his father an invalid blacksmith and his mother a common drudge. Such facts as these underlie democracy. That is why, with all its discouraging blunders, we must everlastingly believe in it.

When Borlaug went to Mexico in 1944 little did he know that it was thanks to a decision Dr. Fosdick's brother Raymond had made four years earlier. But that quirky coincidence will find its proper place among dozens of other quirky coincidences as well as the continuing drama, adventure and good Samaritans who pop up in the nick of time to rescue the beleaguered hunger fighter. Those and much more fill the 300 thrill-packed pages of Volume 2 and keep the saga rolling forward toward the point where Norman Borlaug receives the highest accolade of all.

Noel Vietmeyer
October 2008

ACKNOWLEDGEMENTS

The author gratefully acknowledges grants from:

- **The Rural Development Foundation**, Taipei, Taiwan, Republic of China; and
- **The Wallace Genetic Foundation**, Washington, D.C.

Both grants were administered by Professor **Edward Runge** (Department of Soil & Crop Sciences, Texas A&M University), whose efforts I also acknowledge with gratitude.

This biography is not the academic kind compiled from a collection of learned quotes and documents. At bottom, its content is entirely thanks to **Norman Borlaug**. These pages result from discussions scattered over several decades. Many took place while we were on assignment for the National Academy of Sciences.

A number of Borlaug family members also contributed. Norm's wife, the late **Margaret Borlaug**, twice provided hospitality when I visited College Station, Texas and we shared some good talks about old times. Norm's daughter, **Jeanie Laube**, went to a lot of effort to rummage through the Borlaug attic in Dallas and locate the tender wedding photo (page 201). Norm's granddaughter, **Julie Borlaug**, also helped recover that photo. Norm's sister Palma's children—**Ted Behrens** (Minburn, Iowa) and **Judy Reed** (Lehigh, Iowa)—located the striking family photo of Nels and Emma Borlaug and their children (page 34). And Norm's distant niece, **Joanne Lane** (Waterloo, Iowa) provided the historic snapshot showing 8-year-old Norm and his cousin Vilmar (page 67) as well as the stunningly beautiful portrait of her aunt Sina Borlaug (page 80). Norm's sister **Charlotte Culbert** made a memorable contribution by letting me join the family feast she'd prepared when Norm took me to Cresco during the project's preliminary phase.

I must also thank Norm's friend and colleague **Lowell S. Hardin** of Purdue University. Dr. Hardin provided the touching story of the grateful Pakistani farmer that appears in the prologue (page 14). He was present, and (with his permission) I present the episode largely as he recorded it at the time.

As I've said, the text reflects Norman Borlaug's own recollections. However, the overarching historical and philosophical comments and claims reflect my own reading of science and history. Most of Norm's claims (as well as mine) were double-checked via alternate means, including personal contacts, direct requests, library services and Internet sources. This meticulous checking proved the phenomenal quality of his memory.

Gathering the photographs was a separate saga. I'm especially grateful to the individuals who went out of their way to help find the rare pictures enlivening these pages. I sought images that help the reader by supporting the text and by being instructive, but above all, by being moving. Below I present the contributors in the order their photos occur.

The cover shot comes from **Nathan Heath**, an amateur photographer from Evansville, Indiana. My son Rob spotted Nathan's image of wheat heads silhouetted against the setting sun posted on the photo-sharing website called Flickr.

The photos of Herbert Hoover and the Belgian girl (pages 22 and 23) are thanks to

Jim Detlefsen of the Hoover Library in West Branch, Iowa. The Hoover portrait is a soft-focus sepia print, which I had sharpened and converted to black and white for printing. The girl's picture apparently came from some old book and cannot be improved. Sadly, there are no other Belgian-child pictures that exude any sentiment.

Though the wheat crop collapse in 1916 was a huge event, it seems to have attracted few photographers. I despaired of ever being able to show it visually until **Thomas Fetch Jr.** of the Cereal Research Centre in Winnipeg came up with the image seen on page 25. Searching through journals of that era, he discovered this grainy exposure, which was probably taken by Stakman.

Thanks to **Hillary Levin** of the St. Louis Post-Dispatch I can highlight the incredibly brave public-health workers picking up the body of an influenza victim (pages 46-47).

The picture of the Borlaug farmhouse (page 56) is thanks to **Ken Becker** of the Cresco Times newspaper, who drove out on a sunny Saturday afternoon just to take the photo. In the days before distance died, the Borlaugs could undertake that journey only once or twice *a year*.

Even though **Jim Johnson** and **Paul Vasold** live in California and Ohio, respectively, both provided information about the Norwegian immigrants of Chickasaw County, which is only a mile from the Borlaug farm. Paul, for instance, supplied the digitized version of the 1915 property plat map that provides the backdrop on page 65.

The special "World Series of Corn" photo (pages 76-77) proved especially troublesome. It appears in Carl Hamilton's 1974 book (see page 274) and was attributed to Wallaces Farmer. That magazine still exists, but neither Executive Editor **Frank Holdmeyer** nor Editor **Rod Swoboda** could find the original. Archivist **Virginia Wadsley** of West Des Moines, spent a day combing through the magazine's 1930s photo files without success. I've thus resorted to scanning the image in Hamilton's book and using Adobe Photoshop to roughly restore its original appearance.

The picture of Henry Wallace showing his grandfather the new seeds (page 92) came thanks to **Ann Taylor** of the Wallace House Foundation in Des Moines. It's a small section cropped from a group photo. The two Henrys are so absorbed in discussing the new corn that they are oblivious to the other family members who are way off to the left, posing properly for the cameraman.

Henry Ford's mechanical horse might have changed the face of farming but it's hard to find a satisfying photo of one. The images either show rusty wrecks or gussied up collectors' items. Thanks to Google I discovered the image of crouched power seen on page 96. This was taken by **Michael Rawluk**, a Canadian amateur photographer who lives in Prince George, British Columbia.

The outlaws in overalls photo (page 108) proved a huge problem. In his book, Carl Hamilton attributes it to the "Des Moines Register and Tribune," which apparently never existed. The incident was photographed outside Sioux City, but the Sioux City Tribune was sold decades ago and its current incarnation keeps no records. I ended up scanning Hamilton's printed image.

Mel Bashore of West Jordan, Utah indulges in a strange hobby of locating obituaries and cemetery records of lesser-known sports figures from decades long ago. His efforts provided numerous contacts, including the children of Margaret Borlaug's brother George Gibson and those of George Champlin. That's how I found Champlin's daughter, **Jill Newby** of Bella Vista, Arkansas, who provided the photo of her father (page 119). This snapshot was taken about the time he rescued Norm's career from ruin.

Bobak Ha'Eri, spent more than one weekend driving around Dinkytown, looking for buildings that feature in the Borlaug saga. Sadly, many had been torn down in the 1950s to build Interstate 35W (the freeway that collapsed on August 1, 2007). Others, such as the University Coffee Shop, no longer bore any resemblance to the structure Norm knew. None of Bobak's photos made it into the book. However, those of the Kearsarge Apartments (page 123) can be seen at **BracingBooks.com**.

As mentioned, **Fred Hovde** became president of Purdue University. While searching the university website I expected to find only formal photos taken during his tenure in office. However, I was happy to find he'd donated many others, among which was the one (page 127) taken around the time Norm knew him at the University of Minnesota.

For years the low-resolution photo of the sorority dining hall (page 141) featured on the Alpha Omicron Pi website. **Andrea Wegner** took up the challenge of finding the original print. But not even the sorority's past president could locate a version good enough for publication, despite a weekend of digging through old archives in the basement. The dining hall has since been renovated and no longer looks anything like what Norm knew. I've used this poor quality image, though with reluctance.

I was overjoyed to find that the **Library of Congress** had a Henry Wallace photo (page 152) taken the year he went to Washington to quell the rural unrest that was tearing the country apart. It was even more exciting to find that it had been taken during his first week on the job. Sadly, though, the image had been defaced, with white paint crudely brushed around his head. Thanks to digitizing and photo-restoration the image was rescued, though it remains far from perfect.

The picture showing Kharkiv residents strolling past bodies in the street (page 155) was part of a memorial exhibition at Harvard University in 1986. Harvard's **Peter Nestor** scanned the picture for me, but the original apparently had come from an old book and possessed both poor contrast and an embedded printer's screen. **Orest Zakydalsky** of the Ukrainian Canadian Research & Documentation Centre in Toronto searched for a print or negative, but hadn't uncovered one by press time. I persisted with this image because it grabs the conscience and the heartstrings without being gruesome.

Out of many disappointments, perhaps the greatest was the inability to find an original of the prohibition repeal photo (page 176). I still hope to track down the owner of this shot, which is goofy and a little daring but captures the spirit of uplift like no other.

Eben Lehman of the Forest History Society in Durham, North Carolina supplied many pieces of information as well as the Raphael Zon photo (page 168). Eben also put me onto the trail that turned up John Cohen and the Edward Pulaski picture (page 195).

John Phelps, then of Southern Illinois University, led me to the Edward Behre photo (page 172). He'd been given a print by **David C. Baumgartner** of Goreville, Illinois, and posted it on the SIU website fancying that someone on earth might possibly find it interesting. He was right, because I'd spent days trying to find anything whatever about Behre, and finding a photo was a thrill. David Baumgartner provided the print, which I scanned and had slightly restored to improve the contrast and sharpness.

Hank Art and **Andrew ("Drew") Jones** of Williams College in Williamstown, Massachusetts, provided the old photo of the Hopkins Forest (page 174). Hank also supplied the information about Amos Lawrence Hopkins and his house (page 171).

Marlee Wilcomb, curator of the Central Idaho Historical Museum in McCall, directed me to **Richard Holm Jr.** and **Lawrence A. Kingsbury**, also of McCall. They provided the photos of the fire tower and cabin (pages 186-7), the view of the Chamberlain Basin (pages 190-1) and the mountain range Norm traversed (page 198).

A photo of Edward Pulaski ought to be easy to find, right? Not so, and I'd despaired of ever finding a book-quality image until **John Cohen** of Pictorial Histories Publishing in Missoula, Montana came through. His photo of Big Ed (with contrast slightly enhanced) can be seen on page 195. Apparently, not even the Forest Service has a portrait of its great hero.

Mark E. Hughes of the U.S. Department of Agriculture's Cereal Disease Laboratory in St. Paul, Minnesota kindly provided the map showing the area subjected to rust spores each summer (page 210).

Neither photographers nor plant pathologists find rust very photogenic. Getting an image that would work in black & white proved tedious until **Philip Northover** of Manitoba Agriculture in Carman, Manitoba supplied the one seen on page 214.

My neighbor **Ray Murphy**, who grew up in Providence, told me that a local photographer named Adler had taken his high school class photos. Next **Lee Teverow** of the Rhode Island Historical Society provided the name of a Providence camera store that had belonged to an Adler. There, I happened to reach one of two people on earth who knew what I was phoning about. He referred me to his father, **Carl Adler** of Greenville, whose father, Walter Adler, had photographed Rhode Island's capital during the hurricane of '38. Carl had only one print, and it was hanging on the wall of his basement. However, he got it removed from the frame, professionally scanned, and the result can be seen on pages 222 and 223. Thanks to Carl we probably have the finest image of that historic scene.

Alan Marra of Amherst, Massachusetts sent snapshots showing Norm during his stint in Massachusetts clearing tree debris left by the 1938 hurricane (page 225). He remembers Norm organizing wrestling matches with the young workers and calling Minnesota every evening to talk to Margaret. Back then before automatic switching, making long-distance calls was expensive and tedious because you had to wend your way through the operators. Sadly, Chapter 11 proved too tight, for Alan's photos, which will instead appear on **BracingBooks.com**.

David R. Foster, director of the Harvard Forest in Petersham, Massachusetts dug up the dramatic pictures seen on pages 226 and 227. These two faithfully reflect the overnight destruction of New England's forests. The first picture, however, was taken some years before the hurricane struck.

On the day after Hurricane Hanna (September 6, 2008) **Brian Feeley**, whom I'd providentially found through Flickr, the photo-sharing website, took to the streets of Wilmington, Delaware and located the apartment building in which Norm and Margaret lived in during World War II. His photograph is on page 249.

The myriad pieces of data and details that enliven the text are thanks to many sources. For details on the main sources go to **BracingBooks.com**. The following also contributed.

Matt Bryant, Cresco Times, Cresco, Iowa
Jeff Beshey, St Louis Park, Minnesota
Bill Case, Funk Prairie Home, Shirley, Illinois
Michele Christian, Iowa State University, Ames
Karen Cummings, The American Phytopathological Society, St. Paul, Minnesota
Debra J.S. Dietzman, U.S. Forest Service, St. Paul, Minnesota
Bethany Francis, Rockefeller Archive Center, Sleepy Hollow, New York
Susan Jellinger, State Historical Society of Iowa, Des Moines
Bill Kemp, McLean County Museum of History, Bloomington, Illinois
Karen Klinkenberg, University of Minnesota Archives, Minneapolis
Leonard J. Jacobs, Franklin Grove, Illinois
Kewanee Historical Society, Kewanee, Illinois

Janel Quirante, Hoover Institution Archives, Palo Alto, California
Janice Sowers, Howard-Winneshiek Genealogy Society, Cresco, Iowa
Pamela Riney-Kehrberg, Iowa State University, Ames
The Franklin D. Roosevelt Presidential Library, Hyde Park, New York
Carl E. Snow, Purdue University Libraries, West Lafayette, Indiana
Roland van der Gracht, Algemeen Rijksarchief, Brussels, Belgium
Emory J. Westcott, Cresco Public Library, Cresco, Iowa
    The late **George Knaphus**, a soldier during the Battle of the Bulge and subsequently a botanist at Iowa State University, supplied *Successful Farming* magazine's cautionary quote about hybrid corn (page 91) as well as his remembrance of dusting DDT onto thousands of refugees during WWII's aftermath (page 243).

    In addition, my National Academies colleague **Mark Dafforn** clued me in on wheat farming and much more. His mother, **Anna Dafforn** of Cunningham, Kansas told me about waking up during the Dust Bowl era with a grimy silhouette on the sheet (page 166).

    The late **Merlin B. Dickerman** happened to live in Alexandria, Virginia, which was not far from my home. Norm took me to hear them reminisce about their time together at the Hopkins Forest (page 175) as well as his days working for Raphael Zon (page 167).

    In one sense, producing this book has been a neighborhood activity. At the beginning, **Arnie Zimmer** and others at the **Lorton Library** helped by obtaining numerous very obscure books via Interlibrary Loan. Then, after 17 publishers sent rejection letters, my Hallowing Point neighbors **Rick** and **Bernadette Raymo** sustained my spirits through their unquenchable enthusiasm for the manuscript. In its final stages, my neighbors **Al Papenfus** and **Dick Kennedy** reviewed the text, exposing several bonehead errors. Another neighbor, **Pat Pascale**, designed the book's frontmatter. My son **Rob Vietmeyer** designed the cover. And my wife **Anne** took care of business while I was preoccupied with Borlaug. Without that, there'd be no book at all.

    Most of the archival photographs lacked sharpness or contrast or both. The images brightening the previous pages have benefited from the talents of **Rob Vietmeyer** as well as of **Chris Ariasaif** of Photo-60 in Woodbridge, Virginia.

PICTURE CREDITS

PICTURE CREDITS (cont.)

FURTHER READING

CHAPTER 1 Hostage
The Life of Herbert Hoover; The Humanitarian, 1914-1917 by George H. Nash (1988, Norton) is a close-up look at Herbert Hoover's efforts to feed the Belgians. The quote from Ambassador Walter Hines Page as well as other details came from here.

Under a Flaming Sky: The Great Hinckley Firestorm of 1894 by Daniel James Brown (The Lyons Press, 2006) is a recent review.

Burning an Empire: The Study of American Forest Fires by forest firefighter Stewart H. Holbrook (The Macmillan Company, 1943) blends beautiful prose with fun and facts.

CHAPTER 2 Mortality
The Great Influenza: The Epic Story of the Deadliest Plague in History by John M. Barry (Penguin Books, 2005) is an exhaustive account of the 1918 epidemic.

The Good Old Days—They Were Terrible! by Otto Bettmann (Random House, 1974) shows photographically just how bad they really were.

CHAPTER 3 Awakening
A Celebration of the American Highway by Phil Patton (Simon & Schuster, June 1986) is a fascinating account of how roads changed American life.

In No Time At All by Carl Hamilton (Iowa State University Press, 1974) is a heartwarming evocation of growing up in rural Iowa in the 1930s. Hamilton is the survivor who never felt free because he had to feed the animals and milk the cows (page 60).\

Saude; A brief history by Kermit Hildahl. This 60-page manuscript tells about the village Borlaug grew up in. The author lives at 608 Huckleberry Heights Dr., Hannibal, MO 63401

Farm Town: A Memoir of the 1930's (The Stephen Greene Press, 1974) is a photographic of rural life before WWII. J.W. McManigal took most of the photos in his hometown of Horton, Kansas. From this interesting volume come the pictures of the boy and horse team (pages 72-73) and of the farmers stringing electric wires (pages 178-179).

CHAPTER 4 Dreamy Days
American Dreamer: The Life and Time of Henry A. Wallace by J.C. Culver and J. Hyde, (Norton, 2000) is packed with details on the amazing life of Henry Wallace.

Only Yesterday: An Informal History of the 1920s by Frederick Lewis Allen (Perennial Classics) is a lively narrative that brings back life as it really was in the '20s.

CHAPTER 5 Nightmares
The Americans: The Democratic Experience by Daniel J. Boorstin (Vintage, 1974) is a Pulitzer Prize winning portrait of the United States as it climbed the heights.

Down on the farm; a picture treasury of country life in America in the good old days by Stewart H Holbrook and Milton Rugoff (Crown Publishers, 1954).

CHAPTER 6 Hunger Pains
Since Yesterday: The 1930's in America, September 3, 1929 to September 3, 1939 by Frederick Lewis Allen (Harper and Row, 1940). A sequel to *Only Yesterday.*

The Big Change: America Transforms Itself 1900-1950 by Frederick Lewis Allen (Transaction Publishers, 1993) presents the first half of the twentieth century in Allen's always colorful prose style.

FURTHER READING (cont.)

CHAPTER 7 Margaret

Famine on the Wind by G.L. Carefoot and E.R. Sprott (Longmans, 1967) vividly describes crop diseases' impacts on history. My version of the story of Joseph and the Biblical rust epidemics (pages 214-5) follows their scholarship.

CHAPTER 8 Heavy Weather

The Glory and the Dream; A Narrative History of America 1932-1972 by William Manchester (Bantam, 1984) is a great source of detail about the America of Borlaug's youth. The quotes of the lady who prayed in the Amarillo street and the man describing the different dusts hitting the Texas Panhandle (both on page 163) are from there.

CHAPTER 9 Wilderness

Year of the Fires: The Story of the Great Fires of 1910 by Stephen J. Pyne (Mountain Press, 2008) is a skillful depiction of the Big Blowup's horror and history.

Fire Lookouts of the Northwest by Ray Kresek (Ye Galleon Press 1998) is just one of a surprising number of books by those who have successfully survived fire lookout duty.

Go Tell It on the Mountain, edited by Jackie Johnson Maughan (Stackpole Books, 1996) presents recollections by fire lookouts, including Edward Abbey (see page 189).

CHAPTER 10 Course Correction

E.C. Stakman, Statesman of Science (American Phytopathological Society, 1984) is by Stakman's colleague and Borlaug's research advisor, Clyde Christensen. My account of Stakman's work in is derived largely from this memorial biography.

The Staffs of Life by E.J. Kahn, Jr. (Little Brown & Co, 1985) recounts the story of Marquis, which, like so many other great crop varieties, arose almost by accident. In Volume 2 of this Borlaug biography we'll revisit Marquis and tell more about its history and its maker.

CHAPTER 11 National Service

The Glory and the Dream; A Narrative History of America 1932-1972 by William Manchester brilliantly describes the 1938 hurricane.

Recent years have seen a raft of books on the events in New England in September 1938. An example is *Sudden Sea: The Great Hurricane of 1938* by R.A. Scotti (Back Bay Books, 2004).

CHAPTER 12 Wartime

World War II: The Home Front: USA by Ronald H. Bailey and Time Life Editors (Time Life, 1978) is one of the surprisingly few books about life at home during history's biggest conflict.

Minnesota Goes to War: The Home Front During World War II by Dave Kenney (Minnesota Historical Society Press, 2004) tells what Norm and Margaret missed while they lived "Out East" in Delaware.

Personally, I like picking up WWII-era issues of Saturday Evening Post and Reader's Digest. Both can be found on eBay for a few dollars, and both allow you to see the world through the same eyes as Americans living through that terrible yet strangely exhilarating era when war and wonderful times just happened to coincide.

Bracing Books publishes information on promising but novel tools for fixing global problems such as hunger, atmospheric warming, deforestation and tropical diseases. Its publications and website expose to world view innovations capable of rapid deployment.

Many global problems persist because there are no practical "tools" with which to build the foundation for a solution. What is little known—even among specialists—is that means for fashioning such foundations exist among the natural resources native to Africa, Asia and Latin America.

In the main, Bracing Books highlights such promising tropical resources. Built from independent thought, its publications provide inspiration and unconventional insight into ways to attack problems that beset the world. Avoiding popular beliefs, faddish trends, policies and theoretical speculation, these innovative publications highlight natural species (and some manmade materials) that possess the promise to be high-impact hammers for cracking open seemingly insoluble global difficulties.

Moreover, the books are all written in a popular style that combines technical accuracy and professional insight with easy public accessibility.

EXISTING TITLES

In addition to publishing Volume 1 of the Borlaug biography, Bracing Books has secured rights to sell books from the National Academy of Sciences' renowned Board on Science and Technology for International Development. BOSTID's "oldies but goodies" include:

Quality Protein Maize. With its milk-quality protein, this special corn offers a simple, universal, natural means for fortifying millions of malnourished lives every day in every way.

Lost Crops of Africa, Volume 1: Grains. The hungriest continent contains hundreds of native food plants that have yet to get technical support. This volume highlights more than a dozen native cereals that are already in place across Africa and poised to help the hungry lift their lives.

Lost Crops of Africa, Volume 2: Vegetables. This volume highlights 18 native legumes, tubers and leafy edibles packed with vitamins and minerals.

Lost Crops of Africa, Volume 3: Fruits. This volume highlights 24 nutritious native answers for the malnourished continent.

Calliandra. A small tree that soars 20 feet per year, calliandra can be cut annually, providing firewood "forever." It promises not only to reduce rainforest destruction but relieve women's daily wood-gathering burden.

Leucaena. This tree probably absorbs more greenhouse gas than any other. As a legume, it rebuilds soil as it grows and its abundance of furniture-quality timber locks up the absorbed CO_2 for decades.

Microlivestock. This large eye-catching book describes domesticated creatures that are sized for poor-people's space limitations. These can provide subsistence farmers in the tropics with both income and nutrition.

Vetiver. This robust grass forms hedges tight enough to stabilize slopes, preventing soil, water and nutrient losses. Also provides simple ways to corral and/or extract pollutants from contaminated sites while also absorbing and burying greenhouse gas in deeply penetrating roots.

Jojoba. BOSTID efforts got this crop going when it was just a wild desert plant. Now jojoba holds promise as an even bigger contributor to arid areas.

Mangium. This stately tree-legume grows 10 feet a year on the red, acid, largely barren, sites that dominate the tropics. Also helps restore rainforests.

Butterfly Farming. Don't laugh: Tropical butterflies are charmers whose worth is measured by the ounce. Their farm is the forest, so their propagation and preservation adds value to the *standing* trees.

These and other BOSTID books offering answers to global problems are available at modest cost (while supplies last). For details visit BracingBooks.com.

FORTHCOMING TITLES
The following are in advanced stages of completion.

Borlaug. Volume 3. Norm donates his super seeds to hungry nations only to meet with resistance, reluctance, disbelief and even professional sabotage. All this opposition arises in the face of a looming famine projected to be the biggest ever known.

Liquid Life Savers; the New Food Revolution. People forget that baby foods must be more than nutritious . . . they must be liquid. This book shows how to turn local staples into tasty and surprisingly nutritious liquids at low cost.

World's Greatest Dilemma: DDT and Malaria. In the 1940s and 1950s DDT was used to eradicate malaria in scores of nations, including the U.S. This book highlights the amazing long-forgotten results and exposes dozens of reasons why the current fear of DDT just might reflect public hysteria rather than public health.

Forgotten Ways to Fight Global Hunger. Following Borlaug's successes hunger-fighting research centers were established around the world. This book presents 300 tangible research advances that offer a veritable smorgasbord of options for helping slow or stop Global Hunger's return.

ABOUT THE AUTHOR

Norman Borlaug and the author at the Environmental Research Laboratory of the University of Arizona in Tucson, Arizona in July 1982. Displayed around them are plant resources Vietmeyer's work had brought to light. These ended up in the Land Pavilion ride at Epcot Center in Disney World. On the right, towers the winged bean, a "supermarket on a stalk" whose edible leaves, tendrils, flowers, pods, seeds and tubers are both prolific and packed with protein.

Noel Vietmeyer earned a PhD in organic chemistry from the University of California. During a long career at the National Academy of Sciences in Washington, D.C. he produced over 30 books describing innovations that can benefit Africa, Asia and Latin America.

Vietmeyer was also a prolific freelance writer, producing some 200 articles for publications such as *National Geographic, Reader's Digest, Smithsonian, Encyclopaedia Britannica, World Book, International Wildlife* and *Ranger Rick.*

His quarter-century of National Academy of Sciences service was noteworthy for the discovery of tropical crops that were little known to science but that possessed qualities for helping the world's poor nations. It was through this work that Vietmeyer met Norman Borlaug, who graciously agreed to chair several of the review panels the NAS appointed to make the final calls on certain extremely fast-growing trees, nutritious food crops, potentially valuable industrial plants and vegetative environmental supports that stabilize tropical lands.

Off and on over the years, the two traveled together, and Borlaug eventually related roughly 300 personal experiences. They included life-and-death adventures as well as coincidences, escapes from financial disaster, squabbles with those who disagreed with his methods (virtually everyone), and farmers who many times came to the rescue just as his program was about to be axed.

These stories make up the heart and soul of this multivolume biography of the mild-mannered maverick who fed a billion people.